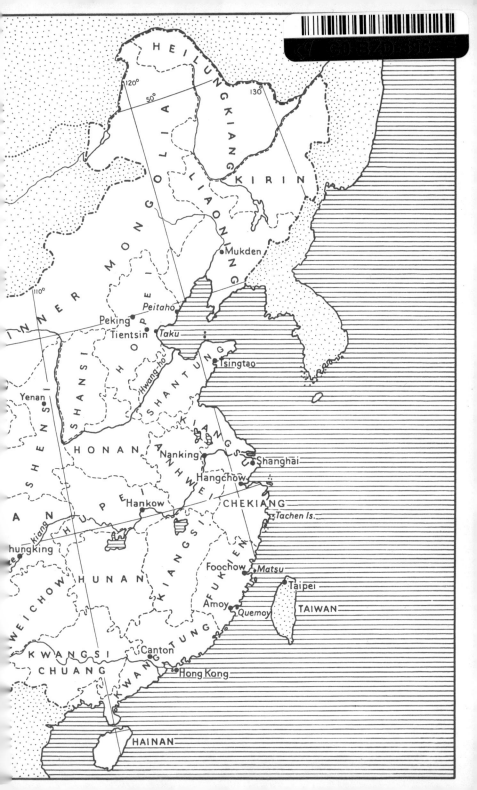

HEILUNGKIANG

MONGOLIA

KIRIN

LIAONING

120°

50°

130°

INNER

110°

Mukden

PEI

Peitaho

Peking

Tientsin

Taku

Hwang-ho

HOPE

Yenan

SHANTUNG

Tsingtao

SHANSI

KIANGSU

HONAN

Nanking

Shanghai

ANHWEI

Hangchow

Hankow

HUPEI

CHEKIANG

hungking

Yangtze-kiang

Tachen Is.

KIANGSI

Foochow

Matsu

WEICHOW

HUNAN

FUKIEN

Taipei

SHENSI

Amoy

Quemoy

TAIWAN

KWANGSI

CHUANG

Canton

KWANGTUNG

Hong Kong

HAINAN

LIVING WITH
THE
COMMUNISTS

By the same author

THE MIDDLE EAST IN REVOLUTION

LIVING WITH
THE
COMMUNISTS

CHINA 1953-5
SOVIET UNION 1962-5

HUMPHREY TREVELYAN

Gambit

INCORPORATED *Boston* 1971

First Printing

Copyright © 1971 by Lord Trevelyan

All rights reserved including the right to reproduce this
book or parts thereof in any form

Library of Congress Catalog Card Number: 70-167958

International Standard Book Number: 0-87645-054-0

Printed in the United States of America

Published in Great Britain as *Worlds Apart* by Macmillan London Ltd

*To the members of the Embassies
in Peking and Moscow
who shared these experiences
with my wife and me*

CONTENTS

PREFACE

T H I S book is an account of my experiences and impressions during the time when I was chargé d'affaires in Peking from 1953 to 1955 and Ambassador in Moscow from 1962 to 1965. I put down my recollections of China in 1957 during my enforced leisure after my return from Egypt, and of the Soviet Union when I returned from Moscow on retirement in 1965. What I have now written is based on that material and not on official records. I am, however, grateful to the Foreign and Commonwealth Office for allowing me to fill out my memory of three talks with Chou En-lai by rereading my initial reports by telegram. I found that, although I had not remembered every detail, my memory had not been at fault.

This is not a study of Chinese and Soviet Communism and it is not written for the expert, who is bound to find points to contest in my opinions or presentation of the facts. Nor is it purely personal narrative, for I have tried to give a fair view for the general reader of the policies, outlook and personalities of the Chinese and Soviet leaders. I have written primarily for my personal satisfaction, but hope that these accounts may be of interest to others who have no personal experience of these great countries. I hope also that any Chinese or Soviet officials who may find it their duty to read them will at least recognise that I have tried to be objective and to avoid any prejudice.

In the first part I have written about the Chinese Communist Government, which we had recognised. The expressions 'the Chinese' and 'the Chinese Government' therefore refer to the Government in Peking. For Chiang Kai-shek's Government I use the term 'Nationalist'. I use the name 'Peking', not 'Peiping' as the Americans do. 'Peking' means 'northern capital' and is the correct name to use if you recognise the Communist Government. 'Peiping' means 'northern plain' and is used by those who still recognise the Nationalist Government which had its capital in Nanking, or 'southern capital'. I use the Chinese name 'Taiwan' for the island often called by the old Portuguese name 'Formosa' in the West. A kind friend has instilled some discipline into the apostrophes generally used in transliterations of Chinese names. If any disorder remains, the fault is mine; but since I am writing for myself and others who do not know Chinese, since any method of transliteration is in any case only a short-hand indication of an approximate pronunciation, and since the experts hold different views, it does not seem to me to matter.

Like my book about the Middle East, this is not my story alone. It is the story of the Embassies in Peking and Moscow and therefore of my colleagues as well as of my wife and me. In both Embassies the work was a co-operative effort, which I express often by using the word 'we'. I am for ever grateful to those colleagues for their wisdom and counsel, without which I should more often have been on the wrong track. We were not by any means always right, but I believe that our approach was sound. I am also grateful to the members of the departments in the Foreign Office who were on the other end and showed us indulgence and understanding. My thanks are due to those who read the manuscript, whether in the line of duty or at my request, and who corrected the more glaring errors. I do not mention them by name, since I do not want to appear to engage them in any responsibility for what I have written.

Finally, I was tempted to call this book 'Through a Glass Darkly', since I do not claim to have seen more clearly than another.

Part I
CHINA 1953-5

I

ON THE WAY TO PEKING

SEVEN days as the solitary passenger on a China
coaster in rough seas was not the best introduction to
Communist China still barred to Western travellers
since the Revolution. I felt as if I had stepped off this
world and was embarked on a voyage to the next. It was
no ordinary voyage. The anti-piracy guards were posted
day and night, for only a week or two before a Danish
ship had been captured by the Nationalists and taken
off to Taiwan. But no incident varied the monotony of
the voyage. I sat in the little saloon reading *The Portrait of a Lady* and tried to avoid unprofitable specula-
tions about the uncertain future.

For three and a half years the British Embassy in
Peking had been in an anomalous and humiliating
position. In January 1950 after the Chinese Communists had expelled Chiang Kai-shek from the mainland
and established their Government in Peking, we had
recognised the new Government, following the Communist countries, the Indians and the Burmese, about
the same time as the Swiss, the Scandinavians, the
Dutch, the Pakistanis and the Indonesians. The Americans seemed to be waiting for the final surrender of
Chiang Kai-shek before recognising the Communists

themselves. Even after the arrest of their Consul-
General in Mukden, the seizure of their consulate in
Peking and their removal of all their officials from the
mainland, they appeared to be waiting on events, until
the Korean War caused them abruptly to change their
policy.

We had recognised the Communists, not because we
approved of them, but because they were in control of
the mainland and it was our normal practice to recognise the government in control, however much we disapproved of it, particularly where, as in China, we had
interests to defend. We had embarked on what should
have been the formal steps preliminary to the exchange
of fully accredited diplomatic missions, but when I
arrived the negotiations had for long been in abeyance.
The Chinese had refused to complete them on the
grounds that we had not effectively recognised Communist China.

Their chief cause for complaint was that we had abstained from voting in the Security Council for the expulsion of the Chinese Nationalist delegate, which they
regarded as implying our continued recognition of
the Nationalists as the legitimate government of China.
They had complaints about the treatment of what they
claimed as their property in Hong Kong and elsewhere
and, after the outbreak of the Korean war, they added
an objection to our having a consul in Taipei, the
'temporary' capital of the Nationalists on Taiwan.*
Our voting in the United Nations on the question
whether the Nationalists or the Communists should be
recognised as representing China had been distinctly
odd. Until the Korean war we had abstained. After
the war had begun, we voted once in favour of the

---

* I have used the Chinese form for Formosa throughout. See Preface,
page 10.

Communists, but reverted to abstention after the 'aggressor resolution' of February 1951.

The main complaint about property concerned seventy aircraft which had been flown to Hong Kong by the Nationalist Air Line and which were claimed by the Chinese Government. They had been sold by the Nationalists to General Claire Chennault and by him to a company which he formed and registered in the United States, the whole transaction having presumably been arranged with the Nationalists in order to defeat a Communist claim to the aircraft. In 1950 an Order in Council had been passed which debarred the Chinese Government from pleading that the case could not be heard by the courts on the grounds that one party was a sovereign government. In 1952 judgement was given in favour of the Chinese Government by a judge of the Hong Kong High Court and confirmed by a full Bench on appeal, but the Privy Council reversed the decision. The Chinese Government naturally regarded the affair as a British political move against them and, as soon as the Hong Kong Government executed the judgement, retaliated by taking over substantial British property in Shanghai.

We told the Chinese that our Consul in Taipei had relations only with the Provincial Government, not with the Government of Taiwan, still less with the rival Government of China maintained on the island by Chiang Kai-shek, which we did not recognise and with which we had no relations of any kind. With these disputes in the way, our mission in Peking remained in Chinese eyes a temporary mission engaged on negotiations for the establishment of diplomatic relations, although no negotiations were taking place and the members of the mission had no diplomatic status or immunity.

My task was not going to be easy. The armistice in Korea had just been signed, but the Korean war had left many troubles in its wake. We were not likely to find much common ground with the new Chinese Government, nor were we going to endanger our alliance with the Americans in order to try to become friends with a régime which was basically hostile to the non-Communist world. Many British subjects were still in difficulties in China. There were British subjects in prison or prevented from leaving the country; British firms were being squeezed into bankruptcy, but were not allowed to close. We were charged with doing what little we could for the American citizens who remained in China in a similar plight, though we could not officially represent American interests, since the Americans did not recognise the existence of any Chinese government other than the Nationalist Government on Taiwan.

Our decision to recognise the Chinese Government in Peking and to keep an unrecognised mission there had been strongly criticised in the United Kingdom. I reserved my judgement, but after a few months in China became convinced that the decision had been right. It would have been easy to declare ourselves insulted and close the mission, though if we had done so it might not have been so easy to get away. But that would have meant giving up any hope of improving the unhappy lot of the British still in China or of re-establishing Sino-British trade in the products in which our China merchants had dealt for a hundred years or more.

A few days in Hong Kong had given me the impression that I was about to enter a strange new world. Escorted by jeeps full of armed police, I had motored along the heavily guarded border, in the wild and beautiful scenery of the Hong Kong leased territories, reminding me in parts of Delphi, when you look from the temple down to the sea. Tough frontier-guards, armed with tommy guns, inspected us through field glasses, a formidable barrier against entry into 'People's' China, but my actual entry was an anti-climax. As we approached the harbour of Taku Bar, the first batch of security police came on board, locked up the charts and field glasses, and took over the ship. In swift contrast to the wastes of the China Sea, we were soon sailing to all appearances on land, sixty miles up the narrow river to Tientsin, looking down on either side on the little plots of neat, ordered farmland – a first sight of the laborious, concentrated cultivation of every inch of ground which is the real wealth of China.

At Tientsin a fresh horde of uniformed police and soldiery invaded the ship; but for me the formalities of entry were few. I was greeted politely by a representative of the Tientsin Municipal Government and was soon on shore. I have often since thought of two friends, husband and wife, who in the early and most difficult days of the Revolution, having with great difficulty obtained exit permits, had reached at this point the haven of a British ship about to sail to safety when the police came on board and took them off again. They stood on shore with the prospect of unknown trials in store, watching the ship sail away without them. It must have been a bleak moment.

Tientsin seemed to me to have attained an intensity of ugliness and desolation achieved by no other town in this world. I have known civilised human beings who lived there with equanimity and even pleasure in the days when the foreign community prospered and managed their own affairs in the Concession. But the immediate impression on the traveller arriving in

China in 1953 was that despair had caught the town in its grip and that decay had eaten it away. Not the romantic decay of fine buildings with a glorious past, but the sordid remains of what had always been ugly; pretentious banks and offices in 'Manchester classical', superimposed on a conglomeration of primitive huts made of mud and old kerosene-oil tins, the mark of a Chinese industrial town where the foreigner had settled, a vivid illustration of the conditions which had helped to cause the Chinese revolution.

My first night was spent in the former Consulate-General, now unoccupied, a building well up to the Tientsin average of ugliness and discomfort, a dying relic of the past, full of stored American office-furniture, with on the one side a neglected patch of weeds which had once been a garden, and on the other side a little church, in which a Chinese priest tried precariously to maintain its Christian services after the departure of the foreign missionaries, in constant battle with a hostile government. Behind the old Consulate stood a dejected block of offices, once the pride of the North China Coal Company and now the seat of the Tientsin Municipal Government. In front, the street, made in the palmy days of the Concession, was full of potholes, with paving-stones lying about in heaps, adding to the general impression of neglect and decay. In the town there remained a small foreign community, struggling against increasing disabilities and restrictions, pressed in by the conquering waves of revolution. The day train to Peking had left, so I stayed in Tientsin for twenty-four hours and my heart sank as I wondered whether this desolate city, exhibiting the worst features of East and West, a shell almost emptied of its former European occupants and seeming no longer to have any purpose, was a foretaste of my life in China.

The same official courteously saw me off at the station on the next day, but it was clear that I was not going to be given any diplomatic privileges on the train. We squeezed with difficulty, on a hot and sticky afternoon, into a coach full to bursting with Chinese peasants and soldiers, their children and their bundles of bedding and pots and pans. The train ambled over the North China plain, stopping at every station, while the all-pervasive loud-speaker battered our ears with the songs which were to become so familiar from daily repetition. Before we reached Peking, I caught my first glimpse of the walls, the most famous city walls in the world, which gave Peking much of its compelling charm. My spirits immediately lifted; the horror of Tientsin was forgotten. Here, surely, was a city in which one could live with pleasure, whatever the trials and difficulties of daily life.

The train slid imperceptibly from a crawl to a halt and, battered and sweaty, I emerged to encounter a formal greeting from an official of the Protocol Department and a warm welcome from the diplomatic colleagues who were to become my close companions and friends in that restricted society. And so I embarked with curiosity but with some misgiving upon my new Chinese life.

2

IN THE EMBASSY

My first impression of life in Peking was that I had been admitted to a superior mental home provided with every comfort, but having no contact with the outside world beyond the limits of the British Embassy compound. This famous compound was a haven in which we could insulate ourselves from all but the sounds of the Communist world outside. These were, however, insistent. Loud-speakers, imperfectly adjusted and of great power, were placed all over the city and were continually in use. They roused the comrades early every morning. At fixed times twice a day they emitted the same tunes to accompany the eurhythmics prescribed for all State employees. Daily they ground out the same songs from their limited repertoire, excerpts from the film-opera, *The White-haired Girl*, the story of a heroic girl Communist during the civil war, folk songs which fitted the Party line, Russian propaganda songs; after a few weeks one knew every note of them. I still seem to hear those loud-speakers exhorting, nagging, penetrating the brain, in the streets, in the trains, in the hotels. But suddenly, a year after I came to Peking, they were damped down. Perhaps they disturbed the comrades at their work. It was a blessed relief.

Our legal title to the compound, or at least to part of it, was doubtful. We still had eighteen acres after the new Government had expropriated the barracks of the old Legation guard, the tennis-courts and the swimming-pool. The Russians had given up their old military compound under the Sino-Soviet treaty of 1950 and were building a new Embassy in the north of the city. So the Chinese made a similar generous gesture to themselves on our behalf. What we had left was quite enough for us. The compound lay in the northern part of the old Legation quarter, and was surrounded by a high wall, the northern side of which gave on to the great east–west street, the Ch'ang-an ta-chieh, running to the south of the T'ien-an men, the main gate of the old imperial palace. Between the wall and the street was a large space, known formerly as the glacis, which the foreign governments in the old days had insisted should be left free of buildings and other encumbrances, in order to provide a field of fire for the defence of the Legation quarter. On the inside of the wall had been inserted a stone inscribed 'Lest we forget', the only visible surviving memory of the siege of the Legation during the Boxer rising. The Chinese, too, had not forgotten.

The foreign missions had lived together, each with its guard of foreign troops, under the conditions imposed on the Chinese after the suppression of the Boxers. They had become consulates during the period of Nationalist rule in Nanking. It was hardly surprising that this foreign enclave, like the international settlements, was bitterly resented by the Chinese who, since the Revolution, had filled the glacis with new buildings for the ministries and had expropriated the embassies of countries not in diplomatic relations with them. The American Embassy was the headquarters of the Peking Communist Party. The Belgian Embassy was being kept warm for them by the Burmese. The French Embassy was used for distinguished foreign guests. The East Germans had inherited the old German Embassy and the Hungarians the Austrian. The Japanese Embassy opposite us was heavily guarded and we assumed it to be the headquarters of some military or police unit. An old resident told me that during the Japanese occupation he saw a motor-cyclist lose control of his machine and smash the sentry against the wall, at which the passers-by roared with laughter. It is a curious characteristic of that most civilised race, the Chinese, that they think pain funny. When the Communists were advancing on Peking, the Nationalists used the glacis as an air-strip and flew out as much of the valuable porcelain as they could get hold of in time from the Imperial Palace. This forms the basis of the collections now in Taiwan. They asked the British consul then in charge of our compound for permission to break our wall to extend the air-strip, but he stoutly refused.

Not being an officially recognised diplomatic mission, we were in continual anxiety lest the whole compound should be confiscated. For the time being, we were left in peace. But we knew that a new road through our compound was being planned and that the whole Legation quarter was doomed. A new diplomatic ghetto was to be built on an unattractive site among the factories on the east side of the city outside the walls. In due course, after my time, the British Embassy had to move there and was burnt during the 'cultural revolution'.

As you entered the main gate of the Embassy compound, past the sour-looking Chinese sentry incon-

gruously inhabiting the sentry-box surmounted by the
Royal Arms, you saw on the right the T'ing-erh, an open
hall with a stone base, built of wood in the Chinese
style, with scarlet pillars and a painted architrave, transformed in the winter into probably the coldest bad-
minton-court in the world. A stone path led from it to
the old Ambassador's house beyond, the core of which
was a palace reputedly built for one of Ch'ien Lung's
innumerable offspring, but which had lost its character
by additions made to suit the European way of life. You
entered through a hall in the Chinese style leading into
a set of reception rooms, three in Chinese, two in
Western style. The house had suffered many vicissi-
tudes. During the Nationalists' rule in Nanking, it had
been used like other embassies for consular staff. In the
war it had housed infirm British internees and had
been looted by the Japanese. It was therefore practically
unfurnished and, since our appeals to the Ministry of
Works for chair covers fell on deaf ears, we were compelled to cart furniture from the other houses in the
compound for our official parties.

To the left of the T'ing-erh, past a ship's bell hang-
ing under a painted Chinese canopy, was the chapel, a
modest plain building, combining happily enough
Georgian style and a Chinese roof. In it the head of the
mission read Mattins once a month to a Protestant congregation from the diplomatic missions – Scandinavians,
Dutch, Swiss, Indians, Pakistanis, Indonesians and
British – for no Chinese priest, not even the Anglican
Bishop of Peking, dared to face the sentry. And so it
happened that the only clergyman to have taken a service in our chapel in three years was Dr Hewlett Johnson, the 'Red Dean', at the insistent invitation of my
predecessor, which he could hardly refuse, though a
guest of the Chinese Government and not anxious to

fraternise with the British Embassy.

In this Western island, surrounded by a sea of Asian Communism militantly opposed to all forms of Christianity, our services were for some of us not so much a profession of religious faith as a reaffirmation of our own values in a city where we would daily read that we were opposing the forces of progress, bent on war for our own selfish ends and oppressing our workers in order to grind out of them ever larger profits for the reactionary capitalists. At Christmas a party from the Embassy went round the non-Communist missions singing the old carols, drinking with their hospitable hosts and helping to keep up the spirits of our little, isolated community.

It was all very picturesque. The comfortable little houses of the staff, with their Chinese roofs and red pillars, were scattered through the compound. My wife arrived in the height of winter, when nothing seems to be alive and the wind from the Gobi Desert sweeps over Peking. We lived in a comfortable, solid Edwardian house with nothing Chinese about it, separated from the Soviet Embassy by a high wall carrying an ominous, but, I believed, uncharged electric fence.

It was a continual delight to watch the Chinese gardeners at work in a country where the seasons behave with disciplined regularity. Each year on the same day the seeds were planted, the little plants placed in deep trenches, covered against the frost and planted out on the day of the spring festival. The northern Chinese peasant and worker are incomparable in their diligence and tidiness. In what other country would the housepainters clear up the mess when they break off for a half-hour's midday rest? Our personal servants were still of the old breed, the most perfect servants I have ever known. We could not deny that we were very comfortable.

We had our own facilities for recreation, a tennis-court, a squash-court, a library and a social club, a hall with a stage in which we held dances, Scottish reel parties, whist drives, film shows and bingo parties, something for all tastes. In Peking there were no social distinctions. One could have ambassadors and Chancery guards happily at the same party. Since the old Peking Club was by now practically dead, gloomily empty with its library of non-Communist books locked up for fear that they might corrupt the comrades, our social club was a centre for the non-Communist diplomatic colony. Our rare films, however bad or old, drew practically every member of it, starved for non-ideological entertainment. Young Indonesians and Pakistanis became adept at Scottish dances, and the Christmas children's parties had to be restricted to the British children when the Asian missions increased to such a size that, with an average of six children to each married secretary, the numbers became unmanageable.

In the Peking atmosphere these activities were of real value. We were living in conditions which, however comfortable, were not unlike an internment camp. We were at the end of the line. The Queen's Messenger, with our letters from home, came by sea only once a month. Owing to the difficulty of getting staff in and out, the tour of duty without leave was two years. To keep up morale among our own staff, to help to build up a sense of solidarity among the non-Communist missions, was an essential task for all of us.

We were very close to our diplomatic colleagues. Nedyam Raghavan, the Indian Ambassador, had been a member of Subhas Chandra Bhose's anti-British Government in Malaya during the war. When I had men-

tioned this to Malcolm MacDonald in Singapore on my
way to Peking, he had sensibly replied, 'So would I have
been in his position.' Raghavan was a sensitive, intelligent man who became a close personal friend. The Pakistani, General Raza, who also became a good friend, was
a first-class product of Sandhurst and the Indian Army,
who went for the Chinese in the best military style when
they were proposing to do something particularly obnoxious. It was important to remember that his cup of
tea had to be filled to the brim. A large part of the
energies of the Indian and Pakistani Embassies was
taken up with a paper battle with each other in the
Embassy bulletins about Kashmir, which achieved nothing except the exhibition to the Chinese of their domestic quarrels. Fortunately, the two Ambassadors
remained good friends. My periodic suggestions to
one or the other that it was rather a fatuous way of
spending their energies was about as much use as making a similar suggestion to the Reverend Ian Paisley and
Bernadette Devlin.

The Indonesian Ambassador considered Indonesian
politics the only proper subject for conversation. On
one occasion, after about forty minutes on this theme, I
asked him about the quarrel between Sukarno and the
Ladies' Club over Sukarno's new acquisition of a second wife. He assured me that Sukarno had taken this
step for medical reasons on doctor's orders. We forgave
him his discourses for the sake of 'Auntie', a house
agent from Djakarta, a most popular figure and a pil-
lar of our church. The Danish Ambassador, who had
started his career selling stamps in St Petersburg, was a
specialist on Iceland, a collector of clocks and a con-
noisseur of claret, which hardly explained why he had
been sent to Peking in his sixties as his first diplomatic
post. He was not happy. He would discourse on the

beauties of Peking and its perfect climate in an obvious effort to convince himself that he was well off. I suggested to him that he might take a few days' holiday in Hong Kong. He fiercely rejected the suggestion. 'Why not?' I asked. 'Because I would never come back.'

The Finnish Ambassador was said to be a Communist dentist, but somehow became an honorary non-Communist, since his diplomatic staff were well on the other side and perhaps also because he had caviar flown in from Moscow and his blinis were excellent. The American wife of the Swedish Ambassador, also close friends, bore with equanimity the torrent of abuse of her country which poured out daily in speeches, in the Press and on the radio. The Norwegian chargé d'affaires was much to be admired, for he had somehow convinced his Government for several years that his post was Shanghai and that he was therefore entitled permanently to draw a special subsistence allowance for being on tour in Peking. One Swiss was musical, the next a formidable hill-walker; so we had much in common with both. It was an agreeable little community.

Four of the old British civilian community had hung on. One, a happy irresponsible child of nature for whom we grew to have real affection, had the task of closing the Peking branch of the Hong Kong and Shanghai Bank. How he had become a banker, no one could understand. He loved Peking and only asked to be allowed to stay. He would potter happily about in his Chinese clothes and in his Chinese house, surrounded by his treasures and endearing himself to everyone by his sheer good nature. Fortunately for him, it took three years to close the bank. The Chinese officials, in pursuit of the policy of never bringing any negotiations with a British firm to a conclusion, spent every day in the consideration of some minute point, magnifying every little difficulty. To a British manager with a family in England whom he had not seen for years, this was a perpetual torture; to our friend in Peking it was a heaven-sent prolongation of a beautiful sunset, which he knew must soon come to an end. When he left, it was like pulling up a plant and he did not live long in Europe. Soon after we left, the old breed of British resident finally became extinct.

There were other British and Australians in Peking, whom we only saw when they came to have the births of their babies registered or in the vain hope of having their passports renewed. I called them the twilight brigade. They were the Communists, mostly old journalists, employed by the Chinese on minor literary tasks. They were pathetic. Who knows what private disturbance or maladjustment had caused them to tear up their roots and plunge into the Chinese Communist world where they could never assimilate themselves to Chinese life and would always be suspect as renegades? There would be the initial excitement, the welcome, the flattery accorded to the recruit from the other side. Then would come the inevitable change to neglect and indifference. They could hardly expect a welcome if they returned home. One at least might have to face prosecution. When later the British journalists began to come in, these old journalists would sit on the bed in the hotel room while the visitors typed their despatches, trying to smell Fleet Street.

While nearly all the foreigners who wanted to leave were being kept in China, nearly all those who wanted to stay were being expelled. When I arrived, there were still two German antique-dealers in Peking. Their characters could not have been more different and they were not on speaking terms. One was an amiable, gentle man who had ambled fecklessly through life and had been washed up in China where he had just stayed on, absorbed in Chinese porcelain, smoking opium, in the hands of an apparently faithful but unscrupulous servant, his affairs always on the brink of disaster. He lived among his collections of porcelain, scrolls, glass pictures, clocks and trinkets, with his little bed in the corner, sharing meals with his servants, dressed in Chinese clothes, only deprived (perhaps not always) by the new China of his opium. He rarely went out except to a meal with a friend in an embassy. Almost every piece of his porcelain was of interest, almost none perfect. I started to learn from him, spending hours in his shop, fingering his shards. He had no place in the new scheme of things. The police took their opportunity. A friend, on leaving China, had left with him an old cabinet. He had never looked inside. A disgruntled servant found a few old cartridges in it and reported it to the police. In twenty-four hours he was out, after his friends had subscribed to pay off, according to law, the servants who had nursed him, provided for his wants and in the end betrayed him.

The other also lived among his collections. No pieces were broken. All, if we could believe it, were of immense value. He was given four months to leave. He wrote to Kuo Mo-jo, the Minister of Culture, hoping to get permission to export some objects against a present of others. But there was no reason for the Chinese to make a bargain with him. They could easily take it all. He overstayed his time, was arrested and was lucky to be deported without a prison sentence. Soon afterwards, the Chinese dealers put it about that many of his tomb figures were on sale in Liu-li ch'ang, the street of the antique shops, labelled as fakes.

During my first months in Peking, the Soviet Ambassador in Peking was Mr V. V. Kuznetsov, whom I afterwards came to know well in Moscow, when he was First Deputy Minister of Foreign Affairs. It was understandable that he should avoid all contact with us in Peking. His business was with the Chinese, who did not recognise us as a diplomatic mission. He appeared to be under instructions to play up to the Asian heads of mission, though, judging by what one of them told us, he rather overplayed his hand. Later, when we had become diplomatically respectable and were giving parties, the Soviet Counsellor, in his normal state of effusiveness after a party, remarked, 'We must break down the wall between our embassies.' So the next day I asked him to lunch and, some days later, after the new Soviet Ambassador had returned from tour, received a refusal on the grounds of pressure of work.

By the time we were recognised by the Chinese, Mr Kuznetsov had been succeeded by Pavel Yudin, a heavy-handed professor of Marxist philosophy; he had made himself particularly obnoxious to the Yugoslavs at the time of Tito's breach with Stalin in 1948, when he was in Belgrade as representative of the Cominform and the editor of the Cominform newspaper. Dedijer, in his *Tito Speaks*, draws an unflattering picture of Yudin cringing before Zdhanov, and quotes the Soviet joke about Yudin as being the best philosopher among the N.K.V.D. men and the best N.K.V.D. man among the philosophers. At this time, my wife and I were included in the category of people to be cultivated. We exchanged dinners amicably enough, though I nearly lost my temper when he chose at dinner at my house to bring out the old Soviet accusation that we had deliberately delayed the second front in order to increase the Soviet Army's difficulties. When I told him that I was leaving to go to Egypt, he asked me why I was leaving a great for a small country and said that he did not know anything about Egypt except that there had been some Pharaohs. I said, 'Have you not heard about the imperialist exploitation of Egypt?' Two years later his line would have been very different. His favourite remark was that he was not a diplomat and, even after a year of it, he had not found out what an ambassador did. Evidently the Soviet Government had the same impression, since soon afterwards he was returned to an institute of philosophy where he remained until his death a few years later.

Russians were at this time swarming over China. In Peking the Soviet Embassy was given precedence over all other missions, and Mao and the other top people were seen regularly at their official parties. They organised vast exhibitions in Peking, Shanghai and Canton, and presented the buildings and exhibits to the Chinese. Russian ballet and opera was seen for the first time in China. A member of my staff was sitting behind two Chinese at the Russian opera. One fell asleep. The other indignantly nudged him, saying, 'Comrade, it is your patriotic duty to keep awake.'

The Russian experts were carefully isolated outside working hours and few were to be seen in the streets. In the suburbs of Shanghai I saw what appeared to be an internment camp, surrounded by barbed wire, with arc lights and armed sentries on high platforms. It was a hostel for Soviet technicians. Even in those days it was not an easy life for members of the East European Communist missions. Some of their commercial diplomats told us later that they were followed everywhere by the Chinese police, to the extent of having a policeman sitting in their room in a Shanghai hotel when they were on tour. We heard, too, that the Czech Consul-General in Shanghai had abandoned his holiday in the hills because he was followed on every walk. As far as we could see, we were never followed inside or outside Peking.

The saddest foreign community in China were the White Russians. Many had grown up there, mostly in Manchuria, having lost all connection with Russia after the Revolution. To most of them, the only hope in life was emigration to Australia or, if that could not be arranged, to Brazil. The Inter-Governmental Committee for European migration did admirable work in helping to get them settled outside China. Australia gave hope to many for whom there was otherwise no light ahead. By the end of 1954 the Soviet Government were putting on pressure to get them back to the Soviet Union to colonise the 'virgin lands' in Central Asia and Siberia, and many, in their desperation and under strong compulsion, responded. It was curious later to meet in Moscow the doctor of the British Consulate-General in Shanghai.

The first few years of the Revolution had been the roughest. During those years, a new Head of Chancery had just arrived. In his first few days a servant came back to the compound and reported that he had seen the Head of Chancery's wife's brother-in-law, an Italian, being paraded through the city bound in a jeep. He was taken to the Temple of Heaven and shot there for alleged conspiracy to murder Mao Tse-tung. If the charge had been true, it would have been a most inefficient and amateur affair. It was alleged that the conspirators, who included the American Military Attaché, had been intending to kill Mao as he stood on the Great Gate of the Imperial Palace for the May Day procession, by lobbing a mortar at him over the roof from a concealed point several streets in the rear. It was certainly a most improbable story.

By the time I arrived, the atmosphere was quieter,

but intense effort was still necessary to ensure our bare existence. It had taken two years after the closure of the British Consulate-General in Canton and the intervention of the Indian Ambassador before an exit permit could be obtained for the Consul-General. It took as long to secure the release of the Consul at Amoy. It is difficult to see why the Chinese wanted to keep them there. These long-suffering officials were compelled to remain idle at their posts for the whole of this time, quite alone without any other non-Chinese left there, their old non-Communist Chinese friends being afraid to associate with them any longer. It must have been a very unpleasant experience.

The Consul-General in Shanghai was not recognised as having an official position, since we were not recognised in Peking. We could not get permission to replace the acting Consul-General and he was forced to stay until we could regularise our own position. It took about six months to get entry permits for our staff in Peking. We had regular contact with only the Protocol Department, and the Chinese Secretariat were occupied in endless petty negotiations about the details of our life. If our stores and luggage were imported free of duty (and we had to import everything except fresh food) it was by favour, which might easily be revoked. Our unrecognised position was precarious, and a move by the British Government interpreted as hostile might at any time have destroyed the shaky foundations of our existence.

Our Chinese clerical staff were mostly members of the old British and American embassies. We could not get rid of any staff, though, particularly in our office in Shanghai, the old employees of the American offices had very little to do. A new-style trade union had been established in our compound in Peking and was determined to exact all it could from our defenceless position. The police were on the side of the union, and the Protocol Department did little to help. A complaint was made by a member of the Chinese staff against one of our British employees. The union demanded an enquiry to which we felt bound to agree. We applied for an exit permit for him. Up to the last moment before he was due to leave, we had no reply. At last, to our relief, the permit came through half an hour before his train was due to leave.

Another member of the staff laid himself open to prosecution under Chinese law. We were thankful when we got him away. In the early days the mission had suffered a number of defeats at the hands of the union. We felt strong enough to give battle on some small issues and at least held our own, but it was all very tricky while we were so vulnerable and we had to be careful not to give the Chinese an excuse to shut us down. In the turmoil of the late sixties, during the 'cultural revolution', most of the old Chinese staff finally disappeared without notice and had to be replaced by men selected by the Government.

We felt a sense of peace on coming back to the old compound from the outside world, but it was important not to get compound-bound and from the beginning I made it a point to leave the compound at least once every day. For holidays we still had our bungalows at Peitaho on the Yellow Sea, which was gradually being turned into an official holiday-resort. We owed their retention during these few years to the Pakistanis who provided a little Asian cover by renting one or two bungalows from us for the holiday season; but we did not keep them for long. Since my day they have gone with the old compound.

And so we lived in Peking, happily enough in spite

of all the trials and uncertainties of our position, within our walls, never isolating ourselves, but with some measure of isolation thrust upon us. We were a strange island. Outside, all the dogs in the city had been shot on the grounds of hygiene. Inside, being a British community, we had a fearsome collection of inbred mongrels, strictly rationed to one per family. Outside was the regimentation of Chinese Communism. Inside was a collection of British individualists who could be led but not driven, who still valued above everything a life which gave you the freedom to buy your own ticket, choose your own amusements, think your own thoughts, miss your train, lose your way, grumble at the Government and turn off its propaganda.

3

THE CITY OF PEKING

PEKING'S reputation as an enchanting city was still deserved. For the first few weeks you could not see it. You saw only a sprawling, rectangular city with straight, treeless streets, lined with blank walls which turned their backs on the passers-by, for Chinese private life is turned in on itself and does not value display. The streets were all north–south or east–west, which made life easier in a country where, if you asked Mr Liu whether he had seen Mr Chou, he might reply that he had seen Mr Chou going south-east a moment ago and where, in the old days, you honoured your guest by placing him at the dinner table facing south.

The visitor to a Chinese house traditionally entered round a corner, so that the spirits could not get in with him, since they could only move in straight lines. So from the street outside you could see nothing of the courtyards surrounded by one-storey pavilions which made up the bulk of the Peking houses. Down miles of these streets, nothing was to be seen but walls, little shops, glimpses of courtyards in the poorer quarters. Suddenly, the eye was met by a great tower, a temple roof, a fine gate, which stood out in the drab uniformity of the little streets. In a month the city had caught you, and it never lost its hold.

The new Chinese Government was gradually renovating with care and taste the great architecture of the past, the landscape compositions formed of buildings, lakes, streams, temples, bridges, courtyards, gardens of rocks looking like sculptures by Henry Moore, always enclosed in walls like a picture frame; the Imperial Palace, the Temple of Heaven, the Summer Palace and many more. A building might easily be of the early fifteenth or late nineteenth century. It made little difference, for the Chinese had had the trick of building in a living style which had lasted for over a thousand years. They had not self-consciously copied the old, nor striven after a new effect, nor tried to improve on the classic models by increasing the size, multiplying ornaments or distorting proportions. Western experience was not relevant to the Chinese scene. In an early stage of their history the Chinese had found a few architectural shapes and colours which satisfied them and they kept on building in the same style, not pastiches of the old, but in a manner which, however ancient, was truly contemporary. Peking was rightly built of houses of a single storey, so that everyone in his central courtyard had the benefit of the glorious sun of northern China. With its sudden contrasts between private modesty and public magnificence, its sense of architectural purpose, its complete absence of vulgarity or ostentation, it was a city admirably designed to form the setting of a great civilisation.

Twentieth-century Europe fortunately had little chance to do more than minor damage, by the erection of a few featureless public buildings, notably the seven-storey French hotel in a commanding position on the great east–west street. But twentieth-century Communism, only five years after its final victory, was already doing its best to destroy the old character of the city in order that it should match the new dynasty's desire to have a modern capital. The Communists erected high buildings on the edge of the Imperial Palace, doubled the Peking hotel, spoilt the famous view from the bridge over the northern lake (the Pei hai), and chose the area of critical importance for the planning of Peking, between the city and the western hills, for the development of an industrial suburb. They have since created their Red Square in front of their Kremlin, but that I have not seen. A visitor to modern London may observe that they are not the only people to make this sort of mistake.

But the saddest story to those who loved the old Peking is the fate of the famous walls. It is a tragedy to our way of thinking that the Chinese Communists have not realised the immense asset which they had in the Peking walls, though they have exploited 200 yards of the Great Wall of China as a tourist attraction to a point where it has become like Brighton beach on a bank holiday. Chiang Kai-shek was no more enlightened. He had been about to destroy the wall of Nanking, I am told, when he was ejected. I once stood with Chou En-lai before a print of medieval Stockholm in the Swedish Embassy in Peking. He asked whether the walls still existed. I replied that I thought they had mostly gone, but that I hoped he was not going to destroy the walls of Peking. Chou said that they might if everyone else destroyed theirs. And so they did.

They started in my time with the picturesque painted wooden or brick gates known as P'ai-lou, which had embellished the main streets, though of no great antiquity. We were told that the traffic required their removal, though at that time there was hardly any. One of these gates was named 'Peace on earth', and there was fear and resentment in the neighbourhood when it went. People were forbidden to walk on the city wall, and we could only get on to it by easing our way through the domestic washing of the soldiers who were lodged by it at the point where there stood in those days one of the famous sights of Peking, the fantastic bronze astronomical instruments erected by the Jesuits for the Emperor Ch'ien Lung. They say that in later years the walls have almost disappeared and that now, doubtless with immense labour, the authorities are pulling down the great gates which dominated the flat Peking landscape and gave the city its striking contrasts, being prepared to destroy some part of the ancient beauty of their famous city in the interests of their concept of modernity or convenience. Of course, they will regret it one day, just as the Russians regret the old churches which were destroyed in the early days of their revolution, but by then it will be too late.

The architects of the new buildings, offices, hotels, barracks, factories, which were to transform Peking into a modern city, did not wholly depart from their old traditions, using Chinese ornamental features which suited the Peking scene. But the practice of the arts was a perilous profession in Mao's China. We could only assume that the architects' plans had been approved by the Party, but they woke up one morning to find themselves unmasked as criminal deviationists who had wasted large sums on unnecessary ornament, on archaisms, on far too costly materials. The architect of the new Peking Hotel was condemned for the expensive decoration of the great hall in which the Party leaders gave their official banquets and which had been unreservedly praised to us by the young members of the Protocol Department. He was even accused of making the reception and dining rooms wastefully large, although he must surely have been working to the requirements of the Party leaders, whose programme for entertaining Asian prime ministers invariably included dinner in the Peking Hotel for at least 800.

This sudden change we could only attribute to the top people wanting to follow the Moscow fashion, for this was the time of the Moscow–Peking honeymoon, as the Russians later called it. A few weeks before, Khrushchev had made a speech in Moscow to the Soviet Master Builders in which, with much justification, he had ridiculed the clichés of Soviet architecture, in particular the indiscriminate use of the Leningrad admiralty spire, and had given a reasoned exposition of the principles of good architectural design. The Chinese architectural storm broke suspiciously soon after this. Local report had it that the leading architect had adopted the old Chinese stratagem of taking refuge in hospital until the storm blew over, or at least until he discovered the form of confession which would clear him and enable him to continue his profession under the new directive, which was not to improve design but to build more cheaply.

Much of the colour had gone out of the Peking streets. Every man and woman, and almost all the children, were dressed in the drab monotony of blue boilersuits, plain cotton in summer, quilted in winter, the jacket buttoned up to the neck in the Sun Yat-sen style, as it was called, made familiar by Stalin and Mao. In 1955 a directive was issued advocating a return to the traditional tight dresses for women in order to save cotton; but a pretty dress could mark a family as capitalist and invite unwelcome attentions from the police or the local Party representative, and we only saw Chinese dresses of the old style being worn at official parties by the wives of high officials who were secure. Asians keep sex under wraps, and the Chinese Communist régime was puritan; so it was not surprising that I only once saw a boy and girl sitting together in a public park.

The shops were empty of all foreign goods except Communist literature and old tins of American food, left over from the days when the Nationalist officials were selling United Nations relief supplies on the black market; they were by this time of doubtful quality. The streets were almost empty of traffic, but under the local rules every car was required to sound its horn when approaching a policeman on traffic duty, or a street intersection, or when overtaking or passing another car. The noise was therefore considerable. There were a few old American and new Russian cars belonging to the Government. No private person dared be seen in his own car. There were few buses and no taxis. The Japanese had introduced bicycle rickshaws, but the poor rickshaw men were only too obviously not a favoured class. They still made some sort of a living with their tattered and ancient equipages, mostly falling to pieces, but there were no new machines nor spare parts to be bought, even if they had had the money for them. They were a pathetic relic of private enterprise allowed to linger on until the State could provide new means of public transport.

Many features of the old Peking life remained. In the early mornings the old men still took their birds in carefully covered cages for an airing, letting them out occasionally to sit on their fingers. Young and old men were still seen shadow-boxing in the parks. Peasant families came in to see the sights. There were the ingenious hand-made toys, the shadow-puppets manipulated on sticks, the fighting crickets in their cylindrical boxes made of gourd with elaborately carved ivory lids, and there was the famous fair on open ground opposite the Temple of Heaven, a perpetual delight with its jugglers, acrobats, trapeze artists, Chinese opera and stalls and booths of all kinds.

The fair was later dispersed as part of a plan for the provision of entertainment in the provinces. My Counsellor, John Addis, was an habitué of the fair and well known to the performers. Some years later he was walking along a street in Central China when he was suddenly clapped on the back by the best trapeze artist of the old fair who urged him to attend that night's performance of his troupe, then on tour. The best actors, jugglers and acrobats performed for important official visitors or became political–cultural exports, and Chou En-lai in all seriousness announced in a speech at the party for the Finnish National Day that the visit of some Chinese acrobats to Finland was an important sign of the improvement of relations between the two countries.

At the Peking fair I used to watch two men engaged in a contest which seemed to illustrate the Chinese Government's tactics over Taiwan. They would each take a long stick and spar for an opening, one seeming just about to crack it down on the other's skull. But it never quite happened. Then they would arm themselves with murderous-looking swords, flash them round each other's faces and take great swipes at each other's legs, the apparent victim jumping at the critical moment so that the sword flashed harmlessly by just under his toes. All the time a barrage of violent backchat was going on, just like the Chinese propaganda against the Americans and Chiang Kai-shek. A little homely knowledge of Chinese customs sometimes helped in the interpretation of politics.

To the foreigner seeking a little diversion there were three important streets: Furniture Street, Embroidery Street and Liu-li ch'ang. The information would go round that number 27 in Embroidery Street had some fine 'tribute silk', or that a Ming table had been seen in Furniture Street. Liu-li ch'ang was at this time still of the company of the famous streets of antique shops round the world, the Musqi in Cairo, the Marché des Puces, the Kaitstrasse in Berlin, Cat Street in Hong Kong, the old Caledonian Market. It was an unpretentious little street. In the front of the shop would be the inferior Ch'ing pots, which form the staple of the English country-house collections. But the shop-keeper could sometimes be induced to produce a good piece of Sung or Ming porcelain, or one could rummage in a cupboard and find, as I did, a fourteenth-century 'under-glaze red' vase, now looking very important in a prominent case in the King Edward VII Gallery in the British Museum.

In the shops the prices were marked and there was no bargaining. It had been very different in the old days. Sir Percival David, perhaps the greatest private collector of Chinese porcelain, told me how he had selected two inexpensive pieces of jade in a shop in Liu-li ch'ang as Christmas presents for friends in Peking. He had offered the price asked. The shop-keeper had looked at the pieces he had selected through a magnifying-glass, compared them with other pieces in the tray, put them down and walked off into the back of the shop. Sir Percival's secretary had explained that this was not a serious transaction, but the shop-keeper was upset because Sir Percival had not bargained. He said he could not see any difference between the pieces selected and the other pieces in the tray. He was unhappy and suspicious. In the end, he took the money, but Sir Percival was never again able to buy anything of good quality in that shop. Confidence had been destroyed.

The best pieces would be brought to the house after luncheon by a small number of dealers, who still expected you to bargain and on whom I look back with affection and regret. It was a recurring excitement as the dirty cloths were untied. An agony of indecision followed as we tried to decide whether the piece offered was genuine Sung or a Japanese fake. It took a year's hard work to begin to train the eye and it was almost too late when, helped by the superior knowledge of John Addis, I learnt that they were all genuine and that the greatest error was to doubt. I still find it hard not to regret the fine pieces which I failed to buy.

The Chinese forbade the export of any piece more than eighty years old, but allowed the diplomatic corps to take out their small collections. We played fair in return. We did not seek to take out any national treasures and displayed our pots in our houses to Chinese official visitors. We were few and what we took without commercial motives for our own delight was a drop in the ocean. Soon after I left China, the supply of good pieces dried up with the extension of the system of joint State–private ownership of commerce, and the enforcement of a rule that all valuable objects must first be offered to the State for the newly organised provincial museums. So much has been lost to China in the last hundred years through sale, looting by foreign armies and removal by the Nationalists, that any sensible government, Communist or not, would have taken measures to prevent the further drain of works of art from the country.

In and around Peking we made the most of our opportunities. We only gave up the attempt to visit a temple if we failed to get past the sentry and then tried but failed to get a pass from the Protocol Department. We observed without surprise that the eunuchs described by Osbert Sitwell had left their temple home, but we could still see there the picture of the famous Ming general who, left behind by the Emperor on his way to the wars to look after the imperial harem, had taken the precaution of castrating himself in advance and secreting the evidence in the Emperor's saddle-bags in order to forestall the inevitable charge of breach of trust on the Emperor's return.

We could mark the sad progress since Sitwell's visit of the gradual destruction of the last vestiges of the old Summer Palace, partly built by the Jesuits, sacked by Lord Elgin's troops, its ruins ever since progressively removed as building material or, curiously, to aid some process in the manufacture of soda water. We found endless delight in repeated visits to the great palace, the 'Forbidden City', with its fine museums showing no signs of the Nationalists' looting of art treasures, the exquisite proportions of the Temple of Heaven, the enchanting lakes and pavilions of the Summer Palace, the superb acrobatics of the Peking Opera, not yet overlaid by the new ideology; also the incomparable Peking restaurants, dirty hovels most of them, with rickety old tables and chairs, the crudest utensils and some of the best food in the world. Each gave the food of a different province of this immense country, the solid and appetising fare of the sturdy men of Shantung, the Mongolian grill, the hot peppers of Szechwan, the birds'-nest soup and sharks' fins of Canton. It was right to be greedy in Peking.

My predecessor had been virtually confined to the city and all foreigners had been prevented from going beyond the approaches to the western hills which begin a few miles from Peking and continue for hundreds of miles to the north-west. The time came when we thought we could venture a little further afield. Great caution was necessary, since China was obsessed by fear of spies. We were still an object of official suspicion and had only the flimsiest of diplomatic cover. We had an obligation to our own Government not to risk arrest and perhaps expulsion for entry into a forbidden area. We knew that if we asked for permission to visit the old temples in the hills we should meet with refusal or, at best, silence. But the western hills, that moon landscape of bare ridges fading into the immense distances of China, dotted with exquisite little temples, were an irresistible attraction.

Each Sunday, with great circumspection, we penetrated a little further, taking the next opportunity in casual conversation to tell the members of the Protocol Department where we had been. The time came when we found that we could walk the whole day in the hills, round the Ming tombs or along miles of the Great Wall. These days in the clear air of northern China, the sharp outlines of the hills, the withdrawn beauty of the Emperors' tombs in their exquisite mountain setting, the inescapable romance of the wall, remain a vivid memory. To sit on one of the high hills on the far side of the wall and look back on it winding over the ridges, up and down precipitous cliffs, never compromising with the ground, in itself compensated for all the stale and unprofitable argument in which we were continually engaged. The new dynasty, in the propagation of its doctrine, was contriving to behave like the old dynasties which had spent so much labour and so many lives in building and rebuilding this wall. My successors have found themselves subject to increasing restrictions in their movements round Peking. The western hills have been placed out of bounds; journeys to the Wall are confined to the spot where the road meets it, always full of comradely and Asian delegations; even the Ming tombs can only be visited occasionally with special permission. Much of the old delight of life in Peking has gone.

Further afield we could not go without a pass, and with a pass only to Tientsin, Shanghai, Hangchow and Canton. My recognition came too late to enable me to take part in the official tours arranged for the diplomatic corps. My successor, Con O'Neill, was able to take part in such a tour through central China and his record of it is a classic in the Foreign Office's archives. Every luxury, down to dressing-gowns, slippers and tooth-brushes, was provided on the special train. For part of the trip the party travelled in buses, the first for ambassadors, the second for chargés d'affaires and the third for lavatories.

The Chinese people were not hostile to us. On the contrary, we invariably met with friendly and natural behaviour from the ordinary people, soldiers off duty, townspeople and villagers, in our walks in Peking and the western hills. They were not embarrassed at being seen talking to us. At first they always assumed that we were Russian and the children would cry after us 'Su-lien'. 'Ying-kuo', we retorted, and were met with the same laughing friendliness. At Peitaho we chatted with the workers lucky enough to be sent on a sea-side holiday. A member of the Embassy once came across a party of school-children on the beach, under the direction of a teacher, picking up insects with chop-sticks and putting them into bottles. They warned him gravely not to walk on the sand, since it was contaminated with American germs. He took off his shoes and walked across barefoot. They all roared with laughter.

In Peking the hand of the new masters was everywhere apparent in the many official buildings guarded by sentries. One section of the old palace quarter was barred to all entry except for large cars, the occupants of which were veiled by curtains from the gaze of the vulgar. We assumed that Mao and the top people lived or worked there. But the old Chinese life went on in the shops, in the markets where even other people's old snapshots had a commercial value and among the crowds of laughing, chattering Chinese, the most good-humoured people on earth, going gaily about their business in the old way. In spite of official efforts to suppress Chinese New Year's Day and the other festivals, they were still celebrated as they had been for so many centuries. With all the new restrictions, it was still, in our time, for most of its citizens, a happy city.

4

FOREIGNERS IN CHINA

THE Chinese Government treated me strictly as 'Ying-kuo t'an-p'an t'ai-piao', head of the British delegation for the negotiation of the establishment of diplomatic relations. I was received at the Wai Chiao Pu, the Ministry of Foreign Affairs, a dreary building in European style, by Chang Han-fu, the Vice-Minister who dealt with the non-Communist world and Huan Hsiang, the head of the West European department. After my first formal call, I could get no more interviews. They made it quite clear that I was not to be treated as *de facto* chargé d'affaires. The Vice-Minister only answered my letters when he wanted to be particularly offensive and to publish his reply; my requests for interviews were simply ignored. I had no formal grounds for complaint, since I had not been recognised as head of a diplomatic mission and could not claim to be treated as such. I could always break off the negotiations which were in abeyance and apply for an exit permit. Our continual Notes were at least accepted and, although we received no replies, we occasionally had indirect evidence that they were not wholly without effect. We were not going to give up and abandon people in trouble for whom we might be able to do something.

There were British subjects in prison: Robert Ford, ex-R.A.F. wireless-operator in the service of the Tibetan Government, who had been picked up by the Chinese Army advancing on Tibet; Bull, a missionary of the Plymouth Brothers, also picked up in Tibet; a soldier who had slipped across the border from Hong Kong, and one or two more from the Commonwealth. We had to do our best for the thirty-two American prisoners.

We had to choose our grounds for protest carefully. We could say categorically that Ford was not working for the British Government, but we could not demand his release without trial from a charge of murder, the basis of which we did not know. We had strong enough grounds for our protests on his behalf, which we repeated many times; that he had been held for years without trial, that we had not been told of the evidence against him, nor allowed either to visit or write to him, in accordance with normal international practice. A campaign in the British press was suggested; but our purpose was not to condemn the Chinese, but to get Ford released. An anti-Chinese press campaign about Ford, which the Chinese would judge to have been inspired by the British Government, would probably result in their staging a formal trial, convicting him and sentencing him to death or life imprisonment. We had little enough success in our efforts on behalf of the British and American prisoners, but it was better to go on pressing the Chinese privately and not to attack them publicly in a way which would cause them to defend themselves by demonstrating the prisoners' guilt.

British firms were in great difficulties and their staffs

in China in an unenviable position. In the early years the treatment of foreign firms had been rough but unsystematic. Later, a plan was carefully applied to squeeze the firms out by indirect action. The Chinese would have justified this as a very small recompense for what they regarded as a hundred years' exploitation by the foreigner. The value of the British property being taken over in this way was put in Parliament as £300 million. So it had been once, but this was now only a paper figure, since there were no longer any private buyers and the Government was gradually taking over all private property, Chinese and foreign, without compensation. Most British firms had written off their investments in China soon after the Revolution.

The method now used was to put every form of pressure on a firm to induce it voluntarily to surrender all its assets to the Chinese Government, so that there could be no claim for compensation. The tax officials would come in and say that they were very sorry, but they were afraid that there had been a mistake in the tax assessment some years before; it had now been discovered that a large sum was still due and, under the law, although the mistake had been committed by the tax officials, the firm was liable to pay not only the large amount still outstanding, but also a fine on the unpaid tax at a half per cent a day from the date on which it had fallen due. The day came for the renewal of leases of 'godowns' for storage. The lessees unanimously decided not to renew their leases. Contracts for cold storage were cancelled. Port dues were increased. Exorbitant demands were made for the provision of amenities for workers or for elaborate repairs to a structurally sound building, with scaffolding on a scale never seen in China, least of all on the State buildings being repaired at the same time. Private firms were in the hands of the

Government, having to get raw materials from them and sell the products to them. The materials would be indefinitely delayed; customary purchases of products would dry up.

Under this treatment no firm could carry on unless the Chinese wanted it to do so for their own advantage, and even then there was no question of its being allowed to remit even the smallest proportion of the profits to the United Kingdom. After a time, firms were only able to pay the wages by remittance to China in foreign exchange. The Chinese would not allow them to dismiss any staff; so, although there was no work to do, the Chinese employees would turn up every morning and spend their time gossiping or playing mah-jong in the offices or vast banking halls empty of customers.

After some time British firms could consider themselves lucky if they were able to give up their property and get their staff out of China without paying for the privilege. The managers, particularly those whose head offices were unwilling to remit money to pay the wages, were in a highly unpleasant position. The Government used as a means of harassment the old Chinese custom of making all foreign firms nominate a responsible person to be a personal guarantor of all the firm's liabilities in China. The Chinese staffs put pressure on the managers to make their London offices give way. The staff would besiege them in their offices, sitting there all day and refusing to move. The manager who tried to make his way out and touched one of them risked facing a conviction for assault.

Meanwhile, very few exit permits were granted to foreigners. The British managers and their assistants were in China as virtual prisoners, unable to do business, unable to leave, with all the privileges and pleasures of their old life disappearing round them. Seven members of the senior staff of the British American Tobacco Company were kept for two years in Shanghai after the transfer of their factory to the Chinese Government. They lingered on without an office to go to, waiting to leave. Exit permits were granted once a week, the list appearing in the Chinese newspapers on Sunday. About Thursday hopes would begin to rise; there would be a wave of optimism on Saturday; then came the rush for the newspaper on Sunday morning and the inevitable reaction until hopes began to revive in the middle of the next week.

In Tientsin the Country Club, in Shanghai the famous club on the Bund, the Race Club and finally the French Club were taken away. The French Club was due to go on 1 January 1954. There was a farewell dance on New Year's Eve. By 10.30 p.m. the Chinese police were in, like vultures gathering over a dying animal, waiting to take charge the moment the old year was gone. It was *Cinderella* in modern terms, and not a convivial party. There was one tennis-court left in Shanghai, in the compound of the British Consulate-General; but there were no tennis-balls. Since the Revolution there had been virtually no imports of consumer goods, and goods left over from before the Revolution were sold at fabulous prices. Import duty on tobacco could be 500 per cent of the value; imported cosmetics were periodically confiscated by the Customs as injurious to public morals. No newspapers and few magazines and books got through the Customs. No foreigner could move out of the city in which he lived. The British in Shanghai had plenty of local currency which they found it difficult to spend. Having little else to do, they spent their time giving each other elaborate dinners. Round and round they went, seeing the same people, unable to avoid the same eternal subjects of conversation. Who had got an exit permit? Was there any sign of hope on the horizon?

There were only about a hundred British nationals left in Shanghai out of the many thousands who had lived there in the old days through internal revolution and counter-revolution, foreign occupation and war. Many of those who remained were married to Chinese, or partly of Chinese descent, and so assimilated into Chinese life. There were sad personal tragedies. An Englishwoman was living with her Chinese husband and children in a little flat which they could not afford, hampered by her European standard of living, while the authorities denied her husband a job on the grounds of unreliability. They said she might return to England, but not her children who were Chinese citizens and would be looked after by the State. She would not leave them, though she must have known that the pressures on her husband would be too strong and that she would be beaten in the end. I was helpless and could only listen.

The British community had very little contact with their old Chinese friends who did not risk going to see foreigners. So we heard very little of what was going on in that teeming city behind the official façade. One story was told to us, which may well have been true. A small Chinese boy came back from school and told his mother that the teacher had said that Winston Churchill had been forced to resign by the British people owing to his policy of following the Americans. He had said: 'But he is eighty.' The teacher replied: 'He could have easily gone on until ninety.' Another little boy asked: 'Did Mr Malenkov resign for the same reason?' The boy summed up by saying: 'Really, it is sometimes difficult to believe what teacher tells us.'

On my first visit to Shanghai in November 1953 there

was no light on the horizon for the British left there. British managers could not get permission to go on leave, nor could the banks and commercial firms send replacements. Both in Shanghai and Tientsin there were men who had been separated from their families for years and who could see no prospect of ever being able to join them. It was heartening to find the morale of the community so high. The British banks, like other firms, had filed petitions for closure, but were unable to make any progress in their negotiations. They had large dollar-balances in the United States to the credit of Chinese banks or individuals, which were carried on the books of their branches in China. The Chinese demanded the use of these dollars. The banks acknowledged their liability, but the dollar balances were blocked by the American Government.

The Boards of the banks in London decided that it was intolerable that they should be held up to blackmail and that they would stop remitting any foreign exchange from 1 January 1954. They hoped that this would show the Chinese that they could no longer be squeezed and would make the Chinese agree to allow the banks to close. In China the managers and I knew that this reasoning was false, that the Chinese would not give way to pressure of this kind and that the position of the managers was likely to become serious. We were virtually certain that unless the Chinese staff were paid there would be no negotiations. I put my views to London. The banks were not moved, but matters turned out as we had expected. Negotiations for closure stopped altogether; pressure on the managers increased and it was not long before, bit by bit, the London Boards found themselves having to give way.

So the old deadlock remained. In April 1954, when I was in Shanghai again on my way to the Geneva conference and prospects for the British in China looked a little brighter, one of the bank managers said to me: 'Please tell my Board that I cannot go through another three months like the last three.' The American businessmen, curiously enough, had been mostly in a rather better position, for the Chinese had no compunction in expropriating their property at an early stage and had expelled the American staffs, before they thought out ways of putting pressure on foreign firms and their staffs in China which would force the firms to hand over their property voluntarily to the Chinese Government.

When the Chinese did something outrageous to British interests in China, there was, very naturally, a cry that we should not sit down under it, but should publicise the outrage and retaliate. But this did not work in practice. I selected incidents suitable for publicity and asked the managers concerned for their permission to use material affecting them. They refused it. They were, they said, in favour of publicity; but if the particular incident were used, they would fear retaliation against their interests or themselves.

In considering retaliation, we were in a dilemma not peculiar to China. The developed country had invested heavily in the underdeveloped country, but the underdeveloped country had no investments in the developed country. What Chinese assets could we seize in the United Kingdom, even if we could find some legal way of seizing foreign assets? The Embassy in London? Did we want to invite immediate seizure of the rest of our compound in Peking and the consular property which we still had round China? If the Hong Kong Government took measures against the Bank of China in Hong Kong, we should be inviting hostile Chinese reaction against Hong Kong which daily received a large supply of fresh vegetables, fruit, meat and poultry from Communist China, whose trade unions were riddled with Communist agents, but which was at that time less troubled by subversive action than in the days of Nationalist power. We should be very unwilling to change our system in order to enable the Government to refuse exit permits to individuals or special categories and so to prevent the Chinese officials of the Bank of China from leaving the United Kingdom. In any case, the Chinese Government would probably not mind if they stayed in London for the rest of their lives. The only result would be that we should never get our people out of China. And were we going to adopt methods which we thought barbarous just because the Chinese used them? Would we not then be on a mounting spiral of reciprocal brutality, a game which we were unlikely to win?

We might refuse to trade with China, so long as British firms and nationals were being so badly treated. But it was by no means certain that British firms would be willing to forego their lucrative trade and see it fall into the hands of their European competitors, or the few British firms which were in the hands of the fellow-travellers and could therefore hope to receive favours from the Communists. One British firm was even negotiating a profitable long-term contract for the sale of Chinese produce at a time when its own business in China was being held to ransom and its manager harassed and denied the right to leave. I did not blame it. If the firm refused the new contract, it would neither help the manager in his difficulties nor improve the chance of getting the Chinese to agree to the old branch being closed without the firm having to pay to give it up.

Hong Kong was an important British interest. A Vice-Minister admitted to me that Hong Kong was useful to the Chinese Government. It helped them to keep in touch with overseas Chinese and South-East Asia in general, since there were no restrictions on entry from the mainland. It provided financial facilities which no longer existed on the mainland, and a growing market for Chinese exports. It was the channel for the large remittances of foreign exchange by overseas Chinese to their families in China. The building of the Bank of China in Hong Kong topped the Hong Kong Bank, the highest building in Hong Kong up to that time, by a few feet, clearly a symbolic gesture. If it was a Nationalist base for spying on the mainland, it was also a Communist base for spying on Taiwan.

The Chinese therefore showed no disposition to challenge the existence of British Hong Kong and kept their reservations and future plans to themselves; but it was not surprising that the existence of a British territory on the edge of the mainland at the mouth of the Pearl river flowing from Canton, gave rise to a series of awkward incidents. On 9 September 1953 a British naval launch was sunk by Chinese gunfire off Hong Kong in the Pearl river with loss of life. The boundary of Chinese territorial waters was in dispute; but in any case we claimed the right of innocent passage. We protested and demanded compensation. The Chinese produced a completely different version of the incident, which we knew was not true. Each side abused the other heartily in public and the matter rested. The Chinese would not admit to a mistake while we had no diplomatic relations.

Although we could not do any serious business with the Chinese, we had diplomatic wireless and a monthly bag, and could therefore do the normal reporting job of a diplomatic mission. We had an outstanding Chinese expert, Ted Youde, a brilliant Chinese scholar, who

had been previously attached to the Embassy in Nanking and had been the hero of a remarkable exploit. He
described it to me as we travelled by train over the
stretch of country which he had had to cover. The
British warship, the *Amethyst*, was marooned in the
Yangtse river. The Communist Forces were advancing
from the north. The diminutive Youde had disem-
barked on the northern bank of the river and walked
on alone to meet the Communist troops, in order to try
and negotiate with their commander. It must have been
a very lonely walk.

In my first week in Peking I had an argument with
the Foreign Office. On my arrival I had found a letter
from a Whitehall official reproaching the Peking Embassy for using the word 'liberation' without inverted
commas. The implication was that my staff were un-
critically lapping up Communist propaganda. We
silenced the enemy, but felt it prudent subsequently
to spatter our despatches with inverted commas to
satisfy the Whitehall purists.

We had little information apart from what appeared
in the Chinese press and could mostly be obtained
outside China. The Americans, who had an embassy
for China disguised as a Consulate-General in Hong
Kong, employed at least thirty alleged vice-consuls to
analyse it. In Washington and London there were
Chinese experts in every field with access to previous
statistics and reports, and in some respects we were in
a less favourable position with our small resources in
Peking. We heard the familiar argument that a mission
in Peking could contribute nothing to an understanding of the Chinese Revolution. But we were convinced
that it did not work out like that. We believed that,
living in the Peking atmosphere, concentrating exclusively on the Chinese scene and picking up information

from our diplomatic colleagues who were in direct
contact with Chinese ministers and officials, we could
give London a reasonably sound picture of the Chinese
scene and the Chinese way of looking at foreign policy,
which it was worth their while reading, however voluminous their reports from the home-based experts with
all their knowledge and access to basic information. It
did make a difference whether your evening walk was
to Liu-li ch'ang or on Hampstead Heath.

We could correct mistakes in western reports. For
some time it was reported in the western press that the
Chinese Government had admitted that 200 million
Chinese peasants were short of food. A Communist
admission that one-third of the population was starv-
ing was important news. But, as we pointed out, what
had actually been said was that 200 million people were
not self-sufficient in food, either because they grew
industrial crops or because they were workers in industry or other city dwellers.

Political analysis in a Communist country requires
the continuous reading of every available newspaper,
magazine and document of importance throughout the
year. It sounds a gloomy prospect, as Communist literature, which achieves its effects by continual repetition,
is not lively reading; but if you look on it as a hunt for
clues, it can give you the same sort of intellectual satisfaction as trying to defeat Agatha Christie. After some
months of practice, the reader should be so soaked in
the Party line that he can spot any new variation and
can forecast with fair accuracy the official reaction to
any projected western move. Those of us who knew
Chinese started the day by reading the Chinese newspapers; the rest of us read the English version put out
by the New China News Agency. We would then meet
and would often find that we had each marked the same

points and had the same interpretation. In time the study of the morning's Chinese news became an exciting game and we positively looked forward to the morning dose of propaganda. I was happy to get back to it later in Moscow.

One of the subjects which aroused continual interest and anxiety in the West was the treatment of Christianity and the foreign missionaries in China. Well-meaning Protestant missionaries, clinging to the hope that all was not lost, were apt to believe the Chinese Government's assertion that religion was free. The Protestant missionaries had almost all left China before I arrived. We did not criticise their decision. Their Chinese flocks were better without them. The Protestant Chinese clergy practically conformed to the Communists' requirements. They could have no communication with foreigners; they had to subscribe to the anti-imperialist doctrines of the Party; they must preach obedience to the Government and Party. If they conformed, they were tolerated as 'superstitious practitioners' and might continue their services to their Chinese congregations. In the summer of 1954 a Congress of all Protestant sects was held in Peking. There was not a word about theology. The Congress limited itself to passing resolutions about American aggression in Taiwan.

The Roman Catholics were a tougher proposition, though more of them conformed than the Vatican admitted. The position of each side was clear. The Communists' purpose, in Chou En-lai's own phrase, was to destroy the modern Christian churches in China as thoroughly as the Chinese Nestorian church had been destroyed in the ninth century. On the other side, the Vatican refused any compromise. In their eyes no Chinese priest could admit any authority of the Chinese

Government over him in matters concerning the Church nor any derogation from the absolute authority of the Pope. The Communists attacked. Many priests, Chinese and foreign, were imprisoned; in the early days some were ill-treated. Later, physical violence was no longer used, according to the reports reaching us, but foreign priests were arrested and expelled. Those who were expelled without prior imprisonment could be considered fortunate.

In order to discredit the Church, foreign missionaries were portrayed as spies and as men of immoral character. In the summer of 1954 the police arrested several American priests of the Order of Christ the King, and one or two Belgian priests. A reliable Canadian priest then living in Shanghai told me that after the arrest the police went into the house with photographers, bricklayers and weapons, and built and photographed the arms caches which they subsequently alleged they had found in the house. These photographs and faked photographs of a Belgian priest in bed with a woman were among the exhibits in an anti-Catholic exhibition mounted soon after in Shanghai. But the Chinese Catholics knew their fathers too well. The exhibition was received with ridicule and was hastily packed up and removed to Hankow.

Chinese Catholic congregations were astonishingly steadfast. When we were in Peking, the police expelled the last European priests, four Swiss. They were escorted by policemen. As the train drew out of the station, members of the congregation who had come to see them off, knelt on the platform in full view of the police to receive the priests' blessing. But the pressure on Chinese and foreign Catholics was continuous and effective. My Canadian friend said, 'The church will take a great beating.' He was right. I am told that its last vestiges were obliterated in the 'cultural revolution'.

By the time I left China, there were very few foreign priests or nuns left in the country, and Chinese priests were being arrested in batches in the autumn of 1955. I had visited a Peking monastery, famous for its wine, a few months before it was dissolved. There were then only two or three foreign priests left, Alsatians, eking out a miserable existence in a vast, almost empty monastery, being allowed no contact with their congregation and remaining only because the Vatican had ordered that no priest should leave China voluntarily. In Peking only the nuns of the Franciscan convent survived my time. The police made several attempts to remove them; but they were saved for a few more years by the energetic intervention of the Asian diplomatic missions, for they managed a school for foreign children in the English language and were thus important for the families of the prolific Asian diplomats. They are no longer there.

Chinese Communism was always strongly nationalist and anti-Western. It was essentially different from Russian Marxism in revolt against an indigenous monarchy and church. To the Chinese, Christianity was historically part of the capitalist exploitation of a weak, sprawling China. Though many generations of missionaries, Protestant and Catholic, had spent their lives selflessly in helping the Chinese, they had been a part of the foreign invasion. The French missionaries, in the wake of the British and French expeditionary force, had destroyed the most venerated Confucian temple in Tientsin and had erected on its site a cathedral which they named 'Notre Dame des Victoires'. When the expeditionary force had departed, they in their turn were massacred and their cathedral destroyed. To the

Chinese of the new generation, Christianity was something foreign in the body politic, an associate of imperialism, and had to be eradicated with all other remains of the time when China lay helpless before the West.

So for eight months we remained an unrecognised mission trying to protect our own people in trouble in conditions of great difficulty, never knowing whether we would not be forced to give up, but making the best of a thoroughly bad situation. My predecessor, Lionel Lamb, had been doing that for more than three years.

5

BEFORE GENEVA

I HAD arrived just after the Korean armistice, which
the Chinese had held up for months by insisting that
all prisoners should be sent back to their own country
as soon as it came into effect. The United Nations had
held out against this on the grounds that nearly all the
Chinese and North Korean prisoners were anti-Com-
munist and would wish to go to Taiwan or stay in South
Korea. In April 1953 the Communists had proposed a
compromise by which all who wished to return to their
own country should be allowed to do so, while the re-
mainder would be held for a period in the hands of a
neutral United Nations Commission. During this time
delegates from their own countries would be able to
see them and try to persuade them to return home.
This was agreed.

Synghman Rhee's release of large numbers of
prisoners in June 1953 naturally infuriated the
Chinese. They would not have maintained their armistice proposals unless they had badly needed to end the
war. But it was not surprising that they first reacted to
Synghman Rhee's action by making a last savage attack
which caused many casualties on both sides. Chou En-

lai told the Indian Ambassador while I was in Peking
that this attack was a deliberate act of revenge. The
armistice started. Even after Synghman Rhee's release
of the prisoners there were still large numbers in the
hands of the United Nations, while there were few
prisoners of South Korean and other nationalities in
Chinese and North Korean camps. When the moment
for release arrived, the Chinese received a severe shock,
for very many Chinese and North Korean prisoners
elected to stay on the non-Communist side.

The explanations began. Still very few could be persuaded to go home. During the Chinese civil war the
Eighth Route Army had probably had little difficulty in
persuading their prisoners to go over to the Communists. Throughout those times generals and private soldiers had often changed sides in accordance with the
fortunes of war, and the consequences of refusal were
not attractive. Moreover, the Communists' revolutionary propaganda was persuasive, and it was the poor
peasants of whom the armies were made up who were
going to benefit from the promised reforms. The
Chinese could not admit that the refusal of so many to
go home was the result of free choice. They alleged that
there was terrorism in the South Korean camps and
demanded that the explanations should be suspended
until the camps were brought under control. It was
worth their while to lose a few hundred prisoners who
might still have been persuaded to go back, in order to
confuse the issue and cover up a major blow to their
prestige. So they stopped explanations. The United
Nations maintained that the prisoners had not been
got at but were free to choose where they should be
released.

We were assailed in Peking by a daily barrage of
propaganda on the question. The Indians supported

the Chinese view, and the diplomatic corps were mostly far from sympathetic to the Americans, who for the Chinese were the villains of the piece. It was difficult for us to get at the facts. Later at Geneva I had an opportunity to talk to people on the non-Communist side who had been on the spot. My conclusion was that it was not a black-and-white affair. There was a tight organisation in Synghman Rhee's camps. Some prisoners were murdered and their bodies flung over the wire. Synghman Rhee had had his agents in the camps for eighteen months, indoctrinating and organising for the day when the prisoners would have to decide where to go. He was as tough as the Communists. But the explanations were given without hindrance and the prisoners were really free to make their own choice. They could safely use the moment of explanations to go north. The South Koreans and Chinese Nationalists cannot have had any hold on them, since nearly all their families must have been on the mainland. The advantage was on the Communist side. In January 1954, sixty days after the beginning of the explanations, the remaining Chinese and North Korean prisoners were released by the United Nations Command.

During the autumn of 1953 attempts were started to arrange a political conference on Korea. The United Nations, on American initiative, passed a resolution that only the belligerent states should take part. The Chinese proposed that neutrals should be included, particularly the Indians who might be expected to support them against the Americans. There was a prolonged deadlock. At last it was agreed that American and Chinese delegates should meet at Panmunjon to discuss the conference arrangements and the interpretation of its scope. The Chinese reserved the right to discuss its composition also.

The delegates met on 26 October. The longer they sat, the less likely it seemed that any conference would take place. There was again complete deadlock. It seemed to us in Peking that both sides had given up trying and only wanted to avoid being the one to break off. The Chinese delegate announced that he was insulted and withdrew from one of the meetings. It was clearly a tactical move. Rumour had it that the American delegate was anxiously watching the approaching date of his daughter's wedding. Be that as it may, he took the bait offered him, suspended the talks on the ground that he also was insulted by the Chinese accusation of American complicity in Synghman Rhee's release of the prisoners and was off home. The Chinese were left in possession of the field, and, in our judgement, had won on points.

In Peking we thought that directly after the armistice the Chinese had really wanted a conference, provided neutrals were to take part in it. No one could expect any end to it other than partition, but the Chinese may have thought that the Americans would withdraw their troops from Korea and that the northerners would then be able to gain control of the whole country by infiltrating into the south. Moreover, they may have expected that a political agreement on Korea might help towards the recognition of the Peking Government as entitled to represent China in the United Nations and a modification of the trade embargo. The United Kingdom and most other non-Communist countries supported them on the inclusion of neutrals in the conference, and they had been assured by the Indians and the Swedes that the Americans would be flexible in the discussions at Panmunjon.

The Chinese were also claiming that they should take part in five-power talks on world issues. But by

December they seemed concerned only to put the blame on the Americans for the breakdown of the talks. The propaganda war was stimulated by the United Nations resolution on Chinese and North Korean atrocities in Korea and the counter-charges made by the Chinese in reply. Tension persisted on the Thirty-eighth Parallel, but the centre of interest soon shifted from Korea to Indo-China.

It was hardly surprising that Chinese propaganda concentrated on abuse of the Americans. The Americans regarded the Nationalists as the rightful Government of China and protected them in Taiwan and the coastal islands. They were trying to surround the Chinese with a ring of non-Communist States strengthened by their support and preventing the Chinese from acquiring satellites themselves. But there was an added bitterness. It was like a love affair gone wrong. Generations of Americans had given their lives to China. American money had been poured out to improve Chinese health, education and agriculture. Generations of Chinese had looked to American-run schools and hospitals in China and to American universities in China and the United States for their higher education. American men, arms and supplies had supported the tottering Chinese effort to throw the Japanese out of their country and to relieve the distress caused by war. America had prided itself on being a non-colonialist, non-imperialist country which had not tried to dominate, but which had saved a moribund China from partition by the predatory European powers. Now the 'open door' had been slammed in America's face. The object of American service and affection had, in American minds, turned and bitten savagely into the hand that had fed it. But to the new Chinese all this seemed to count for nothing and the

Americans were the most powerful and predatory imperialists of them all.

The Indo-Chinese phase began. In February 1954
the Berlin conference of the four powers agreed that a
five-power conference should be held at Geneva to discuss Korea and Indo-China. The other states which had
fought in the Korean war were to take part in the discussions on Korea, and the 'interested countries' –
eventually agreed on at the conference to be the
Laotians, Cambodians and the South and North Vietnamese – were to send representatives for the talks on
Indo-China. The crisis in Indo-China grew more intense as the North Vietnamese forces, aided by the
Chinese in every way except by the open participation of
Chinese troops, pressed their attacks in order to obtain
a commanding military position before the conference
opened. Chinese interest was shown by the flood of
their propaganda on the fighting in Indo-China, slan-
ted to appeal to the Asian neutrals.

In Peking we were still onlookers, but at the end of
March the atmosphere lightened. Our personal lives
became a little easier. One Vice-Minister and some of
his officials came to my house for supper and a film performance of the Coronation. I was now able to get an
interview with the head of the West European Department and to lend him an anthology of Chinese poetry
in English translation, which he accepted and never
returned, my first human contact with a Chinese official.
Then there was a clear sign that the political wind had
changed. The Vice-Minister suddenly gave me the
dinner which he customarily gave to heads of mission
on their arrival. Policy seemed to be moving towards
a partial détente with the British, with the object of
increasing the diplomatic isolation of the Americans.

At about this time the Chinese and Indians signed an

agreement on the Indian trading-posts in Tibet, an event which, though of no great intrinsic importance, marked an important new line in Chinese policy. To this agreement were prefixed the five 'principles of peaceful co-existence', originally an Indian suggestion which was appropriated by Chou En-lai. They amounted to no more than a recital of the normal code of conduct of civilised states in dealing with one another, non-interference in each other's affairs, non-aggression and so on. But they were built up by the Chinese and Indian propaganda into a set of principles which purported to describe something new in the relations between states.

The purpose of the Indians in propounding them was presumably to discourage the Chinese from using Tibet as a base from which to organise subversion in the frontier areas of India. To Chou En-lai they were a convenient peg on which to hang his Asian policy. This was in effect to persuade the Asian non-Communist States that China was not an aggressor, that they had nothing to fear from Chinese Communism, that the Chinese were Asians first and Communists afterwards, that they did not seek to convert the Asians to Communism, and that there was a fair prospect of peaceful co-existence in the sense in which non-Communists understood it, provided the Asians did not join any Western-inspired pacts, did not try to contain the Chinese through a policy of strength, and remained neutral. This approach fell on fertile ground in India, Burma and Indonesia and to a lesser extent in Pakistan. Only South Korea, South Vietnam, Japan, Thailand, the Philippines and Taiwan remained on the Western side of the fence. The rest sat on it, mostly facing the Chinese side. It is strange to look back on this Chinese–Indian honeymoon in the light of all that happened in later years between China and India.

The Chinese took great pains to spread the propaganda line of Asia for the Asians, within the framework of Communist anti-colonial and anti-imperialist doctrine. The Korean armistice enabled them to represent the war in Korea as a successful defence of Asia against imperialist aggression and their own strength as changing the balance of power between Asia and the Western world. They made great use of the pressure in the United Nations to exclude the Asian neutrals from the Korean political conference. They urged India and Pakistan privately to settle their differences and not to allow the 'imperialists' to make trouble between them. They continued to try to improve their relations with Pakistan, while deploring Pakistan's adherence to Western pacts and expressing polite incredulity that Pakistan should barter her Asian soul for Western arms. The Chinese policy was soundly conceived and brilliantly executed.

At the same time, they accepted the proposals of the four powers at Berlin for a conference at Geneva. I travelled to Geneva through Shanghai, taking with me the troubles of the marooned British and hoping that perhaps in Geneva I could begin to do the job which I could not do in Peking. My long-suffering wife, who had left our children in England only a few months before to join me in Peking, now had to stay there without me for two and a half months in a time of crisis in the Far East.

The Earl of Avon, then Mr Anthony Eden, has described in his memoirs the differences between the British and Americans during and after Mr Dulles's visit to London in April 1954, and during their meeting with M. Bidault in Paris before the conference opened. Mr Dulles had two aims: to commit the British pub-

licly in advance of the conference to taking part in an
organisation for the defence of South-East Asia directed
principally against the Chinese, and to obtain a request
from the French and the other allies for action by
American forces in Indo-China. This would give the
Americans the international cover which Mr Dulles
required. The British Government went no further
than saying that they would consider the proposal for
an Asian pact, and refused to join in a request for
American military intervention. The French wavered,
but in the end took the same line. Mr Dulles acted as
if the British were already committed to an Asian pact,
and American correspondents who were in London at
the time told me that he had wilfully misrepresented
the British position. His aim appeared to be to create
another Korea in Indo-China with United Nations support in order to stop Communist expansion in South-
East Asia. If the allies had gone any further towards
meeting his views, the Geneva conference would not
have taken place.

The British did not agree with the Americans' pessi-
mistic appraisal of the situation in Indo-China. They
were not prepared to take a public position before the
conference which would jeopardise the chance of a
settlement and were well aware that the Asian members
of the Commonwealth would not see allied military
intervention in Indo-China in terms of the defence of
freedom against Communist aggression. Mr Dulles was
nervous of the suggestion that if an organisation for
the defence of South-East Asia were to be formed Mr
Nehru would have to be given the opportunity to join.
He feared that a suggestion that the pact should be
extended westwards would subject him to pressure to
extend it eastwards to Taiwan and Korea. He need not
have been concerned. I had worked for Nehru in the

months before Indian independence when he first for-
mulated his position of non-alignment, and I had no
doubt that he would want nothing to do with the pact.

Mr Eden had told Mr Dulles that Americans might
think the time past when they needed to consider the
feelings or difficulties of their allies, but that it was the
conviction that this tendency was becoming more pro-
nounced every week that was creating mounting difficulties for anyone in the United Kingdom who wanted
to maintain close Anglo-American relations. These disagreements did not make for happy personal relations
between Mr Eden and Mr Dulles at the opening of the
conference. Mr Dulles had compared the situation with
Germany's seizure of the Rhineland. Mr Eden did not
accept the analogy. In 1956 the rôles were reversed and
Mr Dulles got his own back when he refused to support
the Suez adventure.

6

AT THE CONFERENCE

Now came the Geneva interlude. An international conference is a painful affair for all except the principals. It consists largely in waiting around. The Under-Secretary from the Foreign Office is in charge of the British secretariat, and the visitor from the periphery has little to do but wait for a call which hardly ever comes. I read with amusement subsequent descriptions of myself as having greatly influenced the course of the conference. In reality, I had nothing whatever to do with it, except to accompany Mr Eden to his meetings with Chou En-lai, in order to bolster up my position rather than in the expectation that I could be of any use. Not all Foreign Secretaries have the understanding which Mr Eden showed of the importance of supporting the position of the man at the other end. I regret to say that my response was to return to Geneva from a week-end in Gstaad too late for Mr Eden's dinner for Chou En-lai through having misread the small print in the railway time-table. Having not been concerned with the substance of the negotiations, I limit myself to the superficial observations of the odd man out, the worm's eye view.

The British delegation in Geneva was split into two parts. Mr Eden and his immediate entourage lived in a villa some miles out of the town. According to his memoirs, it was generously lent by the owner after he had installed himself in the hotel and had been told that meetings in his sitting-room would probably not be secure. It would argue a certain negligence on the part of the Security Department of the Foreign Office if they had not thought of this before. Business within the British delegation was mostly conducted in a levée in Mr Eden's bedroom, on the terrace while sun-bathing, in the drawing-room while he was arranging the flowers, anywhere except in an office round a table. This was his old habit and I remembered being taken to brief him on a complicated financial negotiation while he was dressing in his hotel bedroom in Lisbon. What mattered was that the result was immensely effective. Mr Eden was a superb negotiator. He took great trouble over the way in which his talks were conducted. We were in his car going to see Chou En-lai. I had some paper in my hand. 'Put those papers away,' he said, 'this is a negotiation.' The success of the conference in the face of so many intractable difficulties, so many threats of total breakdown, was largely due to his initiative and skill.

Above Mr Eden's villa on the hill were the delegation's offices, where routine business was conducted and the Commonwealth representatives were kept moderately happy with snippets of inside news doled out to them at delegation meetings. In the hotel Beau Rivage, the home of British delegations for so many years, lived the rest of the delegation headed by the Marquess of Reading, a charming gentleman who appeared to have no influence on the course of events and must have found his position decidedly uncomfortable.

The opening session of the conference was confined to platitudes declaimed in the full glare of publicity. It progressed to secret sessions of the whole, during which each delegate stated his propaganda position at great length and the press officers related everything in detail, on the record, to the assembled correspondents, the most accurate and intelligent press officer, by a long chalk, being Con O'Neill of the British delegation, who built up a crowded salon like a political hostess. After the first deadlock had been reached, the conference went into restricted session, consisting of the principal delegates with at most two or three advisers each, who restated their positions in even more extreme form. The press officers observed each other closely, having their spies at each other's conferences, until one broke silence and all the rest followed suit with great pleasure. Non-Communist press officers dispensed information; Communist press officers dispensed drink and propaganda.

The pretence of negotiation in conference was then given up and a serious possibility of private diplomatic negotiation emerged for the first time. The principal delegates began to visit each other's villas at all hours of the day and night. When both sides had made some real concessions, they emerged into the light of day and announced a measure of agreement to the remaining delegates who might as well not have been there at all and were only wasting their countries' tax-payers' money. This, at least, is how it looked to the outer circle.

The Americans appeared to want people to think that they were not there, like a guest at a party which he thinks is not quite up to his social standing. They were not on speaking terms with the Chinese and were seen to be carefully avoiding contact in the buffet during the intervals. One day Wang Ping-nan, secretary-general of the Chinese delegation and afterwards Chinese Ambassador in Warsaw, cornered Mr Walter Robertson, the American Under-Secretary of State for Far Eastern Affairs, whom he had known when Mr Robertson was General Marshall's political adviser in Peking. Mr Robertson was the most fanatical anti-Chinese Communist in the whole American Government. His approach has been described by Lord Avon as so emotional as to be impervious to argument, or indeed to facts. Colonel Gilbert (now Viscount) Monckton went up to his American counterpart, holding a miniature pocket-camera and remarked as a joke, 'I got a good one of that. I wonder how much *Life* will pay me for it.' The American nearly fainted.

Mr Dulles, who was obviously unhappy, stayed only a few days at Geneva and then beat a hasty retreat from his exposed position, leaving affairs in the capable hands of General Bedell Smith. After his return to Washington, Mr Dulles would fly off every now and again to his favourite 'Duck Island', where he lay incommunicado, while everyone in Geneva waited on his return to work, since until he reappeared the American delegation were powerless to take any decision.

The Korean discussions were doomed to sterility. Neither side wanted the war to start again. The Americans were not going to agree to remove their troops nor to the neutralisation of Korea, if indeed that meant anything. The Communists were not going to give up their hold over North Korea, nor the hope that one day the whole of Korea would come under Communist control. There was no incentive to do more than record the deadlock and leave things as they were; but this negative result was useful. It drew a line under the account and made both sides realise that the situation created by the armistice was there to stay. Tension in

Korea was immediately relaxed and elements of stability began to appear. After what has happened in Vietnam, we can look back on the Korean settlement as a shining success.

The conference developed into the negotiation of an armistice in Indo-China. It opened with a resounding Communist success, well timed, the capture of Dien Bien Phu. It was disrupted for a time by the fall of the French Government. It was beset by the doubt whether the Americans wanted it to succeed. They were not going to propose any concessions. Nor was it clear that it was to the Communists' advantage to make concessions. Their forces were sweeping across Indo-China and they might think it better to let events take their course. That an armistice was achieved seemed almost a miracle. The conference would probably have failed if M. Mendès France had not come to power at the crucial moment and shown himself determined to get out of the mess in which successive French governments had been floundering for so long. It became a race against the time limit which he had publicly set himself. He was greatly helped by Mr Eden's brilliant performance.

The basic reason for its success was, however, that neither side wanted to take the serious risk of extending the war. The Chinese had had enough fighting for the time in Korea. Their attention was turning towards their formidable internal problems and Taiwan. Their aims were probably to establish North Vietnam as a friendly Communist State on their southern border and to deny Indo-China to American Forces, with a good chance of making the whole of Vietnam Communist in the course of a few years. They achieved the first objective and probably thought they had achieved the second, though in this they were mistaken. The Russians wanted to further the Communist cause in South-East Asia without getting involved themselves, since they could not bring decisive force to bear so far away from the Soviet Union.

Mr Dulles afterwards claimed that he had been deliberately 'standing on the brink'. This was a major factor in the situation, since the Communists knew that he was perfectly capable of stepping off it. It can be argued that it would have been better for the Americans to have had their war in Indo-China then rather than ten years later, but that could not have been foreseen. A dangerous situation was resolved, at least for some time. The Korean solution could not then have been reproduced in Vietnam. The Vietnamese had not produced any leader as tough as Synghman Rhee. There was justice in the nickname given to Bao Dai by the *Journal de Genève* – 'le Synghman Rhee des pauvres'.

Although I had nothing to do with the conference, I was at least able for the first time to do what I had not been able to do at Peking. I held regular meetings with Huan Hsiang, the head of the West European Department of the Chinese Foreign Ministry and with Lei Jenmin, one of the Vice-Ministers of Foreign Trade, a cheerful and practical man with an unrivalled capacity for drinking that most potent spirit, Mao t'ai. Many of the troubles of the British community in China were now resolved. Exit permits were granted, negotiations for the closure of British firms began to move forward, a British deserter from Hong Kong was handed over, all British prisoners were released except Ford and one man convicted of murder. It was agreed that the British staffs of British banks and commercial firms could go on leave and be regularly replaced by other employees of the firm, that a trade delegation from the China National Export Import Corporation should visit London and that a return visit by British businessmen to China should follow. Finally, at a dinner party given by Mr Eden to Chou En-lai, at which I was present, it was agreed that diplomatic relations should be established between Britain and China at the level of chargés d'affaires, which meant that I should be recognised in Peking, and a Chinese chargé d'affaires sent to London. To mark the new situation, I was for the first time received by Chou En-lai.

Incidentally, I was something of a curiosity. No British or American visitors, apart from a few Communists, had been in China since the Communists had become the masters of China. I was besieged by correspondents who were in Geneva in their hundreds and, as usual at a conference, for most of the time had nothing much to do. So I said my piece as best I could, though, heaven knows, I had not seen very much. Some of the 'old China hands' had been taking the line that the new Government was more Chinese than Communist, implying that conditions for the foreigner would return to something like the old days. My line was that the new Government were real Communists, orthodox and closely bound to the Soviet Union. I was right about Liu Shao-ch'i and his friends, but wrong about Mao, who had not yet shown his hand and was to come into violent conflict with the Soviet and old Chinese Communists. I was right in thinking that, whatever happened, the old way of life would never come back.

I had one more problem in Geneva – how to help get the Americans out of China. I had got one American and his wife out by telling the Chinese that they were ill and in such a nervous state that they were upsetting the rest of the foreign community, which indeed was true; but I soon found that I could do no more for the rest. The Chinese, not unreasonably, said that they would either negotiate directly with the Americans or would recognise me as in charge of American interests in China, if the Americans would agree to the Chinese Government's appointing another country to look after their interests in the United States. The Chinese knew that the Americans would not agree to this, since it would amount to an indirect recognition of the Communists as the Government of China.

There was another difficulty. Since the Korean war, the Americans had been preventing Chinese students with technical qualifications from leaving the United States, so that the Communists should not have the benefit of their special skills. We had been accusing the Chinese of uncivilised conduct in refusing to give exit permits and now found that the Americans were doing the same thing. The Chinese naturally made great play with this in Geneva. The Americans had the choice of either releasing all the Chinese who wanted to go home to the mainland and then putting pressure on the Chinese to let their people out, or of bargaining body for body. They said that they did not bargain bodies and authorised the Indian Embassy in Washington to make representations on behalf of Chinese wanting to leave. In February 1957 the Indians reported that there was then no case of proved detention.

Meanwhile, there was no hope of getting any American out of China unless American officials were allowed to talk directly to the Chinese. We felt that the interests of the Americans kept in China were more important than the American theoretical position, and said so. As usual, Mr Dulles was on Duck Island. When at last the American delegation were able to get into contact with him, he agreed; but they tried to maintain the fiction that I was convening a meeting at which they and the Chinese happened to be present. They chose

Mr Alexis Johnson, Ambassador in Prague, and asked
me to ensure that the Chinese representative should be
of a suitable status, not less than that of Mr Wang Ping-
nan. I approached the Chinese, who, somewhat to my
surprise, agreed not only to my being present but to
the Americans in effect choosing Mr Wang Ping-nan
as the Chinese delegate.

I introduced the contestants and umpired for two
rounds. The Americans tried to keep me in the ring,
but at the beginning of the third round the Chinese,
with elaborate politeness, delicately indicated that the
talks should be between the two principals. I withdrew.
The talks lingered on at the level of Consuls-General
for a year, were revived on the original level in April
1955 and, with various interruptions, continued their
melancholy and unproductive course until the 'cultural revolution'. As I write, they are still formally in
being and are the only form of diplomatic contact between the Americans and the Chinese Communists.
The original purpose was, however, served. Exit permits were quickly granted to several Americans and,
within a relatively short period, most of the Americans
in Chinese prisons were released.

7

THE CHINESE LEADERS

I RETURNED to Peking. Chou En-lai visited India
and Burma on his way back and expounded to his re-
ceptive hosts the happy future under the banner of
'peaceful co-existence', a phrase soon to be used in
China with scorn as a sign of Khrushchev's revisionism.
Before he returned to Geneva for the final part of the
conference, which I was not required to attend, he spent
three days in Peking, during which I was able to present to him a letter appointing me chargé d'affaires, in
order to formalise the agreement made orally in Geneva. From this time, I saw him on many occasions and
had many spirited battles with him. He had greatly increased his international stature at the Geneva conference, where he had shown himself to be a forceful
orator and tough negotiator, and had appeared to be in
no way subject to Soviet direction.

These were my impressions of him, written when I
was in China.

He is, by any standards, a remarkable man, even if
he has not the qualities of leadership of Mao Tse-
tung, who still stands out as the real master of China,

in spite of the framework of collective leadership.
Chou is an extremely adroit negotiator and displays
in the international field the subtlety and tactical
flexibility which have enabled him to stay in the top
rank of the Party, in spite of his association in his
earlier days with others who fell in disgrace. He has
immense energy and an astonishing capacity for work.
He often works through the night and is liable to
interview foreign delegations at two or three o'clock
in the morning. It is a clever trick, too; it impresses
and most of them love it. He takes great trouble over
his personal relations, particularly with visitors from
Asian countries, in the interests of his efforts, to
which he attaches great importance, to convince the
Asians that the Chinese Communist régime is not a
monster ready and eager to eat them up, but will be
a reasonable and easy neighbour, intent only on increasing the prestige of Asia and destroying the last
vestiges of colonialism.

He has immense charm and vitality and is always
completely at ease. His Chinese classical background
is continually apparent in numerous quotations. He
likes simple illustrations. He was something of an
actor in his youth and is always to some extent acting
a part. He suggests with great skill the atmosphere
which he wishes to convey. He flatters cleverly and
takes care to emphasise that his personal relations are
not affected by his political views. At the same time,
he is emotional, sensitive and suspicious, and however flexible his tactics, his basic thinking is as strictly
conditioned by Marxism-Leninism as that of his colleagues at the top of the hierarchy. He speaks no
French [it had frequently been suggested that he
spoke French, since he was for a time a student in
France], but speaks a little and understands more

English. He travels and works closely with a small circus of assistants, most of whom have served him for many years, and his method of work seems to be to elaborate his ideas in continual group discussion with them.

I would not now wish to alter this assessment, except that I should have written 'the Chinese version of Marxism-Leninism', though this, as we now see, did not apply to all his colleagues, some of whom had little sympathy for Mao's development of orthodox Communist doctrines. Chou has remained at the top under Mao throughout the 'cultural revolution' and, with Mao, has broken with the conservative wing of the party. From his history one might reasonably deduce that he has never sought the position of real power and that he is, to that extent, the Mikoyan of the Chinese Revolution.

I also visited some of the other Chinese leaders, in accordance with a list given me by the Protocol Department, among them Chu Teh, the old Commander of the revolutionary army, a figure of more honour than influence at this stage of his life; P'eng Chen, the Mayor of Peking and member of the Political Bureau, the organ of real power, a cheerful villain whom I could not help liking and who was one of the first to fall in the 'cultural revolution', and Kuo Mo-jo, the smooth 'front man', who had been a considerable literary figure, but had dropped literature for politics and, a notable expert at climbing on band-wagons, has succeeded in surviving the great internal battle of the late sixties. From time to time I was greeted by the top two, Mao Tse-tung and Liu Shao-ch'i, but as a mere chargé did not rate interviews with them.

It was the greatest regret of my time in China that I

had only superficial contacts with the formidable Mao. At the end of 1953 he was probably seriously ill, but by the summer of 1954 he was on the way to recovery and the British Labour Party delegation found him intellectually vigorous and dominating his associates. Revolutionary, soldier, poet, mystic, Chinese nationalist, natural leader, he is, without doubt, one of the great men of our time, however one may judge the results of his influence on world events and the suffering which he, like other great world figures, has caused to attain his ends. The vigour and determination with which this old man started a new revolution in the last stage of his career, hit back at his enemies, turned his huge country upside down and embarked on a collision course with the Soviet Union is surely unparalleled in history. Mao was an aloof, mysterious figure in our days in Peking, immured in his imperial fastness, no longer the guerrilla leader of the Yenan days to whom foreign correspondents had ready access, little seen by the people; but his personal ascendancy, if not his policy, was unchallenged, so that even if his opponents had defeated him they would still have had to do so in his name. His presence was everywhere, even in those days, though the adulation had not reached the height of extravagance of later years. His pictured wart was as famous as Cromwell's.

The claim that Mao had made a major contribution to Marxist philosophy was surely overstated by the propagandists. I suspect that he knew that he was not much of a philosopher, though at least his doctrinal expositions were written in readable style, unlike the turgid and repetitive productions of Liu Shao-ch'i and Ch'en Po-ta. His contribution was more practical, to insist that Marxism must be interpreted in the light of Chinese conditions and to adapt Communist theory to the developing world at the end of the colonial period. He had not forgotten how often Stalin had led the Chinese Communists along the wrong path, through his failure to understand the difference between Chinese and Russian conditions. Mao had switched his line many times to meet a particular set of circumstances and he was sometimes wrong. His works have been revised to conceal past errors. He had luck. He would never have got power without the Japanese war and if the Nationalists had not been so incompetent and corrupt. He had many set-backs during this most complex of revolutions. But his ultimate success was primarily due to his knowledge and understanding of the Chinese peasants from whom he sprang and, above all, to the outstanding qualities which he displayed as revolutionary and guerrilla fighter. His poems have imagination and quality and are derided by the Russians as evidence of his 'idealism' in the pejorative Marxist sense.

Behind the inevitable opportunism of the civil war, the Chinese nationalism in Marxist wrappings, lay the real Mao, determined to use all his moral force to carry on a continuing revolution to remould men's minds. His basic ideas and methods have not changed through the years, but he has finally revealed himself in the 'cultural revolution'. This cataclysmic movement was not primarily a struggle for power by competitors for the succession over the ailing body of the old leader, who appeared during its course to be still vigorous and with his intellectual powers unimpaired. In one sense it can be regarded as the culmination of the central aim of Mao's life, to press forward to another stage of the permanent revolution, but it seems unlikely that he would have embarked on it if he had not thought it necessary to resuscitate a revolutionary spirit which he felt was being stifled by the influence of a 'revisionist' bureaucracy.

In any case, it had a practical objective in the power game. It is probable that for years Mao had failed to get his way among his immediate colleagues and he may at times even have been excluded from their counsels. Since he could not prevail from the inside, he chose to administer a shock from the outside. For this purpose he revived the old revolutionary tradition of the 'Red Guards', the younger members of which were encouraged to attack the power basis of his opponents at the centre and in the provinces where there were signs of separatist régimes appearing under the local Party bosses. By October 1966 Mao had got rid of his principal opponent, the sour-faced, doctrinaire Liu Shao-ch'i, who had at one time been his chosen successor and had had an immensely powerful position in the Soviet-backed old guard of the Party, but he seems to have had greater difficulty in eradicating the influence of Liu's ideas, which are probably still strong in the Party. He seems also to have found it difficult to get rid of the old officials in the provincial administrations, many of whom have probably recovered their former positions, though perhaps tamed by adversity.

When the Red Guards had served their initial purpose and began to get out of control, Mao, however reluctantly, had no alternative but to bring in the Army, also probably reluctant to take on civil responsibilities. As a result, the Army, in the later stages of the 'cultural revolution', acquired a key position in the structure of power through the old provincial commanders, some of whom had held the same commands for many years. The Army was, on the whole, conservative in the use of its new power. One may judge that the 'cultural revolution', as originally conceived, has failed, at least

in some of its objectives, but the issue of this great up-
heaval is not yet clear to the world and it is always dangerous to underrate Mao.

Mao is regarded, at least by his less sophisticated·fol-
lowers, as something approaching a god. The little red
bible of his thoughts is all that is necessary to salvation.
During the height of the 'cultural revolution', a visitor
to Canton remarked to a student that it was pleasant to
see the sun shining again after rain. The student replied, 'It is Chairman Mao, shining down upon us.'
What in the end will be the impact of Mao upon China,
no one, not even Mao, can predict. But his achievements, on any calculation, are formidable. He has laid
the foundations of a modern state which already has a
formidable impact on world politics. He has broken the
Communist world in two. He has inspired new radical
forces in the capitalist world. In one generation the old
China has disappeared.

But this is to go far beyond my story. The top five in
the Party in 1954, by the order of the photographs carried in the great parades, were Mao, Liu Shao-ch'i,
Chou En-lai, Chu Teh and Ch'en Yün. The formidable
Chinese Communist leaders had nearly all been at or
near the top since the early days of the Party and there
had been no purges on the Soviet model. No divergence
of views was then observable. The first sign of disagreement since 1937 appeared in 1954. Kao Kang, an old
comrade of Mao, had been number six on the list and
prominent at the parades on the ceremonial gateway.
He was in charge of industrial planning in Manchuria
and Chairman of the National Planning Commission.
For some months he had disappeared from view. He was
not elected to the National People's Congress in the
autumn of 1954, a sign that something was wrong. In
March 1955 it was announced that there had been a

conspiracy against the Party. Kao Kang was said to have committed suicide. He and Jao Shu-shih, an important Party official and head of the Party's organisations department, were expelled from the Party, Kao Kang posthumously.

We could only speculate on the real causes of the trouble. The indictment of Jao Shu-shih included the allegation that he had been guilty of the policy of 'rightist surrender to the capitalist landlords and rich peasants', in the city and in the countryside. He had been prominent in Shanghai and had perhaps been too independent there. We did not even know whether their crimes were separate or whether they had been engaged in some movement together, though subsequently they have been credited with forming an 'anti-Party alliance'. From slight indications we could, however, roughly reconstruct the stages in the affair. The two men were probably accused at a Party meeting in the spring of 1954. They were under interrogation for about a year, in order to make them confess their mistakes and submit, after which they would undergo penance in the shape, perhaps, of labour in the countryside and would finally be reunited with the Party. But both remained obstinate. The fate of Jao Shu-shih is unknown. Kao Kang finally cheated the Party – this was explicitly stated – by committing suicide.

This affair helped us to understand what one might call the 'religious outlook' of the Chinese Party. I read at the time an account of an incident in English Tudor history which, strangely, had certain elements in common with this domestic quarrel in another continent and century. In the middle of the sixteenth century a crazed renegade monk stabbed the celebrant of Mass in St Margaret's, Westminster. The Bishop of London took him into custody, in the hope of inducing him to repent and be reunited with Mother Church. But he remained obstinate and in the end was handed over to the secular arm and burnt at the stake in St Margaret's churchyard. The Chinese, too, were mainly concerned to secure submission from the rebels, to inflict spiritual humiliation on them, to reunite them in humble obedience with the Party, to reform them through penance. It was therefore logical to regard Kao Kang's suicide as the ultimate crime, the final sign of obduracy. As Roger Vailland observed, the right to suicide has always appeared to be the only, but the irrefutable proof of human liberty.

With hindsight, this incident might be regarded as the first sign of the great schism which was to convulse China ten years later, though at the time it was only the biblical cloud no bigger than a man's hand. In our day P'eng Teh-huai, Minister of Defence from September 1954, delivered in harsh and aggressive tones the keynote speech at the great October parades, standing by Mao on the Great Gate, the T'ien-an men, and apparently secure in a position of power. How little we knew what was happening in the Chinese Party. In 1959 he fell. Later, the world was told that he was a bourgeois agent who had sneaked into the Party, a big conspirator, an out-and-out hypocrite, an opportunist, a counterrevolutionary revisionist, an agent planted in the Army by the 'top Party person in authority taking the capitalist road' (the conventional expression for Liu Shao-ch'i after the split), that he had always opposed Chairman Mao's correct line and that it had been necessary to continue to beat the dog that was already sinking in the water. At the trial of his wife, the judge noted that 'P'eng Teh-huai and his stinking wife Pu An-hsiu were birds of a feather.'

Unlike Kao Kang, he submitted, for his letter to Mao

written in September 1959 has been published and
there is no reason to doubt its authenticity. He said:

I sincerely thank you and my other comrades for
patiently educating and assisting me. It was entirely
necessary for the Party to conduct historically a
systematic criticism of my mistakes. Permit me to
carry on studies or leave Peking for the people's communes, to study and participate in some labour, so
that in the collective living of the working people I
may reform my ideology.

It was also alleged that P'eng Teh-huai joined with
Kao Kang, Jao Shu-shih, Huang K'e-ch'eng, the Chief
of Staff and Chang Wen-t'ien, a Vice-Foreign Minister
who had once been senior to Mao in the Party hierarchy,
in an anti-Party alliance. Of this I am more doubtful.
The real truth is now buried, probably for ever, under
the voluminous documents of the Party line.

A few years after I had left China, a distinguished
British statesman was talking in my house about the
Curragh incident before the First World War. He knew
every detail of it. I suddenly seemed to see what was
wrong with our view of Asian affairs. In spite of our
world-wide interests and experience, we were still
parochial in outlook. Perhaps it was because of our
former power. We had not got out of the habit of
thinking that the affairs of India, for instance, were
still settled in King Charles Street and had no independent existence of their own. I remarked, with, I
hope, a sufficient measure of courtesy, that the trouble
in England was that everyone knew everything about
the Curragh and nothing about the Long March, which
had saved the Chinese Communists from extinction and
provided them with a base from which they could win

the civil war. Yet it might one day be regarded as one of the decisive events in twentieth-century history. The Americans were always much closer than the British to China, but now, at last, the history of the Chinese Communists' struggle for power and its significance for world politics is better understood in Britain.

8

THE INTERNAL SCENE

DURING the first three years after the Chinese Communists had formed their new Government, they had been engaged in consolidating their position. They had waged a fierce campaign against nationalist agents, landlords and 'counter-revolutionaries', which meant anyone who came in their way. Punishment included execution, imprisonment in labour camps, confiscation of property and strict surveillance. Many unrepentant landlords, capitalists and intellectuals were employed in the labour camps alongside thousands of peasants, on ambitious projects for irrigation and flood control on the great Chinese rivers. Two Chinese Ministers, Po I-po in October 1952 and Chou En-lai in February 1953, said that two million bandits had been 'eliminated'. This and similar phrases in other official Chinese statements caused some confusion in the minds of western editors, who were apt to interpret them as an official Chinese admission that they had executed two million of their opponents, one editor going so far as to justify them for doing so. The phrase was probably meant to include other punishments besides execution, but the first few years were in any case a period of ruthless action.

The early campaigns were followed by the 'San-fan' and 'Wu-fan' movements, the so-called Three Antis and Five Antis, directed against corrupt Government officials and businessmen, but doubtless also against the politically unreliable. To the Chinese suicide is a traditional way of release from the troubles of this world, and in Shanghai at this time hardly a day passed without shattered corpses being picked up from the pavements below the famous skyscrapers of Shanghai's capitalist past. In these years it was a young revolution, though its leaders were already elderly. They were united, confident and vigorous in attack, determined to transform China into a great industrial power and to destroy the remaining Nationalist forces which, after being chased off the mainland, remained in being in Taiwan under the protection of the American fleet and continued to declare their intention to reconquer the mainland.

The early turmoil was succeeded by a period of relative moderation, during which the Party concentrated their energies on industrial planning and agricultural and social reform. In industry, except in coal and textiles, they were starting more or less from scratch. They said that it would take fifteen years for the base, fifty years for full industrial development. They made mistakes, but went ahead fast. The Western press were apt to exaggerate their failures which were prominently reported in the Chinese press in pursuance of the technique of public self-criticism, by which they hoped to increase efficiency and drive. The statistics of actual production, which were rare, were probably mostly accurate, but the more common statements of relative increases were, at the least, misleading. It was not very illuminating to learn that production of machinery had been increased by so many hundreds per cent since 1949, a year when China was in the last stages of the civil war and nothing much was being made.

Capital for industrial development had to be found from the profits of the State industries. To increase the profits, wages had to be controlled. Since industrial wages were tied to the cost of living, the Government had also to control essential consumer goods such as food-grains and cotton cloth. The peasants were therefore required to sell to the State co-operative at fixed prices all their produce in excess of what they kept for the family to eat. The result was that they ate more and sold less to the Government, since they could neither hoard nor get a good price and there was nothing much for them to buy. The local officials tried, probably without much success, to dissuade them from spending on weddings and family ceremonies and to get them to buy stock, implements and Government bonds instead. From long and discouraging experience the peasants did not trust Government bonds and they were chary of investing in agriculture, since there were already signs that they would soon be swept up in co-operatives.

Mao's revolution was based on the support of the peasants. He had eliminated the landlords, squeezed the rich peasants, and distributed land to the poor peasants. He now reversed direction and began to organise the peasants into the socialist system, taking from their individual control the land which they had so recently been given. Apart from the need to be able to acquire most of the peasants' produce at low prices, Mao had political reasons for his action. It was repeatedly proclaimed that the time for the most intense struggle in the countryside had now come, that the peasants were natural capitalists and that if they were left alone they would all become little landlords. They had to be brought on to the right path under the leadership of the Party.

It was not all done at once. First came the 'Mutual Aid Group', the members of which helped each other to farm. Then came the lowest grade of co-operative, in which the profits were divided mainly in proportion to the land, stock and implements put into the co-operative by its members and only in small part in proportion to their work. Then the co-operative gradually advanced to the point at which the whole profit was divided in proportion to work and the peasant had effectively lost his land.

At first Mao felt his way carefully. He was not going to have a peasant revolt on his hands, nor use force as Stalin had. When there was trouble, he drew back. Suddenly, at the beginning of 1955, the pace was increased, the pressure was put on and in two years nearly the whole peasant population, probably 110 million families at that time, were in co-operatives. We could only deduce that there were signs of the economic plan breaking down if the State did not get hold of most of the grain harvest, and that Mao had decided that he could carry through this vast revolution in the countryside without serious opposition. He seemed to be right. It was an astonishing feat.

Within a few years Mao again became impatient and proclaimed the 'great leap forward'. Steel was to be produced in the backyard; communes were to manage the whole life of the peasant. New methods of farming had been introduced; new land had been brought under cultivation and irrigated by controlling the great rivers; forecasts of increasing grain-crops were wildly optimistic. Large-scale farming by the peasant communes was to solve the problem of feeding the huge and rapidly increasing population. But it did not work out like that. 'The 'great leap forward' was soon modified and then abandoned; industry reverted to normal methods of production and the communes' farms were again managed by small peasant-groups, though the communes' organisation remained in existence for some other purposes and perhaps as a framework for their later full revival. The agricultural revolution failed to live up to the overconfident estimates and, after a succession of bad harvests, Mao, like Khrushchev, had again to condone private plots. But, while I was in China, the 'great leap forward' was still in the future and Mao still seemed to handle with a sure touch the peasants among whom he had lived for so long.

The State could not take over all commerce and industry at once. The Government first hit the capitalists hard through the 'Five Antis' campaign, which got out of hand like the later Red Guards' attack and had to be called off. Then they started to socialise industry by stages. In the first stage, the State fixed the price of the raw material and the finished product, which had to be offered to Government departments and co-operatives. This gave the Government control. In the next stage, the firm was limited to processing materials to Government order. The remaining British firms were in this position. In the third stage, the foreign firms were finally squeezed out and the Chinese firms, faced with the same squeeze, found themselves with large liabilities to the Government, which were liquidated by the Government's taking over a half-share of the ownership and management. The larger commercial firms were treated in the same way, but the small shop-keepers were left alone for the moment. The final stage, which was not reached in my time, could be foreseen.

The capitalist was not deprived of all his money at once. He had to contribute large sums to Government loans, and his drawings from the bank were restricted to what he might have earned as manager of his firm. If he was intransigent, he would disappear to labour in the countryside. Capitalists were easier to deal with than peasants. Specimens of the tamed variety were occasionally exhibited to the foreigner in Peking. The method of expropriation was very Chinese in its emphasis on the action which the victim was required to take to earn absolution for his past sins. Steady pressure was applied until the Chinese capitalist saw the light; the foreign capitalist 'voluntarily' made some, if inadequate, restitution for his past exploitation of the Chinese people and was finally allowed to depart in peace.

Social reform was to accompany political and economic reform. The Chinese marriage customs, requiring complete subjection of a wife to her husband, were an obvious target for the Communist reformers, but they went too fast and had to draw back. Enforcement of the initial law for social reform, enacted as early as 1950, proved unexpectedly difficult and had to be deferred. The new régime was not the first Chinese Government to introduce measures of social reform, but it was the first with sufficient control to hope gradually to carry it out. As a young man Mao had cut off his pig-tail. It was natural that the new régime should wish to suppress every sign of the old ways. The old women with bound feet still hobbled about Peking, but the authorities forbade the export of any picture which showed this old bad habit or even a baby with a window in the seat of its trousers in the old Chinese way, and amateur foreign photographers were apt to find it as dangerous to photograph picturesque humanity as railway bridges and military installations. The past was to be forgotten; the propaganda image of smiling peasants and workers was now to be the reality.

Internal administration was much stronger than before the Revolution. There was security throughout most of China, a condition of life which no Chinese alive could ever have known. Roads and railways were being built and transport was organised to relieve local shortages of food. There was much less corruption. Public discipline was so strict that when a train drew up at a wayside station the orderly queues of waiting passengers boarded it separately at the signal of a whistle. Free medical treatment was provided for State employees including factory workers, but we knew from our clerks that when they or their relations who were not Government employees wanted treatment they had to pay in advance. An English lady, prominent in public life, who was visiting Peking and seemed determined to find everything perfect, refused to believe me when I told her this. The same evening at an official party she brought up to me two Chinese officials and said that they were in charge of hospitals in Peking and would tell me that what I had said to her that afternoon was not true. She left us and we exchanged polite remarks. I was not amused.

The attention being paid to public health was bound to have its effect on the terrifying problem of the increase of population. We were inclined to believe the new Chinese figures of a population of 600 millions increasing at the rate of 12 millions a year. Chou En-lai said to me that the Malthusian doctrine suited Russia but not China, and that birth control would have to be introduced if the people were going to be fed and have a higher standard of living. The problem was not going to be easily solved. Ten years later, Chinese husbands with children were being urged to accept sterilisation.

The minorities were treated with special attention. Great deference was paid to their customs and culture. They were granted what appeared to be a high degree of autonomy, but at the same time were kept under tight control. The attractive Dalai Lama and sour-faced Panchen Lama were being re-educated in Peking, and were paraded at official parties. The great military road was being pushed through to Lhasa, a formidable engineering feat, and the creation of an autonomous Tibetan area was announced with a flourish. The Tibetans did not appreciate the gifts of the conquerors, no longer content with the shadowy far-off suzerainty of the old China. The set-back was still to come.

The organisation of government under the constitution of 1954 was highly complicated. Mao was Chairman of the Republic. The functions of Head of State, never of much importance in a Communist State, were exercised jointly by the Chairman of the Republic and the Standing Committee of the National People's Congress. This arrangement was presumably intended to give 'face' to the Standing Committee which was a repository for the leaders of the non-Communist splinter-parties and old members of the Kuomintang, who had joined the Government and enabled Mao to exhibit the union of parties under Communist leadership which made up his 'New Democracy'. This symbol of the alliance of the national bourgeoisie with the workers and peasants stemmed from Mao's ideas about the unity of the Chinese people, while being a useful political device during the initial transitional period.

No one could have had any illusion that the old gentlemen who decorated the high table at official dinners in Peking had any real power or influence, whatever their nominal position in the new hierarchy. Later, outside China, I asked a Chinese Ambassador why they accepted and honoured in this way Li Chi-shen, the former Canton warlord, who, in his capacity as Vice-Chairman of the Standing Committee of the Congress, sat at official functions with the Communist leaders. Were they not at the same time erecting a memorial to the Communists who with their wives and children had been burnt alive with petrol by the police, acting under Li Chi-shen's orders, during the Canton Uprising of November 1929? He replied that what I said was true, but that Li Chi-shen had been prepared to fight the Japanese, which I interpreted as meaning that he had joined the Communists and betrayed his old friends at the right moment.

Chou En-lai as Premier, with ten top Communists as Deputy Premiers, presided over the Administration, but real power lay with the Party Political Bureau, headed by Mao, and their decisions were carried out through the organs of Party and Government, on the basis of 'democratic centralism', which only meant that the Party kept a tight control all the way down. There were six million Party members and strict qualifications were required. There was a Party cell in each village, factory and town ward. Residents' committees in each street in the towns were responsible to the Ministry of Public Security for the behaviour of their members. A separate supervisory organisation, taken over from old China, kept subordinate officials under surveillance. Informing was a civic virtue. Everyone spied on everyone else and no one was left alone in Mao's China. The organisation was tight and effective, and it is not surprising that a convulsion was required to break it down, when the men who controlled it fell out with Mao.

The single list elections to the National People's

Congress were probably popular. In the old days, the Kuomintang had not consulted the peasants before declaring their nominees elected and the landlords, often oppressive, had controlled the village elections. Under the new régime, as far as we could find out, teams went round the villages with provisional lists and asked the villagers for their comments. The elections at the lowest level were important to the villagers, for the elected representative was not only a delegate to the local People's Congress, but also the official responsible for assessing the village taxes and the amount of grain to be sold to the State. If the villagers complained that a man was extortionate or cheated them, his name was struck off the list. In this way the villagers had the satisfaction of improving their own lot, and the Government claimed that they had changed a quarter of the village officials during the elections. Each local Congress elected the next one on the Chinese-box principle and the top people were inserted somewhere up the line. The Congress met in the autumn and ratified every proposal unanimously. The official defence against the charge that this unanimity made the Congress a sham was that the delegates were naturally unanimous, since they all started from the same point of view. Cicero, who gave the Roman augurs credit for retaining a sense of humour, would have enjoyed the spectacle.

9

DIPLOMATIC STATUS

THE weeks before the Geneva conference and each deadlock in the conference had bred rumours of 'instant and massive retaliation' by American Forces in Indo-China and perhaps even in China itself. In Geneva, with the aid of an American correspondent, I composed a limerick in honour of my forthcoming return to Peking:

A man who was off to Peking
Said 'For God's sake don't drop the damn thing;
The bomb, you'll allow,
Will hit me and not Mao,
Not Chou, but the tombs of the Ming.'

But, when I returned, the solution was in sight and the brief second session of the conference sufficed to achieve an agreement to which the Americans assented by separate statement, but did not directly subscribe.

I returned to a very different situation from that which we had suffered since 1950. We were now treated as a recognised mission and could do business in the same way as others. The Consulate-General at Shanghai was recognised as an outlying part of my office under an

oral agreement which lasted until it was swept away in
the 'cultural revolution', and we could at last relieve the
acting Consul-General and bring in his replacement.

Chang Han-fu, the Vice-Minister in charge of our
affairs, saw me at my request in the Foreign Ministry,
gave parties for our visitors and came to official parties
in my house. He was jovial enough, but there was always an undercurrent of sarcasm and I did not find him
easy. His wife, Kang P'u-sheng, was Vice-Director of the
International Affairs Department, and rumour had it
that they only saw their child at weekends. Huan
Hsiang, the head of the Western European Department
until he was appointed chargé d'affaires in London, was
a sympathetic character, who seemed to try to be helpful. He had been at the London School of Economics,
became a Customs official and moved into the Communist bureaucracy, much, I suspect, as a British civil
servant moves from the Treasury to the Board of Trade.
He told me that he had been a guerrilla fighter and at
dinner in Geneva Mr Eden, whom I had briefed, referred to him as such, provoking a roar of laughter from
Chou En-lai, which flattened poor Huan. His life in
London must have been difficult. He had to leave nearly
the whole of his large family in China and stay in London for many lean years, during which Anglo-Chinese
relations became no easier. I had great sympathy for
him.

The Ministry of Foreign Affairs appeared to be open
day and night. During my time in China, I was summoned to the Ministry at all of the twenty-four hours except
between 3 a.m. and 6 a.m. We would be told by telephone at about 11 p.m. that I would be summoned
during the night and that they would let us know the
exact time later. At about 1 a.m., I might be asked
to go at half past two. I made a point of treating

the visit as if it were at a civilised hour, would comment politely on the fineness of the morning with a touch of frost in the air and sit down to hear the news of such importance as to require my presence in the middle of the night. It was almost invariably the reading in Chinese and then in English translation of a long statement about American atrocities which had been broadcast an hour or two before and which would appear in full in the press in the morning. I would protest that the attacks on the Americans were wholly without foundation and leave.

These meetings were stiff and formal. The Vice-Minister, who knew English well, spoke only in Chinese. Each of us had his own interpreter. It may seem strange that we submitted to this treatment. The Soviet Ambassador was the doyen of the diplomatic corps, the greater part of which consisted of representatives of Communist states. Neither they nor my non-Communist colleagues had ever protested. As a mere chargé I could not take the lead. In any case, I did not want to protest. If I had done so, the Chinese might have retaliated by leaving me out and I could not afford to run the risk of missing something of interest. I used to be amused rather than annoyed by these nocturnal expeditions and always hoped we might get some real news for a change.

The first business to be done was to follow up the representations which I had made in Geneva. Among these was a request for the immediate return of some British sailors who had lost their way on a holiday sailing trip and had landed in Chinese territory. The Chinese said that this was a matter which could be settled with the local authorities, which meant that they did not intend to hold the sailors in order to be unpleasant. If this had happened before the Geneva conference, the sailors would probably have been held for about eighteen months. They were lucky to get lost just at this time. After a few minor squabbles and a persistent attempt by the Chinese to represent me as apologising to them, we got the sailors out in six weeks. Soon afterwards, a police launch stolen from Hong Kong by a disgruntled policeman was returned by the Chinese with its crew. We seemed to be in for an easier time.

The next incident was much more serious. A British civil airliner of the Cathay Pacific Air Line was shot down by Chinese fighters off Hainan Island, when flying on a scheduled route. Several passengers were drowned, including Americans. The situation in the area became dangerous. The Canton authorities, who probably suspected that the opportunity would be taken to collect a little intelligence on the side, warned Hong Kong that military aircraft sent to search for survivors would be shot at. This was naturally bitterly resented and no notice was taken of the warning. Two American aircraft engaged in the search were shot at by Chinese aircraft and a gunboat, and shot down the aircraft. Units of the American fleet moved into the area, ostensibly to continue the search, though by that time there was no more hope of finding any survivors, and it looked more like a political demonstration than a practical effort to save lives.

I made a strong protest to the Chinese Government and demanded an apology, payment of compensation, punishment of the offenders and measures to ensure that such an incident could not happen again. To my utter astonishment, used as I was to Chinese inflexibility on almost every issue between us, I received a prompt acknowledgement that a mistake had been made, a full apology and a promise to pay compensation.

The Americans wanted to get in a separate protest of their own and I was instructed to deliver it personally. As usual, I sat on the right of the Vice-Minister, on a sofa placed at right-angles to his. On my right was my interpreter, on his left was his. I knew I should have difficulty in leaving my protest, which would undoubtedly be rejected. So I stretched across the Vice-Minister and handed it to his interpreter, who took it. The Vice-Minister took it quietly from him and laid it on the arm of the sofa between us. I left the Ministry, leaving the paper where it was. So far, so good. An hour later one of my junior secretaries was asked to call at the Ministry and was handed the protest with the bland remark that I had left my papers behind by mistake. The Vice-Minister had handled the matter neatly.

After that experience, I got Washington's agreement to deliver their protests by letter. They invariably bounced back, but in this way I could be sure of being able to deliver them. The British Government made me go back to the Chinese with further demands for the punishment of the offenders and measures to prevent a recurrence of the incident. I saw no practical point in doing this and did not want to push the Chinese off their new conciliatory line. The offending pilots had probably been shot; there was an oblique reference in the Chinese statement to their taking appropriate measures and they were clearly not going to allow so embarrassing an incident to be repeated. I carried out my further instructions without effect, as I had expected. But what mattered was the compensation and, after no great delay, I received the amount demanded, a cheque for £367,000.

We now attended official functions. The great processions on 1 May and 1 October were partly military parades, partly popular demonstrations, the ceremonial being exactly copied from the parades on Red Square in Moscow. All the familiar stock effects appeared, coloured balloons, peace doves, millions of paper flowers, minorities, in national dress and a succession of floats recording recent production records; but it was gayer than in Moscow in the clear atmosphere and brilliant sunshine of Peking, among the massed thousands of genuinely happy, smiling Chinese out to enjoy the show. The parades had not yet become stale through repetition and displayed all the Chinese sense of the theatre. Of course, it was all highly organised, even the dancing in the streets in the evening, but that did not seem to spoil the holiday spirit. The diplomatic corps showed signs of wilting after standing for four and a half hours watching the parade, and were visibly relieved when the close was marked by what we called the blessing 'urbi et orbi' given by Mao on either side of the Great Gate. A curious feature of the proceedings was the conduct of an official photographer meticulously photographing each head of mission and then crossing his name off on his list. The photographs were never seen by anyone. Were they, we wondered, for the secret-police files and designed to help an agent to identify and follow an ambassador?

The official dinners for visiting prime ministers or national days were immense affairs. The diplomatic corps were met by Chou En-lai and the other top people and processed into the huge dining-hall containing up to a thousand people, being greeted by the slow rhythmic hand-clap favoured at Communist functions and grand dinners at the Guildhall in the City of London. The top people took their places at one side of a long table, facing down the hall, looking like a painting of the Last Supper. The visiting dignitaries were interspersed among the hosts, and since only one interpreter was allowed behind the principal guest most of the people at this table were unable to say one intelligible word to their neighbours. They stared rather mournfully down the hall, munching their food, drinking the toasts, clapping to order and obviously not enjoying the proceedings. The diplomatic corps, with a sprinkling of the appropriate Vice-Ministers and the watchdogs of the Protocol Department, sat at separate tables, carefully segregated from the bosses and the proletariat. Our food, the customary cold first course, was laid before us, but we could only look at it until the speeches were over.

The speeches were given in Chinese, Russian and English, with additions to taste. Both Chinese and Russians were careful not to omit the magic formula about the camp of peace and democracy headed by the Soviet Union, though by the autumn of 1954 the Chinese People's Republic had crept into it. Frequent clapping was prescribed, the only safe rule for the ignorant foreigner who was not a Communist being not to clap anything you did not understand, since it was almost certain to be a nasty crack at your allies or a glancing blow at your imperialist self. At this time the rule was not to say anything about us which was unpleasant enough to make us get up and leave in the middle of the English version. Meanwhile, the non-Communists, not having been brought up to endure the rigours of the Chinese official party, grew hungrier and hungrier. At the Indonesian National Day party, I was sitting next to Mr Aneurin Bevan. After submitting patiently to three-quarters of an hour on economic developments in Indonesia since the 'liberation', while Mr Attlee slept peacefully at the next table, I said to Mr Bevan, 'Now you know that the members of the British Foreign Service earn their pay.' He replied, 'Now I know what happens to them when they get old. It's not that they are stupid; they are just dazed.' I used to dream of getting my own back by celebrating the liberation of the English from the Danes with a ten-hour speech about our economic developments since that date, including an hour or two on Cromwell's draining of the fens.

It was not always easy to know when to go and when not to go to an official function. My first invitation was to a dinner for Pham Van Dong, the North Vietnamese representative at the Geneva Conference. We did not recognise the North Vietnamese, but the party was to celebrate the Geneva agreements which had been signed by, among others, Mr Eden and Pham Van Dong. I went to it, but not to the Soviet Ambassador's party for Sino-Soviet treaty day, since the pact did not concern us and the Chinese would not have attended a NATO dinner in London. The next morning, the Peking news-sheet reported that the British Ambassador in Moscow had attended the comparable party there. In a difficult case, there was much consultation between the non-Communist colleagues. It was no good consulting the Indians who went to everything. So did the Danes who had nothing else to do and disliked refusing any invitation. The Swiss liked to wriggle out of the dilemma by sending a junior secretary, which in official terms made no difference whatsoever. My Swedish colleague, a man of sound judgement, nearly always reached the same conclusion as I, often on totally different grounds from mine, which did not matter.

We could meet no Chinese except officials, whom we had to invite through the Protocol Department, a member of which always turned up at our parties. How many came was decided by the Foreign Ministry and appeared to depend on the state of political relations at the moment. No wife came unless she was there in her own right by virtue of her own post in the Government, or unless her husband ranked as at least a Vice-Minister. Our guests arrived in a bunch at exactly the hour named, talked English, were friendly provided we kept off politics, and left in a bunch as soon as dinner was over.

I only managed to meet other Chinese twice. With our last remaining British banker I visited the university formerly known as Yen-ching, by the simple expedient of driving through the gate past the sentry, in order to call on 'Red' Winter, the only American on the teaching staff who had stayed on into the Communist era. He was not so red, I thought, merely a beachcombing type who did not want to change his habits of life and was prepared to conform to the extent required of him, in order to avoid having to go home. While we were there, a Chinese professor came to visit him. He told us of the indoctrination course for teachers and of the current fight between the Ministries of Education and Culture over English teaching.

English was taught as a shock course with a limited vocabulary in order to train enough students to translate propaganda into English and political and technical material from English into Chinese. English literature was still taught in only three universities, Peking, Shanghai and Canton, to a strictly limited number of students. But the students on the shock language-course demanded to be allowed to read some English literature, since, they said, without some knowledge of the literature they could not understand the language properly. The Education Ministry had given way. The professor was employed on the translation into English of the writings of the Chinese leaders. I said that the language seemed very stilted to us. He replied that there were strict restrictions on the English words which could be used. He told us with evident amusement of the choice by the World Peace Council of the year's 'cultural heroes'. They would never have chosen Leonardo da Vinci if they had known about his morals and that year it was to be Fielding, solely because *Tom Jones* was Marx's favourite novel.

The newspapers told us the amount of floor space in the new colleges and schools, that the educational system had been reformed by the application of 'advanced Soviet technique', that the aim was to train technicians to the level and in the numbers required by the Government's 'construction work' and that Russian was to become the first foreign language, being required for the study of Russian text-books not translated into Chinese. But we had no idea how this 'battery' system was taken by the people subjected to it. This conversation was a tiny chink of light through the thick curtain of official information.

The second meeting was with a university teacher who had found what he hoped would be a peaceful billet doing translation work, for he found university life distasteful in these days. The courses were changed over and over again and teaching had become impossible owing to perpetual interference. However, he had coped with the Japanese and could probably manage this time too. He told me that in the early days of the Communist Government the Chinese intellectuals were so disgusted with the corruption and incompetence of the Nationalists that they felt that anything else must be better. For a time the new régime had dealt lightly with them, for their co-operation was needed; but recently the line had changed and most intellectuals had become disillusioned by the rigid uniformity of thought imposed on them. He expected that there would be a long campaign to subdue them. We know now that he was right.

Some Western writers had maintained that the Chinese Communists had the intellectuals on their side and that this was one of the important elements in their success. In Peking we thought that this was going too far. Some had been converted, many were apathetic, most were probably sympathetic at first but were soon alienated. They were not active in opposition; that was physically impossible. What little evidence reached me suggested that none of them wanted Chiang Kai-shek back in any circumstances, but it became clear a few years later that most of them were not converts to Communism, when Mao's encouragement of debate in the words 'Let a hundred flowers bloom' led to such a flood of criticism of the basic doctrine that it was quickly transformed into a campaign against them, accusations of rightist deviation and the despatch of many to forced labour in the countryside.

Either Mao had thought that by that time criticism could be safely allowed, since it would be based on a genuine acceptance of Chinese Marxism and would be limited to a discussion of defects in the execution of policy, or perhaps he was giving the unconvinced enough rope to hang themselves. They must have known what Mao meant, that his metaphor depicted not the disordered profusion of an English herbaceous border, but the discipline of a Chinese garden, in which every chrysanthemum is made to produce blooms of the same size, height and colour as its neighbours and where the flowers are ranged in ordered ranks like soldiers on parade. Perhaps it was just that they had been suppressed for so long that they could not help letting themselves go. In either case, they suffered a crushing defeat.

IO

FOREIGN RELATIONS

V ISITORS now poured in. A British Labour Party
delegation arrived with the representatives of the
British press trailing along behind in extreme disgust,
having persuaded themselves that the members of the
delegation were earning large sums by writing articles
for the press and did not want to have competitors too
near them. The most notable event of the visit was Mr
Aneurin Bevan's brilliant speech to the People's Con-
sultative Committee, then still the provisional Chinese
parliament, probably the first live non-Communist
speech delivered in Peking since the Revolution, on the
theme that Communism was not the only way to achieve
a social revolution in our time and that the historical,
political and social circumstances of Britain made it
necessary to use different methods. The Chinese translation was listened to with complete attention; while
he spoke in English, there was a buzz of comment. I recall, too, the miners' leader, Mr Sam Watson, holding
up the wish-bone of a chicken and proposing before the
vast gathering at dinner the toast of the 'four freedoms'
coupled with the name of Mao Tse-tung.

To meet the delegation Chou En-lai and a number

of Ministers and officials came to dinner with me in the old compound which they had never before visited. It was a cheerful evening. Chou En-lai asked Mr Bevan whether the British Labour Party practised the Chinese system of criticism and self-criticism. 'Well, Clem,' said Mr Bevan, turning to Mr Attlee, 'we are so busy criticising each other that we have no time for self-criticism. Isn't that right?' The only disservice which the visit did us was the result, we thought, of the banter in the British press about Dr Summerskill feeding luxuriously on plovers' eggs in lotus leaves. At later banquets to visiting notabilities the food became severely plain.

In a Western capital it does not matter whether British visitors come near the Embassy or not. In Peking when non-Communist visitors from Britain were coming in for the first time since the Revolution, their relations with the Embassy might be taken as evidence supporting the favourite Chinese theory that there was a gulf between the British people and their rulers. The Chinese must therefore have been somewhat confused when observing that while a trade-union delegation did not come near us, a party from the Labour Left, apparently including one or two fellow-travellers, were scrupulously polite to the Embassy, called formally on us and issued a public statement thanking me and the Consul-General at Shanghai for their help. To confuse further the Chinese picture of the British Left, there came Mr Desmond Donnelly who, having started by going to sleep on the aircraft at Ulan Bator and having his passport stolen, paid his own way, which enabled him to have a good, honest political row with the Chinese officials looking after him. For all their subtlety and intelligence, the Chinese did not understand the British political scene at this time. They had, of course, totally disbelieved me when I told them at Geneva that most people in Britain looked on the Red Dean as a joke.

They got some good change out of the British 'cultural giants', as we nicknamed them in the Chinese manner, who accepted the pocket money offered to them by their hosts and went through the fatuous performance of offering Kuo Mo-jo a message of peace signed by a long list of sincere but misguided British intellectuals. Kuo Mo-jo, a wily old bird, one of whose principal functions was to exploit the word 'peace' for political ends, was doubtless gratified. The party were greatly entertained at hearing Mr Stanley Spencer guilelessly expatiating to their hosts on the delights of Formosa, which he did not explain was not Taiwan but at Cookham on the Thames.

Two parties of British businessmen came separately, those who followed official advice and came on their own and those who accepted the sponsorship of entrepreneurs claiming a special relationship with the Chinese. I doubt whether the party with political cover did any better than the others. Both parties did some business, but we expected trade to develop slowly so long as China was short of foreign exchange and the embargo was not at least assimilated to the Russian version. There was no ground for maintaining a special embargo imposed by the United Nations for the Korean war, after it was over. In 1957 the British Government summoned up their courage to ignore American pressure and modified it. We continually pointed out to the Chinese that they would profit by doing business with us. They were bartering their produce for the industrial goods of East European governments which were passing it on to China's traditional West European markets at a discount. We even heard of Chinese produce going all round the world by this route and being finally sold at world prices in Hong Kong.

What seemed to impress the English visitors most was that there were no flies in Peking, which became a catch phrase like Hitler's motorways and Mussolini's trains running to time. Indian visitors were especially impressed by the factories in Manchuria full of new Soviet equipment and the accompanying propaganda about Soviet aid and 'advanced Soviet technique'. This, they said, showed the tremendous advantages of the Communist system. Could they not have Communist economics without Communist politics? It would have been discourteous to suggest that the Chinese were better workers than the Indians. The more sophisticated Indians retained their critical sense, notably Nehru, and, incidentally, one Indian lady, a member of a party which had an interview with Chou En-lai. 'Tell us,' he said, 'what you find wrong. We want to be told. We want criticism.' There was an impressive silence. The party filed past Chou, shaking hands. When this lady came up, she said, 'You asked for criticisms. We are on a good-will mission, and so I was silent. If we had been on a fact-finding mission, I should have had a lot to say.' Chou roared with laughter. He was never put off balance.

The visits of Asian prime ministers, of India, Burma and, just as I was leaving, Indonesia, were superbly stage-managed as demonstrations of Asian solidarity and peaceful co-existence. So far as we could judge, Nehru was disposed to accept the Chinese line, since it fitted with his conception of Indian neutralism, but he gave the Chinese some good advice, in particular to show restraint over Taiwan and not to press for another conference on Korea. U Nu appeared rather naïve in his acceptance of Chou En-lai's assurances that he would not interfere in Burma's internal affairs, but showed courage in his public speeches in Peking and, at our request, tackled Chou about the imprisoned American airmen. He was perhaps right in thinking that Burmese neutrality was the best available defence against Chinese infiltration.

The Chinese made a serious attempt to dispose of one major difficulty between them and the countries of South-East Asia with large Chinese communities who had been regarded by successive Chinese governments as remaining Chinese citizens, for however many generations a family had lived outside China. They offered the Indonesians an arrangement by which their Chinese would be required to choose whether to remain Chinese or accept Indonesian nationality, without having the option of dual nationality, and undertook to dissuade those who chose to remain Chinese citizens from interfering in the internal affairs of Indonesia. An arrangement was signed in the spring of 1955 and the Indonesians seemed wholly satisfied with Chinese policy towards them. Later it lost its credibility as a result of Chinese support for the abortive coup in which the Indonesian Communist Party was involved and the subsequent deterioration in Chinese–Indonesian relations wiped out the effect of the nationality agreement.

Having made headway with the Asians, the Chinese were able at the end of the year to obtain an invitation to the Bandoeng conference of Afro-Asian states to be held in the spring of 1955 and thus to establish themselves as full members of the Asian community. At the conference, Chou En-lai played a leading rôle, exploiting to the full the opportunities offered for demonstrating China's new position as a powerful state and incidentally stealing the limelight from Nehru. Taken as a whole, Chou's Asian policy was a brilliant performance. He made only one false step. On his visits to India and

Burma after the Geneva conference, he made tentative approaches towards an Asian collective security pact, which would put a ring fence round an ostensibly neutral area, with a warning to the Americans to keep out. But he soon found that this was going too far and withdrew to the 'five principles', which were more effective for his purpose, since they aroused no suspicions of Chinese policy. It is curious to recall that Chou En-lai and, more recently, Brezhnev, have made the same mistake of thinking that they could recruit the Asian neutrals into a security pact under their dubious umbrellas. Dulles, was at least, realistic enough to want only Asian members of his pact who would toe the American line.

Chou can hardly have expected to bring the Japanese into the neutralist camp, since they were too dependent on the Americans, but his Japanese policy made sense. Thousands of Japanese prisoners were released, unofficial trade and cultural missions were exchanged and the Japanese were given to understand that they would get all the advantages of the Chinese market if they would only throw out the Americans and take up a tenancy in the half-way house of neutralism. The official aim of China's Asian policy was to 'enlarge the area of peace'. We in Peking never thought that there was any likelihood that Chinese divisions would cross frontiers and add by force to Chinese territory, nor that the theory that they must get hold of the South-East Asian rice bowl made any sense. They could much more easily exchange the rice for Chinese products. We judged their aim to be to enlarge the area of their influence near their borders, at most to convert the neighbouring states into satellites, nominally independent, but in fact dependent on Peking.

It was not surprising that the Indian–Chinese honeymoon did not last. The historic rivalry in South-East Asia had not disappeared. The growing rift between China and the Soviet Union coincided with Soviet moves to extend their influence in India. Tibet was in revolt and could only be kept down with the help of Chinese forces moving in from Sinkiang along the road which they had built under the Indians' noses in the disputed territory of Aksai Chin. Chinese claims on the undemarcated frontier were met by Indian rigidity and the self-righteousness which characterised the first years of Indian independence. The Indian forward policy was in excess of their army's capabilities in supply and organisation, and tension built up along the frontier until in October 1962 the Chinese drove the Indians back and the 'panch shila' disappeared in the battle, leaving as their only Indian memorial the name of a road in New Delhi, though they are still trotted out on occasion by the Chinese. Chou En-lai's persistent attempts to arrive at frontier negotiations with the Indians, which did not merely mean submission to India's claims, showed a natural reluctance to diverge from the Asian policy which he had executed with such success.

After the fracas between the Chinese and Indian Forces, southern Asia might be rather more sceptical of China's assurances of her peaceful intentions, though the demonstration of Chinese strength on the borders of India was perhaps a more effective instrument of foreign policy than the fair words of the past. An immediate Chinese gain was the blossoming of a new friendship with Pakistan whose foreign policy was governed by hostility to India. It had all seemed so clear in 1955. The Chinese mountains are seen through the swirling mist. All those clear patterns of policy beloved of the China watchers dissolve in a moment and new patterns appear. You can only hope to distinguish the mountain ridges if you adopt the old mountaineering trick of facing the other way and looking at them upside down through your legs. And even then you should beware of seeming to see too much.

The celebration of the first five years of the Chinese People's Republic was held in October 1954. A few days before, without warning, Government delegations began flying in from all parts of the Communist world. A telephone call would be received from the Soviet Embassy that a delegation was arriving in half an hour. The Western heads of mission struck, and most of the delegations were met at the airport only by the Communist ambassadors. We all managed to turn up for the Russians, since by that time heat was being engendered by our refusal to be bulldozed into observing the local protocol without notice. It was a surprise packet. Out stepped Khrushchev, Bulganin, Shvernik, then Head of State, and shoals of lesser fry. The next few days were spent in an orgy of speeches and toasts, and my wife had the pleasure of celebrating her birthday by listening to three and a half hours of speeches in Russian and Chinese. It was more than a courtesy visit. It marked a new Soviet policy towards China and produced the third and most important of the agreements made between the Chinese and Soviet Governments since the 'liberation'.

Mao's proclaimed policy was to 'lean to one side', though he was careful to maintain his balance. In Stalin's day his bargaining power had not been strong and he had not got much out of it. Loans and supplies of industrial equipment were on the lean side and were almost certainly given on condition of strict Soviet supervision. Sino-Soviet companies were formed to exploit minerals and oil, to develop Sinkiang in which the

Soviet Union had a close interest, and to manage civil aviation. Under the 1950 agreement Port Arthur and the Soviet interest in the Manchurian railway were to be returned to the Chinese on the conclusion of a Peace Treaty with Japan, but in any case by the end of 1952. Mao had to recognise the independence of Mongolia in return.

In 1952 the Korean War was going on and the Russians obtained the deferment of the transfer of Port Arthur. Though on the face of it a set-back for the Chinese, it was represented as resulting from a Chinese request and may have been due to the fear that the Americans would try to seize the peninsula if the Russians removed their forces during the war. Now, in the autumn of 1954, it was agreed that the joint Sino-Soviet companies should be wound up, Port Arthur was to be returned immediately to exclusive Chinese control, and the only special advantage kept by the Russians appeared to be the retention of their facilities at the port of Dairen.

Every mark of inequality was now sedulously eliminated. The Russians could no longer be accused by the West of keeping a special position in China of the kind which, when held by Western countries in other parts of Asia, was attacked by the Communists as being imperialist and colonialist. Plans were announced for building railways linking China and the Soviet Union through Mongolia and Sinkiang, and it was revealed that the line through Mongolia was already being built. Economic aid was increased, and it appeared that the old conditions had been dropped. There was a generous programme of technical aid, including the training of Chinese technicians. The Chinese showed every sign of being grateful and appeared to be convinced that by 'leaning to one side' they had been well repaid.

Judging by public pronouncements, the status of China in the Communist world was now to be almost equal to that of the Soviet Union, and Soviet support was given to every Chinese political position. But even at this time it was not easy for the Russians. We knew from comments dropped by them elsewhere that they found the Chinese exacting and difficult allies. The Soviet Union had a strong position by virtue of their aid and political support, but the Chinese knew that the Russians had every incentive to maintain the alliance and could no longer carry out an Asian policy without taking account of Chinese interests.

China aimed at the leadership of Asia or at least of the Asian Communists. North Korea had been an exclusive sphere of Soviet influence before the Korean war and that war had probably been the result of Soviet initiative, but the Chinese, having come to the rescue at a critical moment, were, for the moment at any rate, gaining a strong position in North Korea. They were giving substantial help in reconstruction; their troops swarmed all over the country and there was evidence that Koreans from China were replacing the Koreans who had fled to the South. They had played the major rôle in supporting the Viet Minh rebellion and in giving the North Vietnamese economic aid after the armistice. They were taking the lead in promoting the policy of peaceful co-existence in Asia and did not encourage Soviet attempts to get an invitation to the first Bandoeng Conference by virtue of their Asian territory and population.

The Soviet Union had not, however, abdicated in Asia to the Chinese. The visits of Khrushchev and Bulganin to India and Burma in 1956 showed the importance which the Soviet Union attached to their growing influence in the mid-Asian countries south of

their border. The Indian Communist Party still received its funds and literature from Prague. But we felt
that, whatever internal difficulties there were between
them, the interests in Asia of the Soviet Union and
China were predominantly the same. We thought that
they needed each other too much to quarrel and that it
was wise to accept at its face value Mao's remark to the
Labour Party delegation that China was very close to
the Soviet Union.

How wrong we were. But so was Khrushchev, and
even Mao probably felt that he would be able to secure
Soviet acceptance of his basically nationalist aim to develop China's power and influence in the world. The
Chinese have never been able to understand why other
people should not accept their own valuation of themselves.

11

TAIWAN CRISIS

AFTER Indo-China, Taiwan. The target was switched. There was to be no détente. On 11 August 1954, Chou En-lai, in his report on foreign affairs to the Government Administration Council, reiterated the Chinese intention to recover Taiwan; a violent campaign opened, coinciding with the Labour Party delegation's visit. The Chinese line was clear and logical; it never varied. In their view, Taiwan was Chinese territory. They therefore had a right to recover it. If they used force, it would not be aggression, but an internal police operation against a rebel. Their dealings with Chiang Kai-shek, whether by force or negotiation, were their own business and no one else's. The Americans were intruding into an internal Chinese matter by supporting and encouraging Chiang Kai-shek. Without them, the matter would have been settled long before. There was no question of a Chinese–American negotiation on the future of Taiwan, since it was not an international question. The Americans should withdraw their Forces and leave Chinese waters. It seemed sometimes to us in Peking that the argument was not understood in the West and that mistakes were therefore made in the handling of the dispute.

For the Chinese Government it was a national question of the first importance, though it served also as a basis for political attacks on the United States and as a stimulus to harder work at home. It was not only the armed Forces who had to be ready to take Taiwan. It was the industrial workers also, who had to produce more in the Taiwan context. An overwhelming response to the Government's appeal was reported. We even read that the makers of piano-accordions had doubled their output to help in the liberation of Taiwan. Some observers regarded the campaign as merely a dodge to whip up internal support, or as a means of diverting attention from difficulties at home. We saw no ground for such suppositions.

To 'liberate' Taiwan and thus complete the revolution was a serious aim of the new rulers, both because they considered it to be a part of Chinese territory unjustly withheld from them by foreign interference and because, so far as we could judge, they genuinely feared a joint invasion of the mainland by American and Nationalist Forces. This was not surprising in the light of the threats published in Taiwan and sometimes even in the United States. In the first years of the new Government, before the Communists had consolidated their hold on the country, they must have felt that they would not be secure while Chiang Kai-shek remained on Taiwan as a focus for disaffection. Chiang's claim to be the legitimate Government of China was still recognised in the face of the facts by the United States and other governments following their lead. Even when the prospects of a Nationalist invasion were obviously waning, the American press were describing Chiang as an essential element in plans for a revolt on the mainland. Chiang was holding the islands just off the coast and was even maintaining on Quemoy a provincial Government of Fukien in exile. With the help of various American organisations, whether official or unofficial was not clear, he was sending agents onto the mainland for subversion and sabotage, and was trying to arm his supporters who had been left behind. His Forces were making the China Sea unsafe for Western trade with the mainland and were continually attacking merchant ships, British among others. The Chinese Government's attitude needed no special explanation.

The propaganda campaign raged all the autumn and winter and was accompanied by frequent bombing and shelling of the Nationalists on the islands and by Nationalist counter-bombing and shelling of the mainland. It was not always the Communists who started it. Since the Korean war, the strongest attack had been by the Nationalists on a Communist island, and from the evidence which we could get in Peking we could not say that the Communists were solely to blame for the renewal of hostilities after the Geneva conference.

For us, the post-Geneva honeymoon ended in a quarrel almost as soon as it had begun. Chinese propaganda after the conference had exulted at the new isolation of the United States. They seemed to underestimate the strength of the Anglo-American alliance, which was of much greater importance to us than our relatively small interests in China, and to expect from us much more than they had any hope of getting. What they expected was indicated by Mao, who urged the Labour Party delegation to modify American policy on China, to press the Americans to remove the Seventh Fleet from Taiwan, to refuse to join the South-East Asia Treaty Organisation and to refuse to agree to the rearmament of Germany and Japan.

We were not going to abandon the American alliance

in favour of a neutralist position, nor had we as much influence on American policy as the Chinese seemed to think. We did not even press, against American opinion, for the recognition of the Peking Government as the Chinese representative in the United Nations, nor for a modification of the special trade embargo. The Chinese failed to understand our position correctly. If they had realised what little they were going to get out of us, they might have stuck to the pre-Geneva position.

On bilateral Anglo-Chinese questions, the Chinese maintained the position reached in Geneva, though things moved slowly. British firms were still being squeezed out, but there was no difference between the treatment of British and other foreign nationals. At an autumn interview with Chou En-lai I faced complaints on our failure to vote in favour of the Chinese Government in the United Nations and on our part in the establishment of the South-East Asia Treaty Organisation, which the Chinese described as the organisation of a militaristic bloc in Asia and naturally viewed as threatening their interests. They maintained that the Manila Treaty violated the Geneva agreements on the grounds that although Laos, Cambodia and South Vietnam were not members of the organisation the signatories of the treaty pledged themselves to defend the integrity of the three states, and that the United States were giving military aid to South Vietnam. They soon began to realise that for a crumbling French colony had been substituted three independent states, able, at least for a time, to defend themselves against Communist infiltration through the assurance of powerful American support.

But the main cause of Chinese anger was the American Mutual Security Treaty with the Nationalists. Mr

Dulles represented his purpose to the British Ambassador in Washington as an attempt to lower the tension by showing the Chinese that they had no chance of capturing Taiwan. In the long run this was a correct calculation, but we warned from Peking that in the immediate future it would have the opposite effect. The signature of the treaty occasioned a torrent of invective from Peking and the treaty was represented as a new and formidable step in American aggression against China.

Feeling against the British Government mounted at the Foreign Secretary's statement in Parliament that it was clear that the treaty was essentially defensive in character and provided for close consultation which 'should surely be welcome to all of those – and this very much includes us – who want to see cautious policies pursued'. This was taken by the Chinese as a statement welcoming the treaty. The feeling was increased by Mr Nutting's* statement in a television interview in New York suggesting that the United Nations would be fighting with American Forces in defence of Taiwan against Chinese attack and that British Forces would therefore inevitably be involved. The Chinese official press now openly attacked British policy. The British Government were accused in violent language of insincerity in their recognition of the Chinese Government, of action tantamount to a recognition of the 'Two Chinas' theory, of a breach of faith and of an extremely unfriendly act against the Chinese people in following and vigorously supporting the 'United States' policy of aggression against China'. Our relations had sunk to a lower level than at any time during my stay in China, even including the early freeze.

* The Rt Hon. Anthony Nutting, then Minister of State at the Foreign Office.

For some time in the late autumn I had been out of touch with Chou En-lai. I had asked for instructions which would have enabled me to see him at the time of the Manila conference at which the South-East Asia Mutual Defence Treaty was signed, but the British Government were not disposed to send him any message at that time. At the end of December, while the Chinese were pouring out a flood of abuse against us and the press was full of vicious cartoons of Mr Nutting, the Foreign Secretary, after asking my opinion, decided to take the initiative and make our position clear to Chou En-lai. On 5 January 1955, I delivered Sir Anthony Eden's message.*

I said that we were disappointed that the Chinese Government thought our attitude had changed since the Geneva conference. It had not changed. We were always working for the relaxation of tensions and an improvement in Anglo-Chinese relations. We had not been guilty of bad faith; we had no relations with Chiang Kai-shek; but nothing was to be settled by fighting. We believed that the American–Nationalist treaty would induce restraint. In any case, no one could expect the United States to give up her ally. We had to deal with the situation as it was.

Chou said that a difference of opinion need not upset our relations, but since the Geneva conference Britain had taken up an attitude of opposition to China which could only harm them. Our actions hurt the Chinese people. We never criticised the Americans and always condemned the Chinese. The Americans supported and armed Chiang Kai-shek who was attacking the mainland and Chinese islands and capturing merchant ships, including British ships. Was this right? If China took counter-action and liberated her own terri-

* Mr Eden had been given the Garter in the previous autumn.

tory, that was apparently wrong. This was an unfair attitude. Taiwan was Chinese territory, as had been recognised in the Cairo and Potsdam declarations and in the Japanese surrender terms, to all of which the United Kingdom had subscribed. Ch'en Yi had accepted the surrender of Japan in Taiwan, and China had exercised sovereignty there. All this was recognised by the United States Government in their White Paper, and by the British Government. But the United Kingdom supported the treaty between the Americans and Chiang and American encroachment on Chinese territory. An attempt was now being made to deny that Taiwan was Chinese. Even Chiang would assert that it was.

Chou went on to attack Mr Nutting's statement, and said that we expected China to forget the merits of the question and to keep silent about them. Restraint was necessary, but appeals for restraint should be addressed to the Americans, who planned to consolidate their hold on Taiwan and the Pescadores and would then prepare for an attack by Chiang on the mainland, so that he could 'resume his reign'. It was another Munich. The Chinese Government had many complaints against the British Government's behaviour during the autumn, but he had been very restrained and had not said anything to me. Mr Eden had told him at Geneva that he was thinking of trying to create a Locarno Pact in Asia. He had said that it was a good idea, but on his return to Geneva Mr Eden had said that he had dropped the matter because the Americans did not like it. The Americans and British had then created the South Asian Pact, which could create division in Asia and was directed against China. In Parliament and New York Ministers had said bad words about the Chinese Government having exercised their sovereignty by condemning American spies, but the British Government had never said a word when Chinese prisoners were forcibly abducted without a chance to hear the explanations.

I said that it would have been better if he had put his complaints to me rather than broadcasting them through the press. Chou replied that he would do so, but that if the Chinese people felt matters deeply their views would also appear in the press. By this he obviously meant that he was not going to be jockeyed by us into promising not to attack us in public. I said that Sir Anthony Eden believed that the American treaty would induce restraint and was not a new stage in an American plan to restore Chiang to power. I reminded him that Sir Anthony had told him at Geneva that President Eisenhower was a man of peace. When I denied that there was an American plan to attack the mainland, Chou replied that he was an older man than I was and that I should find out that he was right. I countered that Sir Anthony was of about his age and a man of great political experience and that I was only repeating his views. Chou had compared the situation to Munich, but he knew Sir Anthony's record in 1938. He need not think Sir Anthony would ever countenance another Munich.

Chou then said that it was like the position of a householder who had been invaded by a robber and driven upstairs, while the robber took possession of the ground floor. I had said that the robber would not pursue the householder upstairs. That might be true for the moment, but how could I tell that he would not do so in a year or two? I said that it was not a bit like that. It was like the position of a householder who had been driven out of his house by a new man and had taken refuge in one room, the pantry. A friend from outside had come and put a large padlock on the door between the pantry and the rest of the house. It was true that this would prevent the new man from getting into the pantry and finally ejecting the old owner; but it would equally prevent the old owner from trying to recover the rest of the house. Chou retorted that it was like a servant who had been guilty of breach of trust and was being protected by an outsider, who was preventing the rightful owner of the property from recovering what had been stolen. And so we went on at it.

I repeated that we did not recognise Chiang, nor two Chinas. What we recognised was the facts of the situation. Mr Nutting's statement had only meant that an attack on Taiwan would involve the danger of a wider conflagration. We had no obligation to defend Taiwan, only an obligation to act as a loyal member of the United Nations in accordance with a United Nations decision. The Manila Treaty was purely defensive. They had their treaty with the Soviet Union. We had our own defensive arrangements which were our business. Chou retorted that their treaty was different from the South-East Asian Treaty which involved people from outside. He ended by saying that we should improve our relations and return to the spirit of Geneva. It had been a good-tempered quarrel.

The argument went on for months in talks with the Chinese, in the press and on the radio. How would you like it, I was asked, if an enemy were in control of the Isle of Wight or the Isle of Man and were supported there by a powerful outsider? How would the Americans like it if the same thing happened on Long Island? A dangerous situation developed over the coastal islands. The Chinese seemed determined to liquidate the remaining Nationalist strongholds on them and the Americans had taken a position which might oblige them to intervene in the islands' defence. The risk of a clash between American and Chinese Forces seemed greater than at any time since Dien Bien Phu. American statements suggested that atomic weapons would be used against a Chinese attack. The Soviet Government implied that their alliance with China would oblige them to aid the Chinese to defend the mainland against American attack. The Chinese talked about retaliation by atomic bombing against American cities for American atomic attacks on China, and took up a defiant attitude. Suppose the Americans killed 200 million Chinese, they said, that would leave 400 million, quite enough to fill China.

In mid-January 1955 Chinese Government Forces took by assault the most northerly of the islands held by the Nationalists, Ikiangshan, and were poised for an attack on the next group, the Tachen Islands. But at the beginning of February the Americans induced the Nationalists to withdraw from the Tachen group and the Communists occupied them. The story current at the time was that the Nationalists were only induced to withdraw from the Tachens by Mr Dulles's undertaking to defend the remaining coastal islands in their occupation as well as Taiwan, but that the President refused to confirm the undertaking. Whatever truth there was in this story, the American statements on the coastal islands remained equivocal. Their line was that they would intervene if it appeared that the forces collected for the attack were intended for an attack not only on the coastal islands but also on Taiwan itself.

Nobody could make much out of this, since it would almost certainly be impossible to tell in advance what the Chinese had in mind. We guessed that the Americans were concerned that a Chinese success in the coastal islands would seriously affect morale in Taiwan and cause a Nationalist collapse. They therefore wanted to warn the Communists that if they attacked the coastal islands they might find the Americans against them in force, but did not want to give an undertaking to the Nationalists which would encourage them to bring on a fight in order to involve the Americans. The Americans were in something of a dilemma.

Meanwhile, the British Government stated their view of the legal status of Taiwan in Parliament. We did not contest that the coastal islands were Chinese territory nor the Chinese right to them. We regarded Taiwan as having a legally undefined status. It had been Japanese territory before the war. Under the Japanese Peace Treaty the Japanese renounced all right, title and claim to it. We held that the Nationalist Government were exercising power in it on behalf of the Allies pending a final decision on its sovereignty, and that the Chinese assertion that we were in breach of the decisions of the Cairo and Potsdam conferences could not be sustained. The Chinese were not in the least impressed by our acceptance of their point of view over the coastal islands, for it was a part of their case that Taiwan and the islands must be considered together and their objective was Taiwan.

On the legal status of Taiwan we were following the American view as expressed at that time and subsequently. Most people assumed that if there had been no quarrel between Communists and Nationalists, or if the Communists had captured Taiwan before it was placed under American protection, Taiwan would have become Chinese territory long before this; therefore our view of Taiwan's status, even if legally sustainable, was asserted only for political reasons. The Cairo conference had declared, 'All the territories that Japan has stolen from the Chinese, such as Manchuria, Formosa (Taiwan) and the Pescadores, shall be restored

to the Republic of China.' The Potsdam conference
had declared that the terms of the Cairo declaration
should be carried out, and the Japanese in the peace
treaty had accepted the terms of the Potsdam declaration. Whatever the lawyers might say, it was difficult in
common sense to contest Chou's view that these declarations meant that Taiwan was at that time considered
to be Chinese territory. On 5 January 1950 President
Truman said that Taiwan had been handed over to
Chiang Kai-shek 'in keeping with the Cairo and Potsdam declarations', and Mr Dean Acheson writes* that,
as far as the United States Government was concerned
in 1950, Taiwan was Chinese.

At some time before the autumn of 1955, the Americans had changed their view, presumably because they
then saw no prospect of Chiang's return to the mainland. The odd feature of the situation at the time of my
talks with Chou En-lai was that both the Chinese Communists and Nationalists disagreed with us and the
Americans in regarding Taiwan as Chinese territory,
while the Nationalists and the Americans disagreed
with us and the Communists in regarding Chiang Kai-
shek as the Government of China. It was the kind of
situation which Alice found so confusing.

* *Present at the Creation*, p. 351.

12

TAIWAN DEADLOCK

Since the late autumn the Americans had been pressing for British support in putting the question of Taiwan and the coastal islands before the Security Council. From Peking we opposed this, since we thought that the Chinese either would not accept an invitation to attend or, if they did accept it, would go to New York only to make hostile propaganda. With the Nationalists occupying the Chinese seat on the Security Council, a debate would only heighten the tension, while demonstrating the helplessness of the United Nations in dealing with a situation, one of the protagonists in which was not a member.

It looked as if the Americans wanted to get United Nations cover for their position, as they had before the Geneva conference, and that they aimed to get the United Nations to threaten the Chinese with sanctions if they attacked the coastal islands. Sir Anthony Eden felt he could not refuse to support the Americans in putting the question to the United Nations, though he recorded his serious doubts about the wisdom of the proposal and made it clear that the British Government agreed to nothing beyond the initial step. The faint prospect of China's acceptance of an invitation was further diminished by American statements that the purpose of the proceedings was to put the Chinese Government in the dock and especially by President Eisenhower's message to Congress on 24 January asking for advance agreement to the use of American Forces in the area, if it should prove necessary.

I was instructed to put our views to Chou En-lai on 28 January as soon as the proposal was put in the Security Council. I was to emphasise that the Chinese Government were to be invited to take part in the discussion and to urge them to accept the invitation. I was to say that we had not changed our views on the legal question, but that the question of the coastal islands was a most dangerous issue and that both parties should be prepared to discuss the matter and abjure the use of force.

I knew that this would be the bleakest interview I had ever had with Chou. It was. Every now and again I tried to lighten the atmosphere a little, but he was in his most emotional and bitter mood. He said that the liberation of the coastal islands had caused no trouble until the Americans intervened. The President's message to Congress was a war message. The Americans had raised the matter in the Security Council in order to get United Nations' cover for aggression against China. They were saying, 'You must either accept our occupation of your territory or fight.' He did not agree that we should leave aside the rights and wrongs of the question. That was what Hitler had suggested at Munich, and both Sir Winston Churchill and Sir Anthony Eden had opposed it. The United Nations had no right to intervene in the exercise by China of her sovereignty. The threat to the peace was an American threat and should be dealt with under chapter seven of the Charter. The United Nations should condemn the Americans and get them to remove their Forces, but they were giving in to the Americans. The British Government's declaration reflected the people's desire for peace, but the support of the measures proposed to Congress by President Eisenhower would not lead to peace.

I argued that the Americans wanted the pacification of the Taiwan area. The proposal for a discussion in the Security Council was not a hostile move against the Chinese Government. A dangerous situation existed and we wanted the Chinese Government to be present at the discussion of it. We were not pressing the Chinese Government to withdraw their claims nor trying to prevent the discussion of the merits of the question. If tension could be reduced, a solution could be found to the problem of the islands. We understood that the Chinese Government considered it to be an internal question, but it was an international question which should rightly be discussed in the Security Council. The British Government were sincerely trying to find a solution.

Chou repeated his arguments. He added that the Chinese Government were indignant that the British, who had been a partner in the war, would not recognise the international documents on Taiwan. China's place in the United Nations had not been restored to her and Chiang Kai-shek sat there. It was absurd to ask the Chinese Government to sit down and discuss Chinese questions with the Nationalists. This put the British in an awkward position, since they recognised the Chinese Government. Chou could not take part unless American aggression was to be the subject of the discussion. The Chinese Government was not like the British Government at the time of Munich. Perhaps he

thought I had not quite absorbed the blackness of the
atmosphere which he was deliberately trying to convey,
for he ended by saying, 'Thank you for coming, but I
must say it has been a most unpleasant interview.' As
I had expected, the Chinese Government refused to
attend the United Nations except on the conditions
that China's seat was given to them and that only the
Soviet resolution on American aggression was discussed, conditions which they knew would not be
accepted. The proceedings in the United Nations collapsed.

Each side then made further attempts to press their
case. The Soviet Government proposed a ten-power
conference in which the Nationalists would not take
part, which was obviously only a tactical manœuvre. Sir
Anthony Eden suggested that on his return from a conference at Bangkok in March he might meet Chou En-
lai on the China–Hong Kong border. Chou replied
that he would welcome Sir Anthony to Peking. He was
not going to appear to be weakening. All kinds of solu-
tions were canvassed, such as a bargain that the Chinese
Government would be recognised as the representative
of China in the United Nations, while Taiwan would
be declared a separate independent country and a new
member of the United Nations, the so-called 'two
Chinas' proposal, or a United Nations' trusteeship and
plebiscite, suggested by the Ceylonese in Bandoeng. We
in Peking never believed that these ideas would have
any attraction for the Chinese. They were convinced
that in the end they would get Taiwan and the Chinese
seat in the United Nations, regarding both, with some
justification, as their clear right and not as matters
which could be the subject of a bargain.

On 28 February I delivered a message from Sir
Anthony Eden to Chou En-lai, enquiring whether the

Chinese Government would state privately or publicly that, while maintaining their claims, they did not intend to prosecute them by force. There was a suggestion in the message that if they could do this it might be possible to find a peaceful settlement of the question of the coastal islands. The British Government were at the same time repeatedly urging on the Americans the importance of evacuating the coastal islands, which were the immediate danger point. The proposal to the Chinese was as much as to ask them to give up Taiwan for the coastal islands. I did not expect them to agree, since the threat of force was their principal bargaining weapon; the basis of their position was that both Taiwan and the coastal islands were part of China and their aim was the recovery of Taiwan and the liquidation of Chiang's alternative Chinese Government.

Chou's reply, as I had expected, was completely uncompromising. He said that the Americans wanted to trade their intervention in the islands against Chinese acceptance of their occupation of Taiwan. It was a dirty deal and the Chinese would have nothing to do with it. The Americans dared to bully people, because the British supported them. They had abducted 15,000 Chinese from the Tachen Islands, because they could not hold them. He regarded the British attitude as strange. They had fabricated a fantastic report about Chinese savagery towards British prisoners. I had said that the Manila Treaty was defensive, but the final communiqué at Bangkok was obviously directed against China. He supported the Soviet proposal for a conference and Nehru's efforts. They would not be intimidated by American threats. I denied that we proposed a dirty deal and defended our publication of the report about the treatment of British prisoners, which was not a pretext for action against China. Chou ended by saying that it took two sides to make a friendship. The British action was suspicious, and China was disheartened by our action. Sir Anthony Eden replied immediately regretting that a common basis did not yet exist on which to reach a peaceful settlement.

In the event, the Chinese did not at this time pursue their objective any further by force. American policy had been successful. It was not, as Mr Dulles had made out, an attempt to reduce tension in the immediate future. It was a deliberate heightening of the tension, an example of Mr Dulles's brinkmanship. The Soviet attitude must also have influenced the Chinese. The Russians in Peking gave me the impression that they did not want to risk becoming involved against the Americans on an issue which was not of the first importance for their security. By their obligations under the Sino-Soviet treaty, they were in danger of having to fight the Americans on a purely Chinese question as a result of a Chinese decision. The Americans still had the advantage in atomic weapons. The Russians must surely have advised restraint, though the Chinese were probably satisfied with Soviet political support, since in less friendly days their public attacks on the Russians about their attitude over the islands were confined to the events of 1958. In addition, Nehru and U Nu in Peking and the Asians in Bandoeng were advising caution and Chou had to think of the credibility of his Asian policy. Mr Dulles's calculation of the balance of forces had been correct.

The Chinese now had to get off the hook. They had carefully left themselves a way of retreat. They had never said that they would attack Taiwan by force. They had always said that they would liberate it, without specifying the method of liberation, only that they had the right to use force. At this stage, therefore, they developed this line by beginning to talk more about negotiation with Chiang Kai-shek to settle a purely internal question. It had been implicit in their attitude all along that Chiang was just another warlord who would eventually surrender to the new dynasty, as many warlords had before him. It was a change of emphasis, not a change of policy.

From the time of the civil war the Communists had always been prepared to welcome the adhesion of individual Nationalists. After all, the Communist leaders had themselves been working with the Nationalists for long periods and the 'New Democracy' was based on the principle of coalition. Fu Tso-yi, for instance, the Nationalist Commander of Peking, had given up the city and was now in the comfortable job of Minister of Water Conservancy in the Peking Government. Other Nationalist generals, too, had come over since that time, and appeals were continually broadcast to those still in Taiwan, doubtless supplemented by private messages, to come back to their homes and families on the mainland, in the expectation that they would be given good jobs by the Government.

The Chinese are a very patient people. Their time scale is much longer than that of the impatient Europeans. The Communists might calculate with some reason that, in the end, Taiwan would come to them peacefully, if only after Chiang's death or retirement to enjoy the family's wealth in the United States. So it looked to us at the time. But China was to go through its time of dissension and unrest, and no Nationalist leader can have been tempted to return to the mainland during the 'cultural revolution'.

In 1958, after I had left China, the Chinese created a new crisis over the coastal islands, perhaps believing that Chiang, who still pledged that he would invade the mainland and still kept large forces on the coastal islands, would make a last attempt to draw the Americans into an attack on the mainland. It was at least partly shadow-boxing, with P'eng Teh-huai, then still Minister of Defence, announcing in the later stages of the affair that he was bombing the islands on alternate days, so that the people could get their supplies on the other days. The heat was taken out of the situation as soon as the Americans made it clear that they were not going to allow Chiang to invade the mainland. The assessment of American intentions which I had given Chou En-lai was proved correct. For the Chinese Communists it was no longer a matter of survival and they were not going to be so foolish as to attack Taiwan and bring in the American fleet, especially as by this time they were much less sure of Soviet support. They have since described the Soviet attitude as being verbal support only, given after the crisis was over.

It would surely have been better if the Chinese civil war had at an early stage reached what, without the Americans, would have been its inevitable outcome. In those days the Americans were not disposed to intervene. Their prestige was not heavily involved and the capture of Taiwan by the Communists at that time would not have materially sharpened the repercussions felt in South-East Asia as a result of the Communist capture of the mainland. The prominent Nationalists would have again escaped, and though the Taiwanese would have had to submit to a Communist régime they would no longer have had the Nationalist and not always friendly invaders sitting on their heads.

The entry of the Chinese Communists into the United Nations and the establishment of diplomatic relations between them and most non-Communist governments would, I believe, have helped towards a resolution of the difficult problems in the Far East and South-East Asia. It would at least have made the Chinese Government accountable in the United Nations for their international actions, and though they would have been arrogant and intransigent there as elsewhere the Security Council could hardly have been more ineffective than it has been without them. The Americans' ability to support the non-Communist governments in South-East Asia would not have been materially weakened. But the onset of the Korean War made it impossible for the Americans to leave the Nationalists, the allies of the South Koreans, to be gobbled up by Peking. All thoughts of American recognition of the Chinese Communists were then swept away and the trend of events was roughly reversed. By 1954 the situation had radically changed. The Americans' prestige was by that time so heavily involved in the defence of Chiang Kai-shek on Taiwan that they could not have abandoned him without losing immensely in prestige and influence throughout the Far East. Militarily, the odds were against the Chinese Government. By not extending their victory on the mainland to Taiwan in early 1950, they had lost their chance.

In 1926, when Chiang Kai-shek was not dependent for his existence on the Americans, he said, 'The Chinese revolution is part of the world revolution. We want to unite the partisans of the world revolution to overthrow imperialism. . . .'* In 1944 the Chinese Communists proclaimed that 'Democratic America has already found a companion, and the cause of Sun Yat-sen a successor in the Chinese Communist Party and the other democratic forces. . . .'† In 1954 the Russians

---

* Quoted by Stuart Schram, *Mao Tse-tung.*
† Ibid.

and the Chinese were apparently the closest of friends, in 1968 apparently torn apart by dissension and rivalry. The Chinese were closer to the Americans than any other people. Perhaps, in spite of appearances, they still are. The pattern has changed and will change again. Who knows whether we shall not see in this century the ticker tape on Fifth Avenue streaming down on the head of a Chinese leader, and an American President standing on the Great Gate of Peking to receive the welcome of a thousand million Chinese?

13

AIRMEN IN TROUBLE

O N 23 November 1954 the Chinese People's Court sentenced, on charges of espionage, eleven American airmen shot down during the Korean war, to terms of imprisonment ranging from four to ten years. In the same trial, on similar charges, the Court sentenced two American civilians, also shot down, one to life and the other to twenty years' imprisonment, four Chinese tried with them being sentenced, one to death, two to life and one to fifteen years' imprisonment. In Peking we did not know the full facts. We had only American and Chinese public statements which did not corroborate each other. What we could gather from these statements was as follows.

The Chinese said that at the end of 1952 they had shot down the two Americans over China. They had captured the men and their C47 aircraft. The equipment which they alleged they had found in the aircraft or on the men was consistent with the Chinese statement that the men had been on an intelligence mission. According to the Chinese account it included weapons, ammunition, wireless sets, maps of Chinese territory, parachutes, forged passes of the Chinese Army, gold, paper money and an apparatus for picking up men from the ground, with instructions attached. They alleged that the men had been sent by the American Central Intelligence Agency to bring an American agent back from China to Japan. If, as the Chinese stated, the aircraft was shot down over China, they were justified in not treating the American captives as prisoners of war. The Americans issued no statement about these men, at the time of their capture.

On 12 January 1953, according to an American account, an American B29 aircraft commanded by an American Air Force colonel and with a crew of eleven American airmen in uniform with United Nations identification papers, was on a mission to drop leaflets over North Korea. Its crew were members of the 581st Air Supply and Communications unit of the 13th United States Air Force, based on the Philippines, but operating on this mission from Yokota base, Japan. According to the report of a United Nations' radar operator, the aircraft was attacked over North Korean territory, fifteen miles south of the Yalu river, by twelve enemy fighter-aircraft. Six minutes after this, international distress signals were radioed from the aircraft and it was abandoned. The crew baled out. Three were killed. The Chinese captured the rest.

Ten days later, on 22 January, Chou En-lai made a public protest, saying that the aircraft had been brought down fifteen kilometres north-west of Antung, the frontier town at the mouth of the Yalu river, well inside Chinese territory. He claimed that the crew had admitted that their aircraft was a refitted B29 bomber used for strategic reconnaissance. He admitted that the crew were held as civil prisoners, not as prisoners of war, as they should have been, since they were in uniform. The Chinese said subsequently that one man had admitted that he had previously conducted reconnaissance flights over southern China.

There was one discrepancy in the Chinese versions of this incident. In January 1953 they had said that the aircraft had been shot down by Chinese fighters taking off to attack it, which would not be inconsistent with the American version of the location. In November 1954 they said that it had been shot down by anti-aircraft fire, which would fix the location over China. Chinese suspicions would certainly have been aroused, since the crew belonged to an unusual unit, the aircraft had just come from the United States Command in the Philippines, it was not engaged on a combat mission and there was an extra-large crew on board. The reason for the large crew was that one crew was briefing another. It was possible that the aircraft and some members of the crew had been previously employed on reconnaissance missions over China, but we had no reason to doubt the American statement of the purpose of this mission. One obvious hypothesis was that the Chinese altered the location of the incident to suit their case, but even if this was true it is highly probable that they genuinely suspected that the aircraft was on its way to conduct an intelligence mission over Chinese territory.

The names of the crew were included in the list of Americans held in China which the Americans gave to the Chinese in Geneva, being placed in a separate category as 'military prisoners'. The Chinese made great play with this, alleging that it showed that the Americans themselves did not regard them as prisoners of war. But the Americans pointed out that they had included the names also in the general list of missing prisoners of war and that their being included in the other list had no significance other than that the Chinese had admitted holding them and claimed that they were in a category other than that of prisoners of war. The two civilians' names did not appear in any list.

At Geneva the Chinese had told me that the eleven airmen were still held and were all in good health. Nothing more was heard of them until their conviction was announced. The trial had been in the usual Communist form which, as we found from an account of Chinese customs in the early part of the nineteenth century, was very like the old Chinese trials. Before the formal trial there were long private interrogations designed to make the accused confess, other evidence not being considered as of any importance. When the accused had confessed, the formal trial was held, being limited to a recording of the confessions, the conviction of the accused and the sentence. When the airmen had confessed to 'intrusion over Chinese air space', the trial was begun and their statements formally recorded, but in their case the Chinese had deferred conviction and sentence and had held the men for later action in the light of political developments. Chou En-lai admitted to the Indian Ambassador that in easier political circumstances they might have dealt with the case very differently.

By November tension had risen and feelings against the Americans had become bitter. It was known that they were negotiating a mutual security treaty with the Nationalists. On 12 November Mr Dulles accused the Chinese of starting a 'free Thai' movement in China, doubling their forces in North Vietnam since the armistice, dominating two provinces of Laos, massing a substantial military force in Yunnan (which was based on false information) and fomenting Communist agitation in Singapore (though the British had made no complaint of this to the Chinese). All this, he said, indi-

cated an aggressive intention which belied Chinese pro-
testations of peace. This statement did not help the
American airmen. The Chinese reacted by issuing a
long statement about alleged American espionage and
subversion in China through Nationalist agents, with
full details of the number of agents caught after being
landed and the amount of arms and ammunition dropped in China and picked up by the police. With this
statement came the announcement of the trials and
convictions of the airmen.

The news created a furore in the West. The Americans sent a strong protest which I delivered and which
was returned to me in a few hours. British Ministers in
Parliament and Mr Nutting in the United Nations
supported the American protest, which increased the
anger of the Chinese against the British Government.
The United Nations General Assembly passed a resolution at American instance condemning the Chinese
for contravening the Korean armistice, demanding the
release of the eleven airmen captured in the B29 aircraft and appointing Mr Hammarskjöld, the Secretary-
General, to act under the resolution and report to the
Assembly.

The Chinese maintained that the airmen were spies
acting against China, who had been rightly tried and
condemned after due process of law. They condemned
the resolution as unwarrantable interference in their
internal affairs, but wisely took the advice of the
Indians and others in agreeing to receive Mr Hammarskjöld 'to discuss pertinent issues'. The Americans said
no more about the two civilians who, after the initial
protest, were dropped from further polemical statements. Meanwhile, the Chinese mounted an exhibition
in Peking, in which they showed photographs of the
B29 aircraft, the crew, their statements and their cap-

tured equipment. The standard equipment of the B29 may have appeared suspicious to the average Chinese from its elaborate scale. The equipment of the C47 on display consisted of many of the objects mentioned in the Chinese Government's statement, including the hazardous-looking device for picking up a man from the ground without landing, with the instructions for its use. What the C47 had been used for was clear enough. The Chinese had put it and its civilian crew in with the others in order to confuse the issue and suggest by the association that the eleven had been on the same sort of business.

Mr Hammarskjöld arrived on 5 January 1955, accompanied by Professor Humphrey Waldock of Oxford as his legal adviser. He held several meetings with Chou En-lai. His first aim was to persuade the Chinese that he was objective in outlook and that his mission was based not on the United Nations' resolution which had annoyed them, but on his position as Secretary-General under Article 99 of the Charter, which gave him the right to take up independently matters which might lead to a danger to the peace. He wanted to get over the effect of the United Nations resolution, to convince the Chinese that they could release the eleven airmen without loss of face, to make them see that they were regarded by the world as finding the eleven airmen guilty by association and to leave the way open for political action leading to the airmen's release. He achieved all that was possible during his visit and arranged for direct contact to be continued between him and Chou En-lai.

The Chinese were not going to release the airmen until American–Chinese tension was relaxed, which required a gesture from both sides. During the Bandoeng Conference, Chou En-lai stated publicly that the

Chinese Government were willing to 'sit down and enter into negotiations with the United States' Government to discuss the question of relaxation of tension in the [Taiwan] area'. This statement did no more than repeat the previous Chinese position. Mr Dulles first replied by again refusing to attend any conference at which the Nationalists were not present. A few days later, however, he admitted the possibility of bilateral talks with the Chinese on the problems of the area. In consequence of these statements, the American–Chinese talks, formerly held in Geneva, were revived between the two protagonists for whom I had initially acted as umpire, Mr Alexis Johnson and Wang Ping-nan, now Chinese Ambassador in Warsaw. As a prelude to these talks, the Chinese Government, in August, released the eleven airmen. Some months before, they had also released one Canadian and four American airmen who had come down in China during the Korean war.

I was to have one more sensational affair on my hands. On the morning of Easter Day, 10 April 1955, the acting head of the European Department summoned my Counsellor, John Addis, and told him that the Chinese Government had information that the Nationalists might 'make trouble' for a party of Chinese officials when they left Hong Kong the next day by an Indian airliner for the Bandoeng Conference. He asked that appropriate precautions should be taken.

Mr Addis sent an immediate telegram to Hong Kong before playing the harmonium for the Easter service. The arrangements in Hong Kong for deciphering immediate telegrams on holidays were odd. The telegram was only dealt with twenty-four hours later at 10.30 a.m. on Easter Monday, 11 April. This was, however, time enough for the Hong Kong authorities to do what was necessary in the light of the information given

us by the Chinese. They were ready before the chartered Constellation, the 'Kashmir Princess', arrived,
placed a police guard on it and arranged for the Chinese
party to motor straight through to the aircraft without
passing through customs or other formalities and to
board it without delay. No unusual incident occurred.
The aircraft was serviced and loaded under the supervision of the Indian crew.

On the evening of the same day the aircraft crashed
in the sea 108 miles north of Kueling in Sarawak. Only
three Indian crew members survived. On the morning
of 12 April the acting head of the West European
Department asked me to see him, told me that the aircraft had exploded, that the Chinese Government had
reason to believe that it had been sabotaged in Hong
Kong, that they wished to know what precautions the
Hong Kong Government had taken following their
message and that an investigation should be held and
the guilty punished. I asked what evidence they had
that the aircraft had exploded as a result of sabotage;
there were many causes which could lead to an aircraft
crash. It would be better not to make such allegations
until we knew the facts. On the same afternoon I told
him of the action which the Hong Kong Government
had taken.

The next day, at 6 a.m. before leaving for Shanghai,
I saw, at his request, Chang Wen-t'ien, a senior Vice-
Minister, who was acting for Chou En-lai during his
absence at Bandoeng. He said that the Chinese Government had warned us of a sabotage plot and that the
Hong Kong Government had failed to take the action
required to prevent its being carried out. Those responsible were American Special Service officers and
agents of the 'traitorous Chiang Kai-shek clique'. The
Chinese Government held the Hong Kong authorities

responsible and demanded that they should suspend the airport staff, place them under surveillance and investigate the plot. The Chinese Government had evidence that the plot had been carried out in Hong Kong and that the airport staff was involved.

I replied that we could not accept any responsibility for the affair. The Chinese Government had not told us that there would be sabotage, only that the Nationalists might make trouble for the party when they left. The Hong Kong Government had taken fully adequate precautions in the light of the information which the Chinese had given us. If the Chinese had evidence of a sabotage plot, they should give it to us. We deeply deplored the accident, but there would presumably be an enquiry into its cause, and until that had taken place it was premature to form any conclusions about it.

The Hong Kong Government at first thought that the possibility of a bomb having been placed in the aircraft at the Hong Kong airport was remote, but as time went on, after the wreck of the aircraft had been salvaged, it transpired that the crash had been due to sabotage, that a time-bomb had been placed in the right wing of the aircraft and that this must have been done in Hong Kong. We stuck to our point that we took grave exception to the wholly unjustified accusations against the Hong Kong Government and that, if the Chinese Government wanted the Hong Kong Government to take effective action, they had better tell us what they knew.

There were several questions unanswered. Only a few hours after the aircraft had crashed, the Chinese had told us that there had been sabotage and an explosion. How had they known? Why had they chartered a large four-engined aircraft and then only put nine minor officials on board? Chou En-lai had travelled to

Bandoeng by a long, roundabout route through Burma. Had it been intended that he should travel on the Indian aircraft and had he then changed his plans? If so, was it on account of the information which the Chinese had given us, or because they had had information that an attempt was to be made to sabotage the aircraft? If they had known of a sabotage plot, why had they not told us or cancelled the flight? Had they been prepared to risk the lives of their officials on the calculation that if the sabotage plot came off the incident could be exploited politically at Bandoeng? The essential fact which needed explanation was that they had very carefully told us only that the passengers might be interfered with as they left, whereas immediately after the information had been received that the aircraft was missing they had claimed that it had been sabotaged and had exploded. We worked out our own answers to those questions.

On 9 May Chou En-lai saw me and promised to give us the evidence which the Chinese had obtained, making five conditions, not all of which were acceptable. However, agreement was reached and the Indian C.I.D. Inspector whom the Government of India had sent to Peking to investigate the affair took the Chinese evidence to Hong Kong. The Chinese took the line that they believed we would deal with the affair in a wholly political manner, that our object would be to cover up American and Nationalist guilt and that only the immediate arrest of the whole ground staff of the Hong Kong airport would prove our sincerity.

Mr Krishna Menon, who was in Peking at this time, was helpful in persuading Chou En-lai to give us his evidence on reasonable conditions, telling him that if the British said they would investigate the affair they would do so thoroughly and impartially. He told Chou that the Indians knew the British. They had their peculiar ways, but if they said they would do something they would do it in accordance with their own procedure. As might have been expected, all this argument gave time for the principal suspect to escape to Taiwan, allegedly as a stowaway in an American–Nationalist aircraft, though this seemed hardly possible without the collusion of Nationalist members of the crew. The Chinese evidence was not good enough to secure a conviction, there was no chance of getting the fugitive back from Taiwan and this unfortunate affair subsided in grumbling and ill-feeling on both sides. If the Chinese had not been so suspicious and had told us what they knew at the beginning, we should have been able to prevent the sabotage or at least to arrest the culprit. I have no doubt that they believed to the end that the Hong Kong Government was only intent on sweeping the whole affair under the carpet.

14

FAREWELL TO PEKING

During my last visit to Shanghai, I found a very different scene from what I had found during my previous visit before the Geneva conference. By this time the British community were down almost to the hard core of those who had some personal reason for staying on in China. One or two whom we had extracted with difficulty from China were trying without success to get back. Even fewer foreigners were giving each other even more elaborate parties. But the black cloud had lifted. They knew that they could leave. From Shanghai we visited the enchanting southern Sung capital, Hangchow, with its willow-pattern scenery of hills, lakes, pavilions and temples carefully restored and with Buddhist monks still officiating in them. Hangchow was an organised centre of religion and tourism, designed to impress the Asian delegations in particular that the Chinese Government allowed the free practice of religion and supported Buddhism with State funds. It was very effectively done.

My time in Peking drew to its close. I was determined to get Robert Ford out of prison before I left. This remarkable young man has made his story known in his book *Captured in Tibet*. He had spent almost five years in a Chinese prison, accused of espionage and the murder of a Tibetan holy man, a so-called 'living Buddha', who had indeed been murdered in the house in which he had been staying, but not by him. The victim had been an emissary from Peking to the Dalai Lama and was therefore murdered by anti-Chinese Tibetans. Since it was a political crime, the Chinese could not believe that Ford was not implicated up to the hilt. During Ford's imprisonment, he had decided, as most people do in those circumstances, that he must confess to something and get himself convicted, if he was ever going to get out. So he confessed to being a spy, which he was not, but not to complicity in the murder.

I had done my best to convince the Chinese Government that he was not a spy and that his radio links with enthusiastic amateurs round the world were what every wireless operator does in his spare time. They could not believe that a man who had been in the R.A.F. and had then entered the service of the Tibetan Government was not in our secret service. I was not surprised. It was an improbable career and the Chinese were bound to be suspicious. Since he had confessed to being a spy, they presumably thought I was lying, or perhaps that I had not been told. Ford's imprisonment, during which he performed the astonishing feat of learning Chinese from a Tibetan who spoke no English, in no way affected the balance of his mind, in spite of the conditions which he had to endure and the sustained attempts to break down his mental resistance to Chinese Communism. When he was released, he was sane and moderate, neither leaning towards Communism nor using language which would prejudice future British prisoners in China It was a remarkable achievement.

Some foreign prisoners made statements on their release which they must have regretted as soon as they recovered their mental balance. Whatever may have happened in the early days, we heard no reports of physical violence being used on foreign prisoners in my time. They were, however, subjected to continual lecturing and interrogation, and each member of a group in a cell was required to instruct and inform on the others, until each one was wholly conditioned by the warning, driven into him incessantly, that he must either reform himself, bring his thought into line with Mao's thought and thus earn an easier life and finally release, or remain obdurate, steeped in sin and therefore justly condemned to continuing punishment. It was a form of Puritan fundamentalism, with its Heaven and Hell firmly placed in this world, in the China of today. It was astonishing to hear of the immense trouble that the Chinese would take to reform Chinese or foreign unbelievers, of the amount of time, effort and money which would be expended in the work of remoulding the thought of one man over a period of years.

At Geneva, I had thought that Ford would be released in a few weeks and so, I was inclined to suspect, did Huan Hsiang, with whom I was negotiating. Then something went wrong. The Security authorities must have raised objections. My impression, though I had no evidence for it, was that the Ministry of Foreign Affairs was doing its best to get him out, but was overruled. I continued to press the matter, but was put off from month to month by absurd excuses, such as the necessity to translate the evidence from Tibetan into Chinese. And so, towards the end of my stay in China, I changed my tactics. I took every opportunity to raise the matter in my interviews with Chou En-lai and finally, when I told him I was leaving, asked for Ford's release as a parting present.

It was not an easy time to ask for favours. The British attitude over Taiwan, the South-East Asia Treaty Organisation and the American airmen was still a major grievance. There was the affair of the sabotaged aircraft; there was the publication of the record of maltreatment of British prisoners of the Chinese and North Koreans during the Korean war. Chou said, 'You ask me to release Mr Ford, and your Ministry of Defence produces this publication which is clearly timed to be an attack on the Chinese Government. How can you expect me to have any Englishman released in the face of this?' At last, I thought I was getting near it. Chou promised that the matter would be considered. Then another little bomb burst. This time it was the decision of the Hong Kong High Court to execute a judgement stemming from the old aircraft case, which meant the eviction of officials of the Chinese Government from some buildings and yards in Hong Kong and the transfer of the property to an American company. I tried vainly to explain the unavoidable requirements of the British legal system.

On my last afternoon in Peking, I went to say goodby to Chou En-lai. He could not spare much time, as he had to take the Prime Minister of Indonesia to see Mao. He had five points for me. The first four were the familiar complaints about the British attitude. The fifth was that by the time I reached England Ford would be in Hong Kong. I thanked him, but not more than formally, for the Chinese conduct towards Ford, according to our ideas, had been outrageous. Still, Chou had probably had hard work to get Ford out and I was grateful to him. So ended my talks with Chou En-lai, one of the most remarkable men whom I have known. We had had good personal relations, whatever our disputes. In one of our blackest interviews Chou had said, 'It is not that I have any complaint against you personally. We regard you as accurately reporting the views of the Chinese Government to the British Government and the views of the British Government to the Chinese Government.' I took this as a compliment, since accurate reporting is the basis of diplomacy.

I feel sure that Chang Han-fu, the Vice-Minister in charge of our affairs, enjoyed his farewell dinner to me. He used the opportunity to make a violent attack on the Hong Kong Government for restricting the passage of Chinese from the mainland and made it clear that he believed my statement of the position to be untrue. It was his usual technique. His farewell dinner to my successor went exactly the same way. I left China happy to feel that, apart from one convicted murderer, there were no British left in Chinese prisons. My aircraft was delayed for twenty-four hours by heavy storms. Mr Ford, then in Canton prison, had been told to be ready to go by train to Hong Kong on the morning of the day on which I was due to leave. Nothing happened. It must have been a bad moment for him. He left on the following day, the day on which I actually left. I presumed that the order was that he should leave as soon as I had left Peking. It was carried out in the usual meticulous Chinese fashion.

My wife and I left with many regrets for our surroundings, for the atmosphere of the old Chinese culture, for the interest of the new Chinese political, economic and social scene, for our friends in the diplomatic corps, who had shared with us our little non-communist island in Peking. I tried to decide for myself how far we in the Peking Embassy had succeeded in keeping our balance. We had tried to be objective, to see both the charm and the ruthlessness of the Chinese, to record impartially the successes and failures of the new régime, to understand the pattern of Chinese thought and so to assess Chinese policy correctly, to view with scepticism a lightening and with equanimity a darkening of the political atmosphere, and to gain what practical advantages we could from even a temporary improvement in Anglo-Chinese relations, without deluding ourselves that British and Chinese interests, save in trade, were likely to converge. We were sometimes critical of American policy, but recognised that, though it was often tactically clumsy, it was generally effective. I hope we were loyal to our own Government, even if we did not always agree with its views. We could not do much, but we did what we could and nourished no illusions. It was a memorable experience.

Part II
SOVIET UNION
1962-5

15

PRELUDE TO MOSCOW

SEVEN years had passed since I had left China. The Earl of Home (now Sir Alec Douglas-Home) said, 'Where would you like to go?' I said, 'Moscow.' He replied, 'That is what I was going to suggest.' Of course, I had known what he was going to say. It suited me well enough. I wanted to be back in the main stream of world politics.

To learn as much Russian as possible in a short time, you go alone to a Russian family in Paris. I had only very little, acquired in Peking. Karl Marx, they said, had learnt it at the age of fifty-six. Could I learn at least something at the same age? I could not suck it in, as a child does; I needed to understand the way in which the Russian verb puts out shoots and branches with new meanings, the key to so much of the language, about which the grammars do not enlighten you. It is probably the wrong way to learn, but I doubt whether that painstaking scholar, Karl Marx, was any more inspired in his method than I was. In learning a language, I find it helps to translate a child's book orally from English. *Alice* suits admirably. It is full of conversation; the tenses are precise; it uses only words of everyday speech. But Madame Bibikova, stern aristocrat who bore with me for two hours every day, would have none of it. 'I don't understand you English. How can you like that silly book full of rabbits and things?' It was exhausting to have to use my brain again, atrophied by years of cocktail parties in the line of duty, but the effort was worthwhile. And there was the great reward ahead, to be able to read the great poets and novelists in the language in which they wrote.

I shall not forget the real friendship which I received from the little Princess, always cheerful and busy, with whom I stayed, and her gentle sister, both of whom took so much trouble to help my stumbling efforts, and from their friends of the old Russian families, who received us in their modest lodgings as if they had still been in the palaces of St Petersburg. It was my first experience of the natural Russian warmth which must capture all but the coldest of hearts.

The Russians in Paris held to their national identity, symbolised by their Nansen passes and the church in the Rue Daru, which was the centre of their life. Only the young generation became really French. Our little apartment was very Russian, full of gaiety punctuated by passionate family disputes, against a background of personal tragedy. There was little money, but there were guests at nearly every meal. It seemed natural for a countess to arrive suddenly from Abijan with her pet monkey and sleep on the drawing-room sofa, though the monkey would pick the goldfish out of the bowl and throw them on the floor. No one went to bed till about three o'clock in the morning. The rooms were small, but several hundred guests had been received at a family wedding by the simple expedient of pushing some out to let others in. As the Russians like saying, 'V tesnote, da ne v obide' ('a squash, but no harm done').

Before some rich friends came to my farewell party, the Princess looked at the drawing-room rug, which was full of holes, and remarked, 'That will not be so good for the millionairesses; still it will be a new experience for them,' and gave it not another thought. It was a lesson in breeding. I thought, it will not be like this in Russia, but I shall know that, underneath, the warmth and friendship will be there.

Back in England we faced the housekeeping problems, taking £350 worth of fresh meat by air, buying fur coat from a predecessor, persuading the highest officials of the Service departments to allow us to take Servicemen willing to work in our household, a requirement of that timesome appendage of diplomatic life, security. It was not an easy time. The Vassall affair, revealing that a member of the British Embassy staff had been blackmailed into becoming a spy, had induced an atmosphere of nervousness which temporarily distorted the judgement of some in responsible positions, afraid of another revelation of a success by the Soviet Intelligence Service. Mr Greville Wynne had just been arrested in Hungary on a charge of spying and had been handed over to the Soviet secret police. Then, a month before we were due to start, came the Cuban missiles crisis, during which we sometimes wondered whether we would ever reach the Soviet Union.

And so, on a cold day in late November, my birthday, my wife and I stood on the Gatwick Airport, waiting to board the R.A.F. Britannia which was to take us on our last official mission together. We were to stop for the night in Copenhagen, since the Britannia could not do the whole journey in one hop and we could not land at Moscow after dark. There were many uncertainties ahead, but I must confess that our only immediate concern was whether all that meat would arrive in Moscow in good condition or whether we should be delayed on the way and have to throw it all away.

In the event, we landed punctually at Cheremetovo Airport to be welcomed by members of our staff, the Commonwealth Ambassadors and a representative of the Soviet Foreign Ministry; the meat was whisked off to the Moscow city cold-store. We motored past the little wooden houses with their forests of television masts denoting multiple occupancy, past the huge blocks of flats built in different styles which denoted the period of construction, like geological strata, the outer circles severe and practical, the Khrushchevian style, the middle circle in dictator's ornamental of the later Stalinist period and finally the inner circle of the old pre-revolutionary city, in the centre of which was our new home. Here we were faced for the first time by the tremendous panorama of the Kremlin towers and domes, which was to be the background of our lives for the next three years.

16

TEST-BAN AND THE WEST

W E were in the wake of the Cuban crisis. The Cuban adventure, like every other major Soviet decision, can only have been the decision of the Party, the collective, though it was probably pressed by Khrushchev and bears the mark of his methods with its gambling element, the bold initiative, the willingness to take big risks. The Russians could argue that after the Bay of Pigs the Americans were bound to invade Cuba sooner or later, that only an intrusion of Soviet power into the Western hemisphere could stop them and that, though the missiles had been withdrawn, Soviet action had been successful in safeguarding Cuba's independence. But their principal aim had probably been to put powerful offensive weapons inside the American guard in order to force the Americans to make concessions under threat of missile attack on American cities. If the Russians thought that they could get Berlin by such threats, they did not understand the Americans, who showed that they would take any risk in order to get the missiles out.

Whatever the Russians' motives, there was evidence that many Russians judged the enterprise to have been a gamble which had not come off. The Soviet leaders became more cautious. In Cuba they had got themselves into the position of having the choice only between a real risk of nuclear war or withdrawal from an untenable position. They were not going to be caught in the same way again. The political atmosphere in Moscow was uneasy. Chinese propaganda attacked the Russians as revisionists conducting a policy compounded of rashness and weakness. Among Communists, inside and outside the Soviet Union, there seemed to be a loss of confidence in Soviet leadership.

Western approaches to a nuclear test-ban treaty made little headway, though both sides tried to narrow the gap. The Americans gradually reduced their demands for on-site inspections and it was hardly surprising if the Russians, perennially nervous of espionage, thought that they had only to sit tight until the demand for inspections disappeared altogether. Then Khrushchev suddenly announced that the Soviet Government would accept three on-site inspections a year. The Americans held out for more and he withdrew his proposal. Even if the numbers had been agreed, I doubt whether a settlement would have been reached on this basis, since it appeared that Khrushchev thought of the inspections as a mere formality, while the Americans intended them to provide a real opportunity to verify the facts on the ground. There was some evidence that the Russians had genuinely received the impression from the American delegate at Geneva that it was only a political question for the Americans and that, having subsequently discovered from Mr Kuznetsov's discussions in the United States that this was not correct, they were aggrieved, felt that they had been placed in a false position and therefore withdrew their offer.

In our discussions Khrushchev deliberately depreciated the importance of a test-ban treaty, which he described as of humanitarian interest only. In Moscow we saw little prospect of any new initiative being successful at that moment when Soviet–Chinese relations were in an uncertain phase of manœuvre. However, Mr Macmillan judged that it was the moment for a Western initiative. At his suggestion, he and President Kennedy wrote parallel letters to Khrushchev, which my American colleague and I delivered jointly to him, in order to give them greater emphasis. We were not hopeful, since the letters did not contain any new proposal. Khrushchev read the letters and said, 'Well, gentlemen, and what is there in this for me?' The written reply, as we had expected, was negative.

But the approach was better timed than we in Moscow had any reason to believe. As we saw it, there were two elements in Soviet thinking about a test-ban. There was the permanent economic inducement to limit the increasing expense of the development of atomic weapons. The Russians could see that a continuation of tests above ground would force them to embark on a fresh generation of weapons on which they would have to spend large sums urgently needed for investment in industry and agriculture. A test-ban treaty could be the first step in a limitation of the American–Soviet race for ever more sophisticated weapons, a race in which the Soviet Union was handicapped by the much greater American resources. The main political obstacle, in our opinion, was Soviet fears of the opportunity which an agreement with the Americans would give to the Chinese. But by the late spring the Russians seemed to have given up hope of an early improvement in Soviet–Chinese relations. They could go over to the attack and exploit a test-ban treaty as a means of isolating the Chinese and drawing most of the uncommitted countries to the Soviet side against them. That, at any rate, was the way in which we subsequently rationalised the Soviet change of front, though it could only be speculation. No Soviet official would ever reveal the real political calculations.

On 10 June, President Kennedy, speaking to the American University in Washington, announced his wish to negotiate a comprehensive test-ban treaty and promised that the United States Government would not resume tests in the atmosphere unless others did. He said, 'Both the United States and its allies have a mutually deep interest in a just and genuine peace and in halting the arms race. Agreements to this end are in the interests of the Soviet Union as well as ours – even the most hostile nations can be relied upon to accept and keep those treaty obligations, which are in their own interest.' In Moscow we judged that this speech had a marked effect on the Russians. It seemed that by this time they had acquired enough confidence in President Kennedy to believe him to be sincere.

When Mr Harold Wilson visited Moscow in June as leader of the Opposition, there were already indications that the Russians might be prepared to agree to a limited test-ban, excluding underground tests, a proposal which had been put to them by the Western governments at Geneva in the previous August and which they had then rejected out of hand. Mr Khrushchev confirmed this view in his conversation with Mr Wilson. Public statements followed and negotiations between the Russians, the Americans and ourselves, as the third nuclear power, were put in hand.

The negotiations were held in Moscow. The Soviet delegation was headed by Mr Gromyko, the American by Mr Averill Harriman and the British by Lord Hailsham. There was never any serious doubt about their outcome, since the Russians had decided that an agreement was in their interests. Towards the end of the talks, Lord Hailsham became anxious lest they should break down owing to Washington's refusal to agree to Mr Gromyko's extraneous conditions, but I assured him that he need not worry. The Russians had made it clear enough that they intended to have an agreement.

In the initial joint American–British interview with Mr Khrushchev, he raised the question of the forty-inch pipe which the Americans had prevented the Germans and other NATO countries supplying to the Russians. He said that he knew that it was the American Ambassador who had been responsible, presumably basing his statement on his intelligence reports, since a short time afterwards the Americans announced that they had found a large number of microphones in their offices. Mr Harriman handled an unpleasant situation admirably. With his characteristic growl, he interjected that he assumed Khrushchev was not speaking seriously. Otherwise, he would have to take the matter seriously in his turn. Khrushchev said no more.

This was the only question on which we had taken a different line from the Americans. We doubted their premise that the pipe was required primarily for the 'friendship' pipe-line carrying oil to other East European countries. It was more probably required for the internal gas-line from Uzbekistan to industry in the Urals. Nor did we regard the 'friendship' pipe-line as being of major strategic importance. We believed that the Russians were perfectly capable of making forty-inch pipe themselves and that the only result of refusing permission for Western firms to make it for the Soviet Union would be to transfer Soviet resources to the manufacture of pipe from the manufacture of consumer goods. It was not in our interest to hinder the development of consumer-goods industries, nor to encourage a reversion to Stalin's policy of concentrating Soviet industry on capital goods. And so it fell out. We offered to provide some of the pipe. The Soviet Government did not accept the offer, but made the pipe themselves, with the aid of small imports from Scandinavia, probably taken for political reasons. Their requirements of pipe suffered only a relatively short delay. In 1970 they made an agreement with the West Germans for the import of pipe, in part exchange for gas.

Mr Harriman had the major rôle on the Western side. Agreement was reached without much difficulty. The Western powers promised to discuss with their allies the possibility of a non-aggression pact between NATO and the members of the Warsaw Pact, the most that Mr Gromyko could obtain in the way of a political bonus in exchange for Soviet agreement to a form of test-ban treaty which had been of Western inspiration. Mr Harriman and Lord Hailsham departed and were succeeded by Mr Dean Rusk, Mr Adlai Stevenson and a party of American Senators, to sign the treaty for the Americans and ensure that at least some members of the Senate were committed to it. Lord Home and Mr Heath came for us. There was much feasting and speech-making, during which Khrushchev was in top form and obviously enjoying himself. The photograph of Mr Dean Rusk and Khrushchev playing badminton without a net at Khrushchev's villa on the Black Sea seemed symbolic, though no one could say of what.

The Russians made all the political use they could out of what came to be known for a brief period of euphoria as the Moscow Treaty or 'the spirit of Moscow'. The French and Chinese, as expected, refused to adhere to the treaty, but almost every other country, however little concerned, got in on the act. I signed it for Trinidad and Tobago and for Western Samoa. The Americans and British duly consulted their allies about the possibility of moving towards a non-aggression pact, having committed themselves no further. The result was negative. It was feared that the Russians intended a non-aggression pact to weaken the allied position in Berlin by enabling the Russians to restrict allied access by the many means open to them, while denying the allies the right of retaliation by force. The climate of confidence necessary for such a pact did not exist. Khrushchev had led British Ministers to believe that the Russians would agree to the stationing of observers in Soviet and other East European territories as an insurance against surprise attack. He had presumably gone beyond his brief, since his officials soon disabused us by attaching the old conditions of the exclusion of nuclear weapons from East and West Germany and the reduction of foreign forces in them, measures clearly designed to improve the relative strength of the Soviet forces. There was no advance on any other of the questions under dispute. East–West relations had reached a stalemate. The 'spirit of Moscow' evaporated and there were soon no more references to the Moscow Treaty.

For the Russians, after the nuclear balance, the central question of their security was Germany. The horrors of the German invasion of the Soviet Union had left a genuine fear of the Germans in the Russian mind. They realised, as Khrushchev admitted, that in the conditions of modern atomic warfare the Germans could not again make war by themselves on the Soviet Union, but they justified their emotional, historical fear by the thesis that the Germans would achieve a dominant

position among the Western European allies, which
would enable them to create 'provocations' and drag
the Western alliance and the Soviet Union into war.
They were, we thought, genuinely convinced that the
Germans would not rest until they had acquired nuclear
weapons and were wholly unconvinced by our argument that the proposed 'Multilateral Nuclear Force',
which had been invented by Kennedy's academics and
was now being actively promoted, would not amount to
a proliferation of nuclear weapons, but would provide
a safeguard against their acquisition by the Germans.
I hope I argued in favour of the scheme with conviction,
though I was by no means enamoured of it, if only because I was fairly certain that it would not come off and
that it therefore created a wholly unnecessary cause of
disagreement with the Russians and blocked our con-
current aim of a non-proliferation treaty.

The essential difference between our and the Russians' assessment of West German policy, as I once
summarised it to Mr Gromyko, was that we agreed that
there were elements of militarism and revanchism in
Western Germany, but that whereas the Russians considered these elements to be dominant with a major
influence on the German Government's policy we regarded them as small and uninfluential and believed
that the West German leaders wanted peace, and that
the best policy was to co-operate and be friendly with
them. There was never the slightest prospect that the
Russians would allow German reunification on other
than terms which would convert the whole of Germany into a Communist state, which they knew was out
of the question. Khrushchev as good as admitted publicly that the main reason for the Soviet refusal to agree
to free all-German elections was that West Germany
would win them. Mr Kosygin told me plainly that they

would never agree to reunification and added that we should be fools if we promoted it. They were never going to allow the Communist frontier to the West to be rolled back. It had been stabilised by the Berlin wall and there it was going to stay.

At the end of 1962 Berlin was in the front of the stage. It formed the centre piece of all conversations with Khrushchev, who was pressing for some form of internationalisation of Berlin's status under the United Nations flag. The situation was tense and we were always on the look-out for incidents and provocations which might grow into really dangerous situations. But gradually the Russians gave up pressing on Berlin. The last dangerous situation in my time arose in the summer of 1963 from a ridiculous dispute. The question was whether the tail-board of an American truck could be lowered under the Four-Power agreements which allowed inspection of its contents at the end of the autobahn. This apparently insignificant dispute, probably local in origin, quickly led to tension and the holding-up of traffic on the autobahn. Contingency plans were brought out and dusted off against a possible serious attempt to stop the use of the autobahn. The technical rights and wrongs of the dispute were obscure, but the Allies took their stand on their basic right of unlimited access to Berlin. It cannot, I think, have been a deliberate test of allied reactions, since the Russians did not pursue it very far, nor try to use it to promote new schemes for altering the status of the allied forces in Berlin.

After this, Khrushchev seemed to tire of Berlin. He negotiated a Soviet Treaty with East Germany, signifying that the Soviet Government no longer wished to negotiate with the Western powers on Germany. The new Soviet line was that German questions were a matter for negotiation between the two Germanies. It was the end of another active phase of Soviet policy on Germany. The West German desire to manifest their presence in Berlin by holding meetings of the Bundestag or electing the President there, caused the routine reflex action in the form of some retaliatory harassment on the autobahn, but apart from this Berlin receded into the background and the new Soviet Government showed no disposition to bring it out of the cupboard again, a state of affairs which my American colleague and I thought to be in everyone's interests. The side which wanted to keep the *status quo* had the advantage, which meant in effect no reunification, but no change in Berlin.

Khrushchev never forgot the realities of world power. For him the most important fact of life was the competition with the Americans, with their nuclear weapons, their production, their wealth and their technology. He was for ever boasting that the Soviet Union would catch up with American production. He implied that the Soviet standard of living would soon be comparable to the American standard, ignoring the immense advantage of the West in capital assets such as houses, roads, mechanised agriculture and all the amenities of Western life, continually increased by massive investment and the revolution in technology. There was no prospect that the Russians would catch up even with northern European standards for a very long time. The other Soviet leaders presumably realised that Khrushchev's boasts were meaningless and made the Soviet Union appear ridiculous. They were dropped on the change of régime.

It was clear that both Khrushchev and the other Soviet leaders increasingly realised the appalling risk of nuclear warfare, the inescapable necessity to keep up with American nuclear power at a time when their resources were severely stretched, and therefore to arrive at an understanding with the Americans which would stabilise the nuclear balance at an acceptable financial cost. In the long run, this would have to override every other consideration. The terrible supremacy of nuclear power had the Russians and the Americans in its grip. When I said to Mr Kosygin that I, for one, would sleep more easily if they and the Americans reached an understanding on the great issues between them, he did not demur. This was the real basis of Soviet and Western security.

The British were relatively small fry in the new power relationships, but the Russians showed no disposition to write us off completely. They had a respect for the British, born of past experience in the German wars and regarded us as the only people able to exercise some influence on the Americans. They were wrong if they expected that a Labour Government, even under the leadership of a Prime Minister who had visited Moscow eleven times, would show themselves to be more independent of the Americans than the Conservatives had been. Under the impact of the Vietnam war, Mr Wilson's Government were vocal supporters of American action in Vietnam, including the bombing of North Vietnam, in contrast to other NATO countries which were more reticent, and relations with the Russians were rather more difficult than they had been when the Conservatives had been in power in easier times. Labour opposition to American proposals for a 'Multilateral Nuclear Force', before they came to power, was translated, when they took office, into the sponsorship of a new proposal for an 'Atlantic Nuclear Force', which was as objectionable to the Russians as the original proposal and as little likely to materialise.

The Soviet press took the line that, beset as the British were by difficulties in their balance of payments, they no longer had an independent foreign policy. There were signs that they regarded the new Government as more interested in their internal political position than in foreign affairs.

It was no harm that the Russians should be cured of the illusion that any British Government would regard the American alliance as anything but the corner-stone of British foreign policy. I was personally doubtful whether it was advisable in principle for us to make statements in support of the actions of another government for which we were not responsible, however much we agreed with them. Later on, the fact that the British Government had declared itself in favour of the American bombing forced them to state their objections when they no longer supported it. But it was right that the Russians should know that, whatever our doubts about the practical outcome of the American tactics, we remained their firm allies and could not be exploited to their disadvantage.

The French were valued in proportion to the prospects of their disrupting the Western alliance, recognising East Germany and helping to remove the Americans from Europe and the Far East. The Russians seemed to us to misunderstand the French position to the extent of expecting that French disagreements with the Americans would bring them much closer to the Soviet point of view. But they had ample reason to be pleased with the turn of affairs as the French began to withdraw from NATO and it became clear that the Franco-German Treaty, which the Russians had at first attacked, was of no great importance and need not concern them. The rest of the NATO powers were classified in accordance with the degree to which they might be weaned away from active participation in NATO activities. Soviet tactics were to pare away at the Scandinavian and Mediterranean edges of NATO, an operation which was not noticeably successful. It was important for the Western Allies' representatives in Moscow to work and to be seen to work together. My American, French and German colleagues and I met every week at each embassy in turn and arrived at a degree of co-operation not always attained by our governments.

Soviet relations with Eastern Europe were changing rapidly. The old political control had diminished, but Khrushchev tried to secure a dominant economic position through 'Comecon,' the economic organisation of Communist Europe, behind a façade of voluntary co-operation. The object was to integrate the economies of the smaller countries under Soviet direction. But the smaller partners refused to play the game under these rules, especially Romania, which was taking a virtually neutral position in the Sino-Soviet dispute, and the Soviet effort collapsed. By 1964 Comecon had become a much looser organisation than the Russians had contemplated and the other Eastern Europeans kept the basic control of their separate economies, at least for the time being.

The Western allies had to define their policy in the face of the new spirit in Eastern Europe. The Americans, with their eye on their public opinion, called it 'bridge building', which made the Russians think that they wanted to split off the client states from the Soviet alliance, to build some bridges and destroy others. This was a natural suspicion, since it was what the Russians were always trying to do with NATO. But this was not really Western policy. It was sensible to take every opportunity to improve our political and economic

relations with the smaller countries of Eastern Europe,
but not to try to split them from the Soviet Union. It
could not have been done anyway and relations with
the Soviet Union and the rest of Eastern Europe
together were what really mattered for the NATO
states.

Khrushchev took great trouble over Yugoslavia,
going some way towards convincing Tito that a warmer
wind was blowing from the East and that he would be
allowed to choose his own way to socialism. And so,
three years after I had left Moscow, the examples of
Yugoslavia and Romania encouraged the Czechs, whose
economy was being rapidly ruined by Novotny's mis-
management, to break loose from the Soviet pattern.
Khrushchev's successors, fearing that the Czechs were
getting out of control and that an admission of the legi-
timacy of the new Czech form of socialism would im-
peril the foundations of Soviet existence and security,
calculating correctly that there was no military problem and that the Western powers would scream blue
murder but not try to play the policeman, took hold
and put more amenable men into power, a violent
action which neither the Czechs nor the Yugoslavs expected, justifying their use of force by propounding a
doctrine which meant no more than that a Super Power
can do what it can get away with in its own backyard.
Even Soviet officials have admitted that it was 'a difficult decision', which implies that there were good
reasons against it, and evidence from Czech sources
suggested that the Soviet Politburo was not united
behind it. For the moment, the Russians stopped the
hole in the dam. In the short term their calculations
were correct; but it seems to a Western observer that
even in terms of *realpolitik* it was a wrong decision, that
even granting that the Soviet premises were correct the

situation could have been handled effectively with greater wisdom and less violence and that in the long term, to use a favourite expression of Khrushchev, life itself will show that it was contrary to real Soviet interests. After the jolt it has received, the Communist movement will never be the same again. But this is jumping a long way ahead of my Moscow story.

17

ASIAN AFFAIRS

THROUGHOUT my time in Moscow, I was in the Soviet Ministry of Foreign Affairs practically every week to discuss South-East Asia. These discussions arose out of the Soviet-British co-chairmanship of the Geneva conferences of 1954 and 1962. They centred on Laos until the Vietnam war put the rest of South-East Asian affairs into the shade. At the time of the 1962 conference, there were three parties in Laos, the neutralists under Prince Souvanna Phouma, the left wing under his half-brother, Prince Souvanavong and the right wing under Phoumi Nosavan. The Neutralists were close to the left wing, the Neo Lao Hak Sat party, with its military wing, the Pathet Lao.

The system set up by the conference which provided that the three partners in the Government, representing the three parties, could only take decisions unanimously was unworkable. The Communists probably calculated that the Neutralists would be drawn into alliance with the left wing, which would then dominate the tripartite Government. The man whom they relied on to carry out their plan was Qinim Pholsena, the Neutralists' Foreign Minister, who was strongly left-wing. Their plans were upset by his murder, almost certainly in revenge for the murder of a prominent Neutralist, Colonel Ketsana, which may well have been his doing. Our attitude to this event was neatly summed up by Osbert Lancaster in a cartoon showing Maudie Littlehampton in front of a poster announcing the murder, saying, 'Restraint, restraint! It's not one of ours.' My interview with Mr Gromyko after this event, in which I had to urge restraint, was, not surprisingly, one of the most difficult of my time in Moscow. There was no doubt that it had hit the Russians hard.

From this time, the Neutralists distanced themselves progressively from the left wing, which, with help from the North Vietnamese, attacked the Neutralists' Forces, but without great effect, since the Neutralists, with help from the Americans and the right-wing Laotians, fought back successfully. The tripartite façade was formally maintained, but the left-wing leaders found themselves increasingly insecure in Vientiane and finally left for the territory under the occupation of their Forces. The situation developed badly for the Communists. The Russians found themselves supporting a party which, for some years at least, made little headway, while they progressively lost their influence over the left wing to the North Vietnamese and the Chinese.

We played paper games with the Russians, each putting forward the view of his side in the form of a draft declaration or message to the Laotian Government and then publishing it with a Note saying that the other side had failed to do its duty as co-chairman by agreeing to the issue of the document. The Russians started this and we were forced to follow suit. But neither side wanted the situation to get out of hand. So the façade of the Geneva conference was maintained, while fruitless attempts were continually made to bring the three Laotian leaders together.

By the summer of 1964 Khruschchev was tired of a situation in which he found himself with responsibility but no influence. He said to Lord (then Mr R. A.) Butler, on his visit to Moscow as Foreign Secretary, that the co-chairmanship in Laos was like being a hook on which you hung dead dogs. Soon afterwards, the Russians virtually dissociated themselves from it. But as soon as Khrushchev fell the new Government re-activated it, being unwilling to leave the field to the Chinese. This became clear when the Deputy Foreign Minister in charge of South-East Asian affairs pointed out to me that the Geneva agreement of 1962 prescribed specific duties for the co-chairmen in respect of Laos, though there was no mention of the co-chairmen in the 1954 agreement on Vietnam. But the Soviet Government were no more able than before to influence the situation in Laos, and the co-chairmanship again became dormant.

The discussions on Cambodia were enlivened by the wayward personality of Prince Sihanouk, who changed his mind twice a week, tempering his irresponsibility with a certain uninhibited charm, so far as one could judge from a distance. He pressed for a conference on Cambodia. The Russians supported him, knowing that the Americans and Thais did not want one and would not agree. We hedged and the proposal died. The next year Sihanouk pressed for his conference again. The Russians again supported him. This time, to everyone's surprise, we and the Americans agreed. The Chinese immediately put pressure on Sihanouk, who withdrew his request to the embarrassment of the Russians, who were left on the hook in the wrong camp.

Nobody took Cambodian affairs very seriously, since Sihanouk was clearly going to continue to float in the middle without coming down on either side and, whatever his political manœuvres, the Viet Cong continued to use Cambodian territory without American intervention. Vietnam was a very different matter. We played the same game with the Russians as we did over Laos, but neither of us showed any signs of being able to influence that intractable situation by diplomatic manœuvring. It was being decided by force on the ground. By the summer of 1964 Khrushchev had decided to have nothing to do with Vietnam either and virtually signed off. But the new Government soon changed their attitude on Vietnam as well as on Laos.

Mr Kosygin visited North Vietnam and North Korea early in 1965. On the day after his return, the Deputy Minister in charge of South-East Asian affairs spoke to me in his customarily oblique manner about the responsibilities of the co-chairman for Vietnam. I reminded him that he had recently pointed out to me that there was a difference between the co-chairmanship under the decisions of the conferences of 1954 and 1962 and that there was no provision in the 1954 agreement for a continuing co-chairmanship for Vietnam. 'I know you said that,' he replied. I retorted, 'You, not I.' He continued, 'When there is a fire, the firemen must try and put it out.' I agreed, since this suited us, and was able in a week's time to propose a joint declaration by the two co-chairmen asking all concerned for their views on how to settle the problem of Vietnam. It was, I thought, a weak proposal, but it was something to offer and was presumably the most that the Foreign Office thought the Americans would take. For weeks, in spite of our reminders, there was no reply. We knew from the Poles, who also thought our proposal too weak, that the Chinese and North Vietnamese had refused to agree to any action by the co-chairmen. We learnt later from Chinese anti-Soviet polemics that the

Russians had wanted to counter our proposal with a call for reconvening the Geneva conference, but that their Far Eastern allies had rejected that idea also.

While we were waiting for the Russians to reply, they took a new initiative towards convening a conference. The Soviet Ambassador in Paris approached the French, who were openly in favour of a conference and the 'neutralisation' of Vietnam. A joint understanding was reached that the two governments would work in parallel for a conference. But there was still no answer from the Russians to our proposal. If they had wanted to reject it outright, they would have 'signed off' by immediately proposing a new message attacking the Americans, which they knew we would reject. They were still trying to clear the ground with their allies.

The time approached for Mr Gromyko's visit to the United Kingdom. Whenever a high-level visit was in contemplation, the Russians were accustomed to issue a statement about any issue which they did not want to discuss, so that during the visit they could merely refer to the statement, when the subject was raised by the other party. When, for instance, Mr Butler was about to visit Moscow in the summer of 1964 they issued a statement on Laos which effectively inhibited serious discussion of the Laotian question. Before the visit of the Pakistani Prime Minister, they set out publicly the Soviet position on the current Indo-Pakistani dispute over the Rann of Cutch, since they did not want to have to take sides. So now they could no longer stay silent and issued the expected 'sign-off' statement on Vietnam, evidence that they were powerless to take any diplomatic initiative. In London, Mr Gromyko did his best to avoid all discussion of the question and refused even to allow the word 'Vietnam' to be mentioned in the communiqué.

From this time, the Russians felt inhibited from taking any action on Vietnam in their capacity as co-chairman. Every attempt by us to raise the matter was met by the reply that it was the Vietnamese who should be addressed, since it was their affair and the Russians could not speak for them. There was no more talk of the duty of the firemen to put out the fire. Suggestions that we might discuss steps towards a settlement, were met by the response that, if they were to talk with the Western side, they might as well talk with the Americans directly, rather than with the British, who only followed American policy. It was therefore no surprise to us in Moscow when Mr Wilson's proposal for a Commonwealth Mission to Moscow to discuss Vietnam, put to Mr Kosygin by the Ambassador of Ghana and myself, was turned down flat. It was not one of Mr Wilson's happier proposals.

In discussion with a visiting British politician, a Soviet Minister said that they were in a delicate and difficult position on Vietnam and a Deputy Foreign Minister repeated this to me. The Chinese found Vietnam a useful issue on which to attack the Russians and even held up Soviet supplies for North Vietnam to show that they only passed on Chinese sufferance. In earlier days, when it was a tidy little 'national liberation struggle', the affair had been politically favourable for the Russians who could help the Vietcong in a small way without trouble and make political capital against the Americans. Now it was becoming, in Russian terms, a 'local war', a much more dangerous affair in which the Russians were becoming deeply involved. In spite of all the supplies which they were sending to North Vietnam, they were unable to give effective protection to their allies against American bombing, nor could they exercise any political initiative on the

Chinese border. The North Vietnamese were able to sit on the political fence and were obliged to accept Chinese aid in the way of political support, equipment and engineer and training contingents. It was a disagreeable situation for the Americans and the Russians, while the Chinese were enjoying themselves fighting, as the Russians were saying in those days, to the last Vietnamese.

As the Vietnamese situation became more difficult and the Americans put in more troops, Soviet–American relations naturally deteriorated. With the American decision to bomb North Vietnam, Soviet propaganda against the Americans increased in vehemence. Moves towards American–Soviet negotiations on nuclear armaments and a liberalisation of American trade with the Soviet Union were halted. Inevitably, Anglo-Soviet relations also drifted downwards, while we proclaimed our support of the American action. I had arranged an exchange of visits between the two prime ministers, but we were not surprised that Mr Kosygin found it politically inadvisable for him to pay his projected visit to England at that time. The French position correspondingly improved, as they made clear their disagreement with American policy. This turn of events was of no great importance. American and British interests in the Soviet Union were not going to be seriously affected by the storm in the South-East.

Throughout these years, Chinese–Soviet relations were steadily deteriorating. The Chinese increased the vehemence of their attacks on the Russian revisionists; the Russians called the Chinese dogmatists, racialists and chauvinists. Both sides thought up the worst names they knew. Both were right if these names meant that the Russians, with rising prosperity and nuclear responsibility, had much to lose and every reason to be cautious, and that the Chinese wanted to become the leaders of the developing countries without subscribing to the Communist club under Soviet leadership. Both countries, apart from their doctrinal differences, were strongly nationalist in policy.

Khrushchev's uninhibited polemics were abandoned for a time, probably as a result of adverse reactions in other Communist parties. The Chinese went on slanging the Russians, who refused to answer back, until the Chinese finally succeeded in goading them into a slanging match again, after the Russians had shown their Communist friends that gentlemanly restraint would not lower the temperature. The tactical battle centred on the proposed meeting of the twenty-six parties, the drafting committee for the congress of eighty-one parties. This meeting had been fixed by Khrushchev for December 1964, apparently to force a split in the Communist camp, to the dismay of the other Communist parties. His successors were unable to get off the hook, but delayed the meeting as long as possible and then made it a relatively mild affair, which did not, however, stop the Chinese from attacking it. The Soviet tactics of moderation paid off and by 1966 the Chinese, who had had a set-back in Indonesia and had made themselves unpopular by their handling of the Indian-Pakistani war, had gained very few adherents in the battle for leadership of the Communist world. They made great efforts to arrange a second 'Bandoeng' conference of the Afro-Asian governments without the Soviet Union. The Russians lobbied feverishly to get themselves recognised as Asians, but failed to get a ticket for the conference. The Afro-Asians disliked getting mixed up in the Soviet–Chinese quarrel, and the fall of Ben Bella enabled them to postpone the conference indefinitely.

There was sense in the Chinese analysis of the correct Communist policy as the surrounding of the cities by the countryside, an analogy from their revolutionary history, if it meant that there was a stalemate in the direct East–West confrontation and that the area of movement in the contest for world influence lay in the developing countries. This was in any case a good description of Soviet policy. The only investment likely to pay dividends was to support the nationalist leaders, even if they arrested their Communists and suppressed their Communist parties. It was no good supporting political friends who had no chance of taking power. So they picked on leaders like Nasser and Ben Bella, whom they regarded as the most hopeful instruments for the enlargement of Soviet influence in the Arab world and Africa. The countries were neatly classified. Algeria and the United Arab Republic were in the first class; Ghana, Guinea and Mali in the second. The Russians attacked the governments which went so far as to kill their Communists, but kept the lines open to them all the same. The exiled Arab Communists were looked after and allowed an annual meeting somewhere in East Europe, being given a little publicity for the occasion, but for sound practical reasons the Russians gave political and material aid to those in power. To explain this policy and defend themselves from Chinese attack, they propounded the doctrine of 'revolutionary democracy', a development of Lenin's anti-colonialist doctrines, which gave respectability to the bourgeois nationalist leaders who 'leant to their side' and away from the West.

It did not all go easily. The old belief that Africa and Asia would progress smoothly towards Communism was not working out in practice, in spite of all the aid, flattery and entertainment given to the Nationalist leaders. The fall of Nkrumah and Ben Bella had been a nasty shock. My old Soviet colleague in Cairo went too fast in Guinea and was thrown out. In the Congo, Lumumba had been killed, and though there was some benefit to be gained from helping to make him a martyr his opponents had got the upper hand, and a coup attempted from Brazzaville ended in the expulsion of the Soviet Mission from Kinshasa. A hopeful little enterprise in Kenya was defeated by the 'old man'. The Chinese, much to the Russians' outspoken disgust, outbid them by extremism in Zanzibar. There was always good propaganda to be made of South African apartheid; but the imperialists were on that side too and it was not politically very profitable. The Africans were too occupied in tribal quarrels and a major effort in Africa would cost too much.

The formula with the Arabs was arms, economic aid and political support against Israel, which could be attacked by the Soviet press and in the United Nations without harm to Soviet interests. But the investment in Egypt fell on difficult days, since the Egyptians had no money to repay their debts and all the training and arms did not prevent their being soundly beaten by the Israelis and losing most of their Russian equipment. The elements of the problem remained after the Six Days War as they had been in my time in Moscow. Neither war nor peace in the Middle East suited Soviet interests, but the Russians found themselves being sucked into a continually deteriorating situation. Despite the apparent threat of the Soviet fleet in the Mediterranean, they could not apply effective force in the Middle East. It was not an area of the first importance for Soviet security, nor worth a serious risk of confrontation with the Americans. The Soviet client was the weaker side, but could not be abandoned. For the Russians it was by no means a pleasant position.

Soviet diplomacy had acquired new fields of endeavour in middle Asia. India had long been recognised as of importance and the Chinese attack had its advantages for Moscow, to which the Indians began to look for political and military support. Pakistan, formerly regarded as an American client state, looked more hopeful after a new and more independent policy had been initiated by Mr Bhutto, though the Pakistanis' rapprochement with China was an awkward complication and the Russians now inherited the British position on the Kashmir tight-rope. Mr Kosygin's appearance at Tashkent to mediate between India and Pakistan must have made Lord Curzon turn in his grave. It was a diplomatic triumph in marking the Soviet Union's new presence in Asia, though it had little effect on the relations between India and Pakistan, equally unable to make war or peace with each other.

On the Soviet Union's southern border, historically and in modern terms of major importance, Afghanistan had for long been a 'good neighbour' and had received substantial economic aid, though some might see strategic overtones in the choice of projects such as the northern road over the Hindu Kush. Iran and Turkey, having successfully maintained their independence against Soviet attempts to undermine it, now became 'good neighbours'. The Shah visited Moscow and the Soviet Foreign Ministry took on the almost impossible task of pleasing the Greeks, Cypriots and Turks at the same time.

Further east, Sukarno's Indonesia had been wooed with political support and arms and even by a visit by Mikoyan, but the Russians, correctly analysing the unstable political condition and economic mess of the country and not wishing to see the victory of the

Chinese-flavoured Indonesian Communist Party, were only lukewarm in their support of confrontation against Malaysia and waited for the inevitable explosion. The Japanese Government were attacked for their subordination to the Americans, but encouraged to develop their trade with the Soviet Far East. The Russians showed no sign of willingness to restore the Japanese islands which they had occupied at the end of the war.

Relations with Latin America were in an elementary stage, except with Cuba. Castro was fêted, supported and given substantial economic aid. It was a risky investment in the American backyard, but after the dangerous missile crisis the local situation was gradually stabilised and Castro, after manœuvring between the Russians and the Chinese, began to see that his bread was more thickly buttered on the Russian side. But the evidence suggested that though the Russians were at pains to discourage his predilection for promoting guerrilla activity in South and Central America as being a form of adventurism in which it was inadvisable to indulge in the prevailing conditions, he paid little attention to their attempts at restraint.

All this added up to a policy of opportunism or pragmatism, if a more respectable name is preferred, always directed towards encouraging tendencies favouring the Left, increasing the influence of Communism and the Soviet Union to the detriment of the West, and at the same time thwarting the Chinese. There was nothing secret about the Soviet aims, which were repeatedly proclaimed in official statements, speeches and articles. It was a contest between opposing ideologies and national interests, though the rules were not always interpreted by the combatants in the same way. There were now three players in the game, which was complicated by the intrusion of the Chinese on the scene.

In the developing world the Russians were impelled by the compulsions of their doctrine to pursue a policy of expansion of influence. It was at least questionable whether they had properly appreciated the conditions of the modern world in which they were operating. Old-fashioned gunboat policy was as out of date for them as for us, and the rise of the new nationalisms had made it far more difficult to gain solid and lasting political influence. If their influence became too strong and apparent, it was likely to engender a nationalist re-action. Influence was bound to come unevenly, and the support of one client was apt to alienate another. The results were by no means certainly advantageous. They might find themselves with risky investments and complicated obligations, with responsibility but without real power, with an increasing economic drain, with a public position from which they could not disengage without unacceptable loss of prestige. The debtor was often in a stronger position than the creditor. Trade no longer followed the flag. There were bound to be many set-backs in the conditions of instability in the newly independent countries. There was always the danger of confrontation with the other super-power in un-favourable conditions. If they won Africa for Communism, what sort of Communism would it be? Would they ever be able to get themselves out again? Perhaps they were being led by memories of an imperial past and hopes of a Communist future into a policy which was against the real interests of the Soviet Union. Per-haps the Russian threat in the developing world would prove in the end to be an illusion, but meanwhile they would cause plenty of trouble for everyone else and for themselves too.

18

INTERNAL POLICIES

TH E Western press took great interest in the African and Asian students in the Soviet Union. The Africans gave the Soviet authorities plenty of trouble. The Lumumba University had been founded when most of Africa was still under colonial rule, largely in order to give political indoctrination to young Asians and Africans who might then be expected to spread the word in their home countries. Most of the students had inadequate educational qualifications, having been selected not by their own governments, but through Communist Front organisations. They liked neither the climate nor the food, nor the fact that they could not buy what they wanted, whereas their friends in London could get African food in the markets and everything else from Marks & Spencer. Some of them wanted to go to Britain. We had to explain to them that dissatisfaction with Russian conditions was not a qualification for entry to a British university. We could only help them to go home, if their governments agreed, and they could try from there. We had to be cautious. Their discontent was damaging to the Soviet reputation and it was always possible that the Soviet authorities might like to accuse a Western embassy of instigating the students to leave. One of them might have come by arrangement to make a case against us. Given the conditions existing in Moscow, one became suspicious, probably too suspicious sometimes, but a member of the American Embassy was expelled on these grounds. Our business was to look after British interests, which included helping Commonwealth students who had no embassy of their own, but not stirring them up to make trouble for the Russians.

Soviet propaganda never admitted that there was any racial prejudice in the Soviet Union, which was absurd. There was about as much in a Soviet as in a British city. There was bound to be some trouble as a result of the sudden influx of Africans and Asians into Soviet universities. We knew about fights between Russians and Africans, generally over girls, and there were one or two murders. Trouble came to a head when the Ghanaian students, after taking possession of their embassy for a weekend, staged a demonstration in Red Square, which outraged the Russians and was therefore ascribed to foreign instigation. The Reuter correspondent, who had sent the fullest reports about the affair, was expelled. There were troubles in Leningrad and Kiev. In the Black Sea port of Kherson the Africans took on all comers with some success. A murder over a girl in Baku, still Muslim in its social outlook, caused so much trouble that all the Kenyan students decamped and most of the other Africans were withdrawn. Many students left the Soviet Union disgruntled, and my African colleagues used to say that their boys had never really settled down there and probably never would.

Most of the African students, having come by illicit means, had no passports. The new African ambassadors had to try to get them under control and insist that the Russians should only take students selected by their governments. They supported the students who objected to political indoctrination, and their governments gave preference to those wanting to take technical courses less susceptible to ideological trimmings. The Russians found it necessary to make the Lumumba University less political, but the political motive remained and they could expect useful dividends from the return to their own countries of even a few dedicated young men, prepared to work and suffer for the Communist cause, some perhaps trained in the delicate arts of subversion and guerilla warfare in addition to the university course. It was right that the Soviet Union should share in the technical training of boys from the less developed countries, but we should have been more sympathetic to their efforts if they had not concentrated so many of them in a special university which, from its name, was obviously intended, at least in part, to serve political purposes.

Another frequent subject in the Western press was the treatment of Jews in the Soviet Union. Anti-Semitism had a long history in Russia. The Soviety Party disliked distinct ethnic communities and there was no doubt that the Jews were subject to disabilities To placate the Arabs, only a few were allowed to emigrate to Israel, obstacles were put in the way of the observance of Jewish customs and synagogues were closed. One class of crime created by the Soviet system, the crime of private enterprise, was punished very severely. Many of the people accused of having small underground factories and selling the proceeds were Jews, and the Israeli Embassy was apt to think that their trials were solely anti-Jewish in purpose. We thought it more likely that Jews, with their commercial instincts and abilities, were to the fore in the attempts to by-pass Soviet social-ism and earn a little money on the side. The official line was that there was no Jewish problem.

The Israeli Embassy used to press the Western embassies to get their governments to protest against the treatment of Jews in the Soviet Union. We had no grounds for intervention in matters of internal adminis-tration in which British subjects were not concerned. The Soviet Government would have rejected official protests which would not have done the Jewish com-munity any good. We argued that a better way of tack-ling the matter was for the Jewish organisations in the West to press the Jews in Communist parties and other left-wing organisations in Western Europe to raise the question with the Soviet Party, since the Party looked to them to support Soviet policies in the West. And there was always Bertrand Russell. The official restric-tions imposed on Jews diminished during our time in Moscow, though the Israeli Embassy was attacked in the press from time to time for the activities of its mem-bers among the Jewish community in Odessa.

The self-appointed friends of the Russian Church in the West were sincere, but sometimes misguided. The Church had greatly improved its position during the war by helping the national war effort, as a result of which the Government established a Committee for the affairs of the Orthodox Church, though the Church was never recognised as a State body. The Patriarch, as its head, attended the annual celebration of the Revo-lution. The Church was not actively persecuted, and Soviet citizens could go to church without penalty, even if it did not help them in their career in the State ser-vice. From time to time a church was closed on the grounds, not always true, that it was the wish of the local people. The Patriarch told me that fifty-four

churches remained open in Moscow. A few monasteries, having theological colleges in them, still kept
their monks, and perhaps about 20,000 churches were
still holding services in the Russian Patriarchate. Every
now and again an attempt was made to liven up atheist
propaganda, but the anti-God museums and meetings
were dull and only sparsely attended. I used to tease
Russian officials by saying that I thought that a higher
percentage of the population went to church in the
Soviet Union than in England. Perhaps this was not so
far out.

The Church rendered unto Lenin the things which
were considered to be Lenin's by his successors, and an
official spokesman of the Church was always found to
support the party line on peace and peaceful co-existence. It was argued in the West that the leaders of the
Russian Church conceded too much. But they had
much to lose and were surely wise not to provoke active
persecution, which might have destroyed the Church
altogether. Interference from outside could only do the
Russian Church harm. Its leaders knew best how to
play the hand.

The internal question which aroused the strongest
feeling in the West was always the Party's treatment of
Soviet writers and artists. It is as well to remind oneself
of the basic thinking behind the Party's actions. They
hold that culture should be organised by the State to
guide people's minds into the right ideological chan-
nels. Art forms which do not contribute to this purpose
are harmful and must be suppressed. The official cultural effort, fine though it is within its limitations, the
immense and devoted labour spent on the restoration of
palaces and churches, the classical ballet, are a retreat
into the womb of the nineteenth century. The unions
of writers, artists and musicians are established to carry

out the Party line. The State publishes all books and licenses plays and films. No dangerous thoughts appear in print, though the official view of what thoughts are dangerous varies with policy at the top. The production of a classic in the theatre in satirical style is taken off. Films, other than the classics, must show the official image of Soviet life, the heroes of Soviet labour. The style of painting of the Royal Academy in 1890 is considered revolutionary and therefore respectable. More modern forms are manifestations of bourgeois reaction; their practitioners cannot show in public nor earn their living by their painting. Music being an abstract art, the musicians are relatively free, though even Shostakovich and Prokofieff were subject to ideological pressure, and Stalin stopped the production of Shostakovich's opera *Katerina Ismailova* for thirty years, saying, 'This is not music; it is chaos.'

From time to time the Soviet Party has found it necessary to loosen slightly the strings of control. After a few years, the painters and writers are considered to have gone too far and party control is tightened again. In the early days of the anti-Stalinist reaction, the intellectuals were generally well disposed towards the régime, which was allowing them rather more freedom, but *Dr Zhivago* was too much for the Party to swallow, though a Soviet official told me that in his opinion they would have been better advised to allow it to appear.

By 1962 the artists and writers were feeling a breath of freer air. Khrushchev had personally sanctioned the publication of Solzhenitzin's *One Day in the Life of Ivan Denisov*, the account, now famous in the West, of a labour camp under Stalin, and had given his patronage to Yevtushenko, one of the young poets who could then command audiences of many thousands for a poetry reading, and who were the real heroes of youth in the Soviet Union. Yevtushenko and Nekrassov had recently published accounts of their recent visits to France and the United States, which displayed a wholly unorthodox objectivity. The authorities had at last allowed the performance of the thirteenth symphony of Shostakovich, a song-cycle with poems by Yevtushenko, including *Babi Yar*, in effect an attack on anti-Semitism. The Ministry of Culture had arranged an exhibition of paintings of Fernand Léger, a confirmed French Communist, but far from an exponent of socialist realism. Bourgeois culture was beginning to seep through.

In the week in which I arrived in Moscow, an exhibition of paintings was opened in the old Manège, the hall used for major exhibitions in Moscow, under the shadow of the Kremlin. It included paintings by living and dead artists which, while relatively academic by Western standards, did not all conform to the strict tenets of socialist realism. At the same time, an exhibition of modernist paintings, including abstracts, was being held in another hall near by. The Old Guard mobilised themselves for the attack. They got Khrushchev to visit the exhibition at the Manège and when he was thoroughly worked up about some of the less conformist pictures there, faced him with a selection of the abstracts which they had brought over for the purpose from the other exhibition. Khrushchev duly exhibited the required Pavlovian reaction, including the 'donkey's tail', an expression which had originated as the name of an earlier Russian modernist school of painting applied to it by its founders. The wind now blew cold on the artists and the writers. They were bidden to Party meetings and there arraigned, but defended themselves with courage. A Plenum of the Central Committee was held on the arts. The Léger exhibition in

Moscow, which had drawn large crowds, was closed prematurely. Yevtushenko, who had accepted an invitation to meet Benjamin Britten in my house, failed to turn up and found it safer to pay a visit of some months to his old home in the Urals. The poet Brodsky was sent into exile from Leningrad. Only the dullest and most orthodox paintings were now shown.

An ideological commission was created in the Central Committee under the Party Secretary, Ilychev, who became the intellectuals' bogeyman. Suggestions were made in the press for the amalgamation of the unions of writers, artists and musicians, in order to strengthen Party control. But, somehow, nothing very much happened. The attack fizzled out. Tvardovsky continued to publish lively and politically doubtful stories in *Novy Mir*, including another story by Solzhenitzin. Ehrenburg continued to publish his controversial memoirs. Yevtushenko made a half-submission, condemned by his contemporaries, and was allowed to publish a poem which obliquely criticised the Establishment, and popular non-conformist poets like Voznessensky appeared again in print. The scientists went on arranging small, semi-private exhibitions of non-realist pictures. Khrushchev had probably decided that it was wise not to push the reaction too far and may have been influenced by the scornful criticism of the Soviet Party's policy by the other Communist parties in Eastern and Western Europe, which needed the support of their *avant-garde* writers and artists and saw no reason why abstract painting should be regarded as subversive. The battle rumbled on, but remained a draw.

The attitude of the writers and artists was neatly summed up in the verse going round Moscow:

Nachinayetsya vse syznova,
Stali vsech rubit splecha;
Slishkom mnogo Ilycheva,
Slishkom malo Ilycha.

It's beginning all over again,
They've started hacking at everyone;
There's too much of Ilychev,
And too little of Ilych [Lenin].

The dilemma for the Party remained. If they suppressed originality and insisted on the old formulas, they ensured that books, films, plays and pictures would be dull and not true to life. Suppression could never be whole-hearted enough to stifle the opposition, which always broke out again. So the policy switched from a light thaw to a severe frost and back again. The leaders after Khrushchev are trying repression. The protests and the publicity given to the trials of writers show that at least some Russians condemn this policy more strongly and boldly than before, even if protest is still confined to a comparatively small minority. It seems unlikely on past form that this new, tougher policy can succeed in the long term, for it goes against the creative genius of the Russian people.

In the last months of Khrushchev's reign, new attempts to reform the Soviet economic system emerged into public view, stimulated by the writings of Soviet economists like Professor Lieberman. The old system had been well suited to the production of the basic capital goods required for an economy in the early stages of industrial development, and Stalin's industrial system had secured the forced development of industry which made possible the Soviet defence against German attack. But the system had become progressively less suitable to a more advanced economy, with a rising standard of living and an increasing demand for consumer goods of greater variety and quality. Goods were produced under a central plan, which tried to embrace every detail, without sufficient attention to consumer demand, often, as was said, 'for the warehouse'. Unsold goods piled up, since the Soviet people were becoming more discriminating and were no longer prepared to buy anything that was offered, as they had been in the old days when there was practically nothing to be had. The pricing system was so rigid that, as the press reported, new and more fashionable models of women's dresses were priced lower than older models which would not sell, since the shops were not allowed to reduce prices to clear stocks.

The basis of industrial production was the fulfilment of the production norm fixed by the planners. To fulfil the norm, the managing director would collect as much labour, material and machines as he could, since he was not responsible for the economic results of his production. In a system of full employment guaranteed by the State, labour was not mobile and the factories were full of under-employed workers. Costs were naturally high. Financial control could be evaded in curious ways. If, as the press explained, a factory manager wanted to carry out improvements and had no allotment in his budget, he got the work done and, by arrangement with the contractor, was sued in the courts for the amount due. The court issued a decree and the manager then paid, meeting the auditors' objection with the unanswerable argument that under Soviet law his primary obligation was to obey the court's decree. Most managers were probably careful not to exceed the norm by too much, for that would only result in its being raised in the next year, and for the workers there was no incentive to increase productivity. Anyone who has employed Russian building-labour in Moscow knows that the Russian worker takes even more tea breaks than the British.

The economists introduced two ideas which were revolutionary in Soviet thinking: that the success of an enterprise should be judged on the amount of goods sold and on profit earned, and that production should stem principally not from a detailed plan, but from demand. Factories and their workers were to receive monetary incentives in proportion to the factory's profit. There was no suggestion in this that the profit motive in the Western sense should be introduced. It was an attempt to improve industrial efficiency, to introduce some elements of the automatic checks and controls of the free-market system, and to adapt the country's economic organisation to the changing pattern of its developing economy. There was much controversy. The conservative planners objected, claiming that central planning in detail of even a complex and developed economy would be perfectly feasible by the use of computers, but the views of the innovators gained ground and, after some pilot experiments, the new system was introduced on a substantial scale. Not everyone was behind it and it has since had a rough passage. But it seems likely that, in the end, the old central planning system will be drastically modified, with consequences not only for the Soviet economy, but also for the way in which Soviet society will develop in the last half of this century.

That is, in some degree, to Khrushchev's credit. He was not so successful in the perennially difficult problem of Soviet agriculture. In a history of Russia in the nineteenth century, I read that industry was making progress on the basis of State investments and that agriculture was stagnating. The same picture was true of the Soviet Union in the early sixties. Khrushchev tried a new nostrum for agriculture every few months, a concentration of effort on fertilisers and the production of chemicals, the opening up of the 'virgin lands', large uncultivated tracts in areas of uncertain rainfall in Kazakhstan and southern Siberia, maize cultivation everywhere, in suitable or unsuitable conditions, hydroponics, reorganisation of the Party into agricultural and industrial 'streams', centralisation at one moment, devolution the next. Industry advanced with the introduction of new Western technology; agriculture stagnated, culminating in the disastrous harvest of 1963.

This harvest produced a stream of political jokes against Khrushchev, until they diminished under the impact of the measures taken by the authorities against their purveyors. The alleged source of these jokes was Radio Armenia, and the Russians loved telling us how the announcement at a radio conference that the Director of Radio Armenia was about to speak caused such a roar of laughter that the Chairman had to declare an interval. Here are a few of the productions of Radio Armenia at that time.

'Khrushchev is to be awarded the Nobel Prize for an outstanding achievement in agriculture. He sowed crops in Kazakhstan and reaped them in Canada.'

'What is the name of Khrushchev's hair-style? Harvest, 1963.'

'Radio Armenia has announced that this year's harvest will be average, worse than last year but better than next.'

'How will Khrushchev be known in twenty years' time? As a literary critic in the age of Mao Tse-tung.'

And they could be bitter:

'Radio Armenia was asked for its comments on President Kennedy's assassination. After a pause it replied, "We shall need to hurry; the Americans have got one further ahead of us."' It was not surprising that these jokes should proliferate at a time when there were bread queues in the cities and reports of bread riots in the south.

When Khrushchev fell, his reorganisations, his nostrums and some of his men fell with him and the Government and Party organisation of 1957, which he had torn to bits, was restored. Agriculture had been his special subject and he had notably failed. Distrusting his haphazard and unscientific methods, the Party would not put in the capital which was necessary if any real improvement was to be made. As soon as the new régime was established, they sanctioned massive new investment in agriculture, devolved more power on to the farm managers, introduced as much incentive as the system would bear and abolished the restrictions on private plots introduced by Khrushchev, an admission that the country's food supply depended to a large extent on the last remains of private enterprise in farming. But the new look was not very convincing. It was relatively easy to socialise industry, but farming cannot be treated like an industry. As an East European ambassador admitted to me, most other East European countries had realised that the collective system was incompatible with good farming, that a predominantly peasant economy was the only satisfactory solution in Eastern European conditions and that the land needs a farmer who will work twelve hours a day seven days a week for his own benefit.

19

SOVIET LEADERS

In his latter years, Khrushchev varied in mood and in health. He needed warming up. He could be abstracted and bored, and if a visitor did not interest him the interview was a failure. With experience, one got to know when a conversation with a British Minister was becoming sticky and it was necessary to intervene and liven it up. Khrushchev had become rigid in his views and in the way he expressed them. He could be rough. He liked to bully us, ridiculing our nuclear armament and threatening to blow us out of the water in five minutes. Patience and firmness were necessary. He did not want to listen to other people's opinions, preferring to air his own, though if one had a specific point to put to him he would listen carefully and make a precise answer. What a personality he was! When on his best form, he radiated self-confidence and could lift the atmosphere of a party to a point at which people would take his most outrageous remarks without offence.

Nearly every week a prime minister or head of state turned up on an official visit. Khrushchev and his colleagues were punctilious in their attendance at every function. At the airport, the formal ceremony with band and guard of honour was repeated on each occasion with precision down to the minutest detail, even to the individuals obliged to leave their warm factory in the height of winter, herded into buses, provided with appropriate flags and ordered to provide a spontaneous popular welcome. This was followed by *Swan Lake*, which Khrushchev must have seen a hundred times or more, the Kremlin party, the return party at the Embassy and the airport farewell. In addition, there were the annual Government parties in the new Hall of Congresses in the Kremlin, nicknamed by the Russians '*stylyaga sredi boyar*,' the hooligan among the nobles, a fine building which in my judgement fits remarkably well into the Kremlin architectural complex.

Politics intruded in these parties, but the speeches were not offensive until the Vietnam war developed to a point at which Foy Kohler, the American Ambassador, found it better not to attend them. The only diplomatic incident was caused by the determination of the representative of the South Vietnamese National Liberation front, who was not on the diplomatic list, to insert himself into the line of ambassadors. The ambassadors below him in the line protested to the Protocol Department who knew that they were right, but were nervous of finding themselves politically on the wrong side. I refused to attend the ceremonies on Castro's arrival after the Cuban crisis, since they were converted into a mass political demonstration and I wished to show solidarity with my American colleague.

The Kremlin parties were held in the great St George's Hall, with its name unchanged and the walls still decorated with the roll of famous Imperial Russian regiments. Khrushchev and his colleagues were ready to talk to any member of the diplomatic corps who approached them. At one party Khrushchev gave me his impressions of British politicians. He had liked Mr Gaitskell and was sorry that he had died, but he said he got on better with Mr Wilson. (At this time, Mr Wilson was still Leader of the Opposition.) 'But that Mr Brown; he was rude and I had to answer back.' The famous Labour Party dinner had not been forgotten. He respected Mr Macmillan but, he said, the best of the Conservatives had been Eden. He had warned Eden what would happen if the British attacked in the Middle East and he could not understand what had taken Eden at the end. At another party, he started ragging the ambassadors. 'Where's the coloniser?' he shouted. 'Here I am,' I replied and we started a half-joking argument. He looked across the room and re-marked, 'Your wife's looking nervous.' In his last months of power, he was increasingly inclined to throw away the text prepared by the Party and start improvising, doubtless alarming his colleagues.

At the New Year parties Khrushchev was at his most ebullient. He was on his feet proposing toasts, making little speeches for over an hour, while my American colleague and I watched each other and made sure that we both either drank the toast or sat through it with-out drinking when it was something like 'the progress of Communism'. The Russians understood the drill well. The press correspondents hovered round the edges of the party, straining their ears to catch Khrush-chev's latest boast or threat. After about three and a half hours at the dinner table, including a concert on the stage behind the 'high table', we adjourned to the immense, revolving, New Year's tree and danced until 3 a.m. to the joggety tunes of a military band. Khrush-chev used his last New Year's Eve party to stage a public demonstration of reconciliation with Bulganin, who was appearing for the first time at a public function since Khrushchev had thrown him out. Alas! After Khrushchev's deposition, Congress no longer danced on New Year's Eve. It was such a personal performance. The New Year party could hardly have existed without him. His successors had had enough of parties, and gradually they were all eliminated until only 7 November, the anniversary of the Revolution, was left. Moscow has now become dull. One can never forget that tubby little figure, showing on his face the emotions of the moment, either happy, amused and showing off or bored and depressed, waddling into a party with supreme self-confidence. And when he let himself go even Mrs Khrushchev was heard to remark that she wished he would stop.

The Cuban set-back was followed by a period of uncertain leadership, during which Khrushchev appeared to be taking personal initiatives, perhaps with the idea of recovering the ground lost by the Cuban gamble. He continued his visits abroad, which he obviously enjoyed. These visits, when he was out of control, must have been a source of anxiety to his colleagues. It was rumoured that he had made Nasser a Hero of the Soviet Union and had offered him extensive new aid without his colleagues' approval, though they naturally had to confirm his actions after his fall. He doubtless aroused violent objections from Ulbricht when he went to the length of proposing a visit to West Germany, at that time about as revolutionary a proposal as he could have made, though it seems unlikely that he had any clear idea of the purpose of the visit or that he would have made any concessions of substance.

In the Soviet Union the struggle for political power goes on much as it does in other countries, but behind a veil of secrecy. The fall of Khrushchev was a most successful operation which appeared to take him completely by surprise. We first heard rumours in the afternoon of the day on which the Central Committee had voted him out, but we knew nothing definite until my private secretary came back from the airport at 11 p.m. and told us that since the time he had left an enormous portrait of Khrushchev put up for a cosmonaut parade on the front of the Moskva Hotel had gone. All thoughts of the British election results, due to come in at any moment, vanished from our minds. We knew then for certain that Khrushchev had fallen. The Army had been squared; the K.G.B. were in the plot; virtually the whole of the Presidium were agreed and enough votes had been secured in the Central Committee. He had been on holiday by the Black Sea. The story went that at the right moment he was asked to come back to Moscow to attend a meeting on agricultural policy and was taken off from the airport. He was not able to turn the tables on the Presidium by getting the support of the majority of the Central Committee, as he had when he had defeated Malenkov. He was wise to resign when he saw that the game was up and thus to secure for himself as comfortable and honourable a retirement as can be secured by a fallen Soviet leader. He had exiled Malenkov to be in charge of a distant power-station and we remembered the story that, when asked whether it was not a post unworthy of a former prime minister, he had replied that it was a very large power-station.

Not many men lost their jobs. Among them were the key men in Khrushchev's publicity machine, the editors of *Pravda* and *Isvestiya*, the head of Soviet Radio, and a few of Khrushchev's men in the Central and Provincial administrations and in the Party machine. Adzhubei, his son-in-law, was relegated to an obscure post on a magazine. A correspondent of the Soviet News Agency

Tass told me that he was in charge of the publication of a type of article which the magazine did not publish. Adzhubei had once boasted to me how he had got an interview with Khrushchev for Lord Thomson. He said, 'This is a revolution requiring discipline. If my office opens at seven o'clock, I am there at seven. But you can always get things done "in the Russian way" [*po russki*].' This time he failed. Khrushchev had given him many favours and Moscow was full of stories about sports cars and special privileges. He had been used as a scout abroad and had visited the Pope and Western Germany. Adzhubei was not popular in Moscow, and the Russians enjoyed the current comment that he had woken up one morning and found that he had married for love.

Khrushchev's fall caused hardly a ripple inside the country, while the world press was treating it as a major world event. My driver said that after all he was seventy and that was an age at which to retire. Deputations came to Moscow from other Communist parties to have it all explained, but there were no explanations to his own people. Seemingly, it was not necessary. The stories were cynical and critical. It was not true, they said, that the Soviet Union had won only thirty gold medals at the Olympic Games. They had won thirty-one, the last having been won by Nikita Sergeivich Khrushchev for the high dive. The most illuminating story was that the reasons for his fall were the six Ks: *Kitai* (China), *Kuba* (Cuba), *Kukkuruza* (Maize, i.e. failures in his agricultural policy), *kult leechnosti* (cult of personality, the current expression for dictatorship), *kumovstvo* (nepotism) and *kuskinomat*, a vulgar way of saying 'I'll see you off' in Ukrainian, and so denoting a vulgar manner of speech. All these elements entered into the dissatisfaction of his colleagues who decided that he no longer represented their collective views and was becoming increasingly wayward and irresponsible. The last charge stemmed from the old inferiority complex in Russian relations with Western Europe. They were always on the look-out for suggestions that their behaviour was *ne kulturni*, not cultivated. So they disapproved of Khrushchev's boisterous manner and did not realise the immense publicity value of his personality, which, as a friend told me, made his name known to everyone in a remote Herefordshire village. I have no doubt that his colleagues thoroughly disapproved of his banging his shoe on the desk in the United Nations, though, as I used to say to them, the British thought this livened the place up and it reminded them of the House of Commons.

Those outside the higher ranks of the Party did not seem to care about the struggle for power. Most people were pleased by the degree of 'destalinisation' which Khrushchev had achieved and were nervous of a return to Stalin's methods under a new régime. But Khrushchev passed in a moment from being a world figure almost into oblivion, brought out to record his vote, since voting in the Soviet Union is compulsory, and to give a fictitious interview to a policeman at the site of a new monument, in order to demonstrate that he was in good health and not wholly under restraint. No foreigner could see him, and his place of retreat in the country was outside the reach of the press and visiting American politicians. I firmly discouraged British visitors who wished out of the best of motives to show that they had not forgotten the man whom they had known in his days of power. They did not understand the Soviet system. The man they had known was the Prime Minister of the Soviet Union, not Khrushchev. When he did appear, he was careful to say nothing of significance. The man who had abolished the midnight knock on the door for the innocent citizen overtaken by vague suspicion, who, in spite of his complicity in Stalin's brutalities, had since done much for his people, passed from the scene without a word of thanks or a sigh of regret. He had done the same to others.

Khrushchev's successor as Prime Minister, Mr Kosygin, was very different in his approach. He had a powerful intellect and, within the limits of his Marxist outlook, an open and enquiring mind. He was always keen to learn something from his visitors, especially on a matter of industrial technique and management. He had a dry and subtle sense of humour and a degree of modesty. He was very business-like and appreciated it if one did one's business quickly. He had a deep knowledge of industry, with which he had been concerned throughout most of his career, but it would be quite wrong to regard him as primarily a technician. He could not have got to the position which he had reached in the Party without being an accomplished politician. When he first became Prime Minister, he was cautious and reserved on foreign affairs, feeling his way, but after a few months he had acquired sufficient knowledge and self-confidence to argue the Soviet case freely and cogently. He was always equable, and interviews with him went easily. He showed his appreciation if he felt that an ambassador was concerned with economic and commercial as well as with political matters. As a Deputy Prime Minister, he had taken great trouble over Anglo-Soviet affairs, and on the occasion of the British Agricultural Exhibition was present at five British functions, at the Embassy and elsewhere, in the space of three days. He was a formidable personality for whom I grew to have a considerable liking and respect.

I knew Mr Brezhnev less well, since in my time he was

Head of State and subsequently First (later General) Secretary of the Party, the real position of power, and there was no reason for me to see him except at public functions. I had only two personal interviews with him, on arrival when I presented my credentials, and when I called on him to say good-bye. At the credentials ceremony, I admired his handling of the proceedings, the right degree of formality and then an immediate lightening of the atmosphere when the ceremony was over. At the farewell interview, at the Party Secretariat, he spoke for half an hour, giving me a straightforward, informative and realistic exposition of the Party's position. By that time, I could understand almost all he said and only interrupted him once or twice for interpretation.

We are, of course, Communists, he said, and we shall continue to act like Communists. He expressed his serious concern over the level of armaments, which I had no doubt was entirely genuine, giving a higher figure than that appearing in the Soviet budget and admitting to ancillary expenditure not coming under the heading of 'Defence'. Of current controversies he said, Some think us weak, because we do not always answer back, but we prefer to wait and then have the last word. I observed that the Chinese liked to have the last million words. He replied that that was only ephemeral paper. He could assure me that there was nothing the Chinese would like so much as for the Soviet Party to resume active polemics. The time was soon to come when the Soviet Party would find it impossible to keep quiet any longer and would revert to the style of the period when Khrushchev talked about the 600 million Albanians.

Brezhnev described the style of Soviet Government after Khrushchev in much the same words as we had used in our reports; cautious, orthodox, with emphasis on the collective, rather unexciting, and referred to Khrushchev's habit of speaking on his own authority without his colleagues' concurrence. He was certainly very entertaining, I interjected, and he replied: Yes, he was a jolly fellow. Some Russians gave foreigners the impression that Brezhnev was regarded as second-rate, and that they did not want an outstanding figure, since that was what they were trying to avoid after Khrushchev; but it would be wrong to dismiss as second-rate a man who had achieved the top position in the Party through all the strenuous in-fighting which marks the rise to the top in the Soviet Union. He seemed at first to be not too strongly entrenched, but as the months passed he appeared to gain in stature and to consolidate his position. His political strength lay in his Party background.

Of Mr Mikoyan's ability there could be no doubt. The crafty old politician had survived all the dangers of association with Stalin. He had been close to Stalin through all the horrors of the purges, apparently without being held responsible for them, and had survived through the milder atmosphere of Khrushchev's régime into the next, until age and ill-health finally brought his retirement. The familiar Russian story went that twenty years on, after the restoration of the monarchy, Khrushchev was on his knees before the Tsar, pleading for his life and crying out, 'God exists! Long live the Tsar!' The Tsar, uncertain whether these appeals were sincere, summons his Lord Chamberlain. In walks Mikoyan. But he was not a weak Vicar of Bray. He was a tough fighter whose strength lay in the fact that he was never a candidate for high office and whose power of survival showed his shrewdness and resilience. Rumour had it that Stalin's death had saved him from a sensational fall. That may well be; he was blessed also with luck. He had never been to England, but had known the British in the early days of the Revolution. He began to tell me at a party about his experiences in the Caucasus under the British occupation; how he had deceived them and how he used to hand out Soviet propaganda to the soldiers in exchange for bully-beef. I remarked, Not a good basis for Anglo-Soviet trade; we have improved it since then. Even the Russians found it difficult to understand his diction. He was a practised conspirator and politician, but never a leader.

The other members of the Presidium we saw only at parties. At the Kremlin party on 7 November 1964, Mr Shelepin, tough and generally on the attack, who had come up through the Komsomol and the secret police, delivered to me and to two other ambassadors an attack on President Johnson's latest speech about aid for Vietnam, which he compared to Churchill's Fulton speech. He was threatening a harder Soviet attitude than in Khrushchev's day and said of Khrushchev, normally never mentioned by the Soviet leaders on public occasions: That old man used to blather away, but we are not bound by what he said. At that moment Mr Kosygin came up and Shelepin said: I was just giving the Ambassador my personal opinion. What, I thought, was the status of the personal opinion of a member of the Collective?

Mr Suslov, the theoretician, looked like a mild university professor. My only contact with him was when he told me about his visit to England some years previously, when he had met my cousin, Charles Trevelyan, who, with Cripps, had been one of the first members of the Anglo-Soviet Friendship Society, in the days when the Soviet idea of the purpose of such societies was not understood. The Czechs said in 1968 that Suslov and Shelepin had been opposed to the invasion of Czechoslovakia. This would seem inherently probable if it was true that they were the members of the Presidium, then again called the Politburo, principally concerned with relations with other Communist parties, though hardly in character with the impression of toughness which Shelepin seemed to want to give. But the Czechs seem to regard Shelepin as more moderate in his views than appears on the surface.

Mr Polyansky was an attractive character, friendly and talkative, though without the incisiveness of Kosygin. He had been the Party member responsible for agriculture under Khrushchev and we wondered at the time of Khrushchev's fall whether he would survive, since the obvious failure of Khrushchev's agricultural policy was clearly one of the reasons for his overthrow. However, Polyansky survived in his position on the Presidium, apparently unscathed. We judged him to be a good administrator, but not a leader. Those who know him well respect his intelligence and find him an agreeable companion.

Mr Mazurov appeared to be able, but is said to be handicapped by his health. He had for me the agreeable attribute of speaking very clear Russian. Voronov, Kirilenko, and Podgorny did not appear to be candidates for the top rank. One had to try to sum up these men on inadequate contacts with them. The free and easy intercourse with Western embassies which marked the early days of their release from Stalin's grip had diminished with time and the multiplication of diplomatic missions. They kept very much to themselves in their offices in the Kremlin, ruling the country through the Party and Government officials in the constituent republics, while they moved only rarely away from their dachas at weekends. Their travels seemed to take them more outside than inside the country. It was no wonder that the people seemed to treat them as 'they', something apart from themselves. The old Russian traditions of government had a persistent life. As Griboyedov said, 'The houses are new, but prejudices are old.'

It was widely believed in Moscow that when Khrushchev was removed the Central Committee passed a resolution that, short of a national emergency, the post of First Secretary should never again be combined with that of Prime Minister. According to this account, it was felt that the combination of so much power in the hands of one man had twice proved detrimental to the interests of the Soviet Union. Doubtless, it was also considered to be a risk to the 'health' of the other people near the top. This resolution would, of course, be easily overturned if one man should prove strong enough to take the whole power into his hands. But there did not seem to be anyone among the principal figures with the will, the ability and the Party support necessary to upset the new balance of power in the Kremlin, at least for some time.

Shelepin, we thought, might achieve it one day, though we could not judge his real ability and, after Beria, a background as head of the secret police, in the opinion of many Russians, was a handicap to the aspirant to power. Podgorny, Suslov, Polyansky, Mazurov – none of these seemed at that time quite to fill the bill. Kosygin was probably the most able, but he appeared to be content to remain as Prime Minister and so in the second place. There was no sign that Brezhnev wanted to oust him. After Khrushchev's fall, the apparatus of political power, to all appearances, remained stable. From time to time, there were rumours of conspiracy in the Kremlin, such as attempts by Shelepin to oust Brezhnev, but there was no real evidence to support these stories of what was happening behind that tremendous façade which faced us across the River Moskva.

There were a host of Deputy Prime Ministers, some having Party status as member or candidate member of the Presidium, all being members of the Central Committee. One senior official on the way out remarked to me acidly that there were so many he did not know what on earth they did. They may be described in our terms as ministers without Cabinet rank, the ministers being more like senior civil servants, but they were at the same time the equivalent of the chief executives of public and private industrial corporations in a capitalist society and were directly responsible for agriculture, scientific research, education and every other aspect of civil life in the country. We were in almost daily contact with the Committee for Scientific Co-ordination and its Chairman who had the status of a Deputy Prime Minister, but only marginally with the others. We met them frequently at parties and some of them in their offices and could therefore make an attempt to form an impression of their abilities. As might be expected, the standard was high, quite comparable to that of their opposite numbers in the capitalist world. Only one gave the impression of being second-rate and he was removed in the economic reorganisation of 1965 after Khrushchev's fall. He had been a Khrushchev man. One of them was a Jew, the only one we ever came across in the higher ranks of Party and Government.

Ministers were relatively low in the Protocol list, but their real power and position seemed to vary with their ministries and the personality of the minister. The Foreign Minister, Mr Gromyko, was very able and had a lifetime of experience in foreign affairs. The depth of his detailed knowledge, extending back for so long, made us think sometimes that the main qualification for a British Foreign Secretary was to have been Foreign Secretary for at least six years, a qualification which few British politicians ever acquire in the musical-chairs system of British politics. Mr Gromyko was a brilliant operator and gave nothing away. He used heavy sarcasm as a weapon when he was on the defensive, in order to disconcert his opponent. It was an effective device, which did not endear him to some members of the Diplomatic Corps; but that was irrelevant, since he was only concerned to use the best weapon with which to promote Soviet interests. One could only admire the way in which he subordinated all other considerations to his main purpose, the absence of any personal weakness, his sheer professionalism. Although we had our battles, I found him courteous and accessible and, in the latter part of my stay in Moscow, progressively easier in manner. It had been tough going before the Test-ban Treaty. In the temporarily improved atmosphere after the signature of the treaty, we found that if we still disagreed with Soviet policy in almost every particular at least we now disagreed in a more friendly way.

Mr Gromyko had clearly had his difficulties with Khrushchev who had once had the bad manners to insult him before Mr Harriman, but I had the impression, though without any firm evidence, that he had a real influence on policy, even if he did not make it. I used to speculate why he was not made a Deputy Prime Minister. Molotov had been Deputy Prime Minister and Prime Minister. Perhaps it was that, if Mr Gromyko had been promoted, it would have been difficult not to give the same rank to the top soldier, who was only Minister of Defence, a sign of the determination of the Party to subordinate the Armed Forces to the Party leadership.

The Foreign Ministry was directed by the Collegium, a body founded by Peter the Great, with powers laid down by law. We knew little about how it worked, but it probably exercised real authority, at least over the administration of the Ministry and the Foreign Service. There was much to be said for the adoption of a similar system in our Foreign Office and there are signs of changes in Foreign Office practice in this direction. The exceedingly able First Deputy Minister, Mr V. V. Kuznetsov, my old colleague in Peking, held the position so long held by Mr Vyshinsky. In my experience Mr Kuznetsov always tried to be helpful within the limits of Soviet foreign policy. One could tell when an issue of foreign policy was considered of major importance, as Mr Kuznetsov was sent to deal with it. I hardly ever found a Deputy Foreign Minister being deliberately difficult. There was only one exception. I quickly learnt to have a real respect for this able body of men as precision instruments executing the Party's policy.

Of the other ministers, the best-known in England were Mr Patolichev, the Minister of Foreign Trade, an immensely hard worker with a likeable personality, handicapped by having to operate within a bureaucratic over-centralised organisation, and Madame Furtseva, the Minister of Culture, a lady of charm and intelligence, who seemed to be as liberal as she dared, though subject to the ideologists in the Party Secretariat. She had been close to Khrushchev and had been made by him a member of the Presidium, but had fallen from that exposed pinnacle to the safer haven of a ministry. I found her helpful, efficient and quick. There were difficulties over the visit of the Moscow Arts Theatre to London at a late stage after all the arrangements had been made. Russians often did not understand that we could not switch such arrangements on and off at a moment's notice, as they could. I waited with her officials for a few minutes before seeing her about it. They said that the new director was obdurate and that there was no chance of getting the visit confirmed. I had better ask for another company. We went into her room. She said, 'Do you want the Moscow Arts Theatre?' I said, 'Yes.' She said, 'Right. I give you my personal guarantee that they will go.' The interview took two minutes. She was as good as her word.

With the Marshals of the Soviet Army I had little personal contact. The array at official parties of famous Marshals with enormous chests plastered with medals took one back into war-time history. There they all were, Malinovsky, Konev, Sokolovsky, Rokosovsky, Gretchko, the famous old Budenny with his long moustaches, not conspicuously successful in the war, but with a long revolutionary history behind him, all except Zhukov, brought out only for the twentieth anniversary of the defeat of Germany. It was an impressive display, like Madame Tussaud's come to life. The only one I found disagreeable was Marshal Malinovsky, who behaved like a bear with a sore behind. I learnt to give him a wide berth.

The twentieth anniversary of the end of the war with Germany was to be celebrated by a special parade. Marshal Malinovsky, who was to take the parade, wrote an ill-tempered key-note article the day before, published in *Pravda*, suggesting that the Allies had deliberately held back in the battle of the 'Bulge' in order to make things difficult for the Soviet Army, and otherwise making insulting remarks about our Forces. I refused to attend the parade, and my NATO colleagues followed my lead, except the French Ambassador who had found it necessary to ask for instructions and was told not to attend. Apart from one slight ironic comment in the Soviet press, no notice was publicly taken of our absence. The French Ambassador went out of his way to tell Soviet visitors that my feelings were strong and very natural. The Russians understood our position well enough. In 1969 President Nasser told me that he found dealing with the Russians very different from ten years before. The Marshals had recently started to give their own opinions and did not always conceal their disagreements with the civilians. In spite of this, I do not believe that, whatever they may say, they have really got loose from subordination to the direction of the Party, which will never take risks with the only force in the Soviet Union capable of overthrowing the Party leaders, so long as they stick together.

20

DIPLOMATIC TECHNIQUES

W E followed the usual routine of an Embassy in a Communist country, reading the Russian newspapers in the early morning and meeting at ten o'clock to go through them and discuss statements of Soviet policy, articles on politics and economics and the treatment of the news. But there were differences from the Peking scene. Most of us could read at least the main articles in *Pravda* and *Isvestiya*. There was far more material to digest than we could get in Peking. In China we depended virtually on one expert, though the younger Chinese-speaking members of Chancery were learning fast. In Moscow we had a number of specialists who had studied Soviet policy for many years, each of whom had their own individual and often conflicting views, for we were surveying a more complicated and sophisticated scene than in Peking.

I, in my ignorance, would say that a point in the latest speech of a Soviet leader appeared to be a new twist in the doctrine. The Minister, Tom Brimelow, whose mind stored facts like a computer and who had himself indexed all Khrushchev's speeches, would point out that Khrushchev had said something on the same lines in a speech in the autumn of 1956. Ted Orchard, the head of the Russian Secretariat, the specialist on the internal scene, looking with his bushy beard like a nineteenth-century aristocratic anarchist, would propound a new theory in order to start an argument. The Minister would succinctly demolish it. The time was not wasted. In these sessions, which I used to call the intra-Party struggle, from the Chinese Communist expression, we came to acquire at least some understanding of the complicated skein of Soviet politics and economics.

The intelligent Soviet citizen understood well enough that their newspapers, in accordance with Lenin's dictum, were essentially didactic, relating Soviet achievements, exhorting the people to fresh efforts of socialist construction, castigating failures in execution of official policy and purveying the official line on everything under the sun which it was considered good for the people to know. The intellectuals sometimes expressed a preference for *Isvestiya*, the Government newspaper, perhaps because they realised that *Pravda*, the purveyor of the undiluted Party line with even less real news than *Isvestiya*, was a bit too much for the foreigner to swallow. But the difference between the two was hardly perceptible. I used to say that the typical headline in the British press was 'Slays six with axe' and in the Soviet press, 'Plant your potatoes early.'

Togliatti, in his last report to the Soviet Central Committee, published surprisingly in the Soviet press after his death, pointed out the deplorable effect on the average reader of the difference between what he read of Socialist success and what he knew from his own experience was the reality. At a lunch for the Managing Director of Reuter's, I told the editor of *Pravda* that we found his newspaper very useful. We got from it up-to-date news of all the railway and air accidents, strikes and natural disasters in Great Britain. A Tass representative interjected, 'Don't you know that there are no railway or air accidents in Socialist countries?' I said, 'Yes, I know that, but I was interested to see that you have just acquired natural disasters.' He replied, 'No, we acquired all natural disasters except earthquakes some years ago, and last year we acquired earthquakes too by the combined efforts of the Academy of Sciences and Tass.' The Tass men seemed to have the licence of a court jester.

In Moscow we had more opportunity than we had had in Peking to check our impressions by talking with political leaders and senior officials, hearing what well-informed press correspondents or diplomatic colleagues had picked up, digesting critically information which we knew had been indirectly passed to us for a purpose by Soviet official sources, assessing the significance of the current political jokes, even talking to the taxi-drivers who contrive to say what they think in Moscow, as they do in other countries, if it is only that your Embassy ought to be shut up because it is full of spies.

It was not our job to engage in minute Kremlinological research, but we had to study the daily evidence and try to determine its significance. Besides the statements of policy in articles and speeches, it included the order in which the photographs of the leaders appeared in the streets, the order of their names at public functions, their presences and absences, the scale of representation at airport receptions and farewells, the way in which foreign visitors' doings were reported, the place of a report in the newspaper. Why had a member of the Presidium not appeared for a month? Why had Khrushchev and Kozlov appeared together at the theatre without the other leaders? Was it to scotch rumours that they were on bad terms? Was a meeting of the Central Committee taking place? Which Soviet ambassadors who were members of the Central Committee were on leave from their posts? In what terms was an official transfer recorded? Was the official merely transferred, i.e. sacked, or transferred, in the usual phrase, to 'other duties'? The Soviet leaders could have saved themselves and everyone else a great deal of trouble if they could have got out of their habit of excessive secrecy.

A particular line of argument or attack was being put over to the diplomatic corps. What was the purpose? Khrushchev, who showed his moods, was ebullient or glum. Was the glumness political or digestive? Was there any truth in the report heard by the press correspondents that an important Communist leader was in Moscow? If so, why was he there? Why was a certain area temporarily out of bounds to military attachés? It was always tempting to speculate, to exaggerate the significance of some indication, but on the other hand it was no use just swallowing the official line all the time. Very often there was a simple explanation. An absent member of the Presidium might have a cold, which would never be officially admitted, since important people were never reported to be ill until they were dead, or he might have stayed at home for a domestic celebration. On one occasion the researchers were beginning to think that the prolonged absence of a member of the Presidium meant that he had fallen from power, when I met him casually in the Kremlin and he told me about his recent holiday. We learnt never to jump to conclusions. The Sovietologists of the Western press, working on the documents in London or Washington, were forced by the nature of their occupation to draw conclusions, not always justified by the facts. But the right answer to the question, what was happening in the

Kremlin, was nearly always that we did not know.

In the difficult days of Stalin's later years the Ambassador could do little except sit in his office and wonder what was going on in the Kremlin. In my time, we were in continuous discussion with Soviet officials, from high politics to matters of trivial administration. The machine worked with great precision and promptness during the week. Requests for interviews were answered immediately, unless there was a political reason for delay. No visitor was kept waiting for a minute. The weekend was sacrosanct and it was very difficult to do business except during office hours. The habit of working at night, so common in new revolutions, had long passed away. Negotiation in the Ministry of Foreign Affairs was normally an agreeable and stimulating experience, in spite of the customary difference in the position of the two governments. I came to have almost an affection for the ugly Stalinist skyscraper on the 'Ring' with its old-fashioned décor and lifts, its heavy furniture upholstered in yellow velvet and the socialist realist landscapes on the landings. The picture on the seventh floor where the Minister and his deputies had their offices was of the Russian spring thaw. This was not an appropriate picture for the Ministry, which seemed to remain politically in a state of permanent Siberian frost. More appropriate, as I used to tell members of the Ministry, was the notice which faced me as I emerged onto the 'Ring' just before reaching the Ministry: 'krasnii svet perekhoda net' – 'no crossing on the red light'.

A visit to the offices of the members of the Presidium in the Kremlin was ceremonious. As one stepped out of the car at precisely five minutes before the appointed time, an officer, a cheerful person who became quite a friend, greeted the visitor, saluting and uttering a formal welcoming incantation. He accompanied the visitor upstairs along endless corridors, fitted with the standard carpet prescribed for V.I.P. offices, of a particularly hideous design. The corridors were always completely empty. I never remember meeting anyone on the way in. The visitor entered the ante-room at one minute before the hour, was greeted by the secretary and, as the Kremlin clock struck, was ushered into a large room, also of standard design, with an office table at the far end under the portrait of Lenin and a long table at right angles to it, occupying the length of the room. There were no papers on the tables. The Minister was standing with his interpreter and accompanying officials, ready to welcome the visitors. On formal occasions photographers were in attendance. The Minister gave the visitor his full attention. No telephones rang; nothing disturbed the conversation. The Russians occupied one side of the table, the visitors the other, in order of precedence. The interpreter sat at the end. Everything – the furniture, the ornaments, the pictures, the bottles of water on the table, the positions during the interview – was precisely to pattern.

Nothing could be less like the breezy informality of a foreign statesman's visit to 10 Downing Street, where Ministers not immediately engaged in the conversation may be seen doing their files, the guests may be seated in easy chairs in the drawing-room and the interview may be abruptly terminated by the overriding demands of the House of Commons. Nor could there be a greater difference between the Foreign Ministry in Moscow and the Foreign Office in London, the one orderly, wrapped in funereal silence, the corridors in the other full of bustle and stacked with old cupboards and furniture, looking like a disused warehouse in the London docks.

There was little real negotiation face to face in the

Foreign Ministry, presumably because detailed control was kept by the Party apparatus behind the scenes, to which everything of the slightest importance had to be referred. At home our own department in the Foreign Office understood this well enough, but other departments were apt to use a language which had no relevance to Soviet conditions. They would tell us that as a last resort we might make certain concessions, imagining a bargain being struck at the table. What normally happened was quite different. The Soviet official presented an 'oral communication', which meant that he read from a piece of paper and then handed over the paper so that we could not get the message wrong. But, being formally oral, the communication would not go into the records as an official Note or Memorandum. I would comment on a personal basis and would promise to convey the views of the Soviet Government to the British Government. When I received instructions, I gave my 'oral communication' to the Soviet official in the same way. He made his comments and promised to refer it to the 'leadership'. He then summoned me again and gave me the Soviet Government's views, using the same procedure. When, as normally, we ended in disagreement, they liked to publish their last 'communication', which had been drafted for the purpose, within a few hours, in order to get in first. Concessions were rare and were apt to be expressed as if there had been no change of position. Inconsistency never bothered them nor required explanation. But, even then, personalities came into it. One man preferred the direct attack, another a delicate irony. Russians like a little play-acting and enjoy the national sport of *vranye*, the game of saying something which the other party is meant to know is untrue, which has been analysed in its use in Russian literature by Mr Ronald Hingley. I once said to a Deputy Minister that a document which he had denied receiving had been handed simultaneously to the Soviet and British Embassies on a specific date a month before. He replied that they had not received it and added, 'Our mails are slower than yours.' This meant, 'You know perfectly well that this document is highly inconvenient for the Soviet Government and that we have no intention of ever acknowledging to you that we have received it.' Another Deputy Minister liked mock surprise. 'I am positively astonished at your statement,' he would say, in order to cover up some weakness in his position. However rigid the procedure, one needed a different 'feel' for each man, if one was to begin to understand what lay beneath the surface.

In a discussion in a Soviet office, an interpreter is always present and takes a complete record for the files of the Foreign Ministry. In a simple discussion, each could speak his own language and dispense with interpretation; but my knowledge of Russian was far from perfect and, however well you know the language, the use of the other man's language is dangerous in a serious negotiation, since it gives him an advantage. The use of an interpreter gives you time to think. The interpreter is thinking only of the language. The negotiator will not be concentrating on the business with his whole mind if he has to think half the time about the inflexion of irregular verbs or to strain himself to catch the meaning of a phrase.

There is much to be learnt from the very competent and professional senior Soviet officials. They are scrupulously accurate. They observe strict discipline. They never stray from the official line. They are never afraid of repetition. They have immense stamina. They will repeat the same things for months on end and will sometimes succeed in wearing down their opponents at the conference table by inducing a feeling of sheer horror at the thought of having to go through it all over again. They will maintain a firm position for years, then suddenly change to their last position which had been prepared from the outset. This has the advantage that they never give away anything unnecessarily, but the disadvantage that the next time they make a firm statement of their position the other party will be less likely to believe them. 'Not one kopeck,' said Mr Gromyko, when asked to help the United Nations' finances strained by the expense of peace-keeping operations of which the Russians did not approve. What he meant was that they would only contribute to an extent which would clearly not compromise the Soviet interpretation of the United Nations' Charter.

Soviet makers of foreign policy analyse their interests and follow the analysis down the line. They do not allow sentiment to divert policy and have no public emotions to distract them. They are ready to take advantage of a weakness shown by their opponents. They base their action on their assessment of the balance of political and military forces and, in the short term at least, are generally right in their assessment. They do not threaten without a specific political purpose which they judge can be achieved by the threat. The threat to use force in the Middle East in November 1956 was intended to stake their claim as the protector of the Arabs, without leaving the field to the Americans, and to divert attention from Hungary. They knew perfectly well that their object would be achieved without their having to carry out their threat.

They do not appear to mind in the least what other people think of them, nor do they mind losing face by being defeated in a diplomatic battle, if they get more in the end from starting from a position which they know cannot be sustained. They appeared to have been defeated in an attempt to unseat Hammarskjöld, but in fact achieved their objective by effectively limiting his power of manœuvre. In the developing world they have the immense advantage of appearing to have shed their imperialist past and are adept in feeding the fears of the newly independent countries that their old masters will somehow get back their former position. They know how to make a good impression on the new nationalist leaders. They have no compunction in abandoning their Communist friends, if those friends cannot deliver the goods. They have the immense advantage, shared only with the Americans, of the backing of immense power. They have developed a formidable diplomatic machine.

Where then does their weakness lie? It is surely in the basis and compulsions of the Communist doctrine. They are securely fenced in behind their ideological spectacles and must therefore suppress the exercise of such imagination as is necessary to understand the reactions of people who do not start from the same premises. Their revolutionary attitude conflicts with their new position in the world as one of the two most powerful 'Establishments', which carries with it new compulsions and new responsibilities. This parallels the American difficulty in reconciling their traditional anticolonialism with emergence as a world power. They think clearly in the short term, but their ideological blinkers stop them seeing where their actions are taking them. They are missionaries for their own brand of Communism, which causes most non-Communists and many Communists to distrust and fear them. They talk about peace, but will use force, where they safely can, to impose their own terms. In their missionary zeal, they will not let people live in their own way. They have got stuck in the period of the wars of religion. They have a long way to go before the world will truly come to trust them. Sir Edward Grey said that the purpose of diplomacy was to enlarge the area of confidence. In this the Soviet diplomats must inevitably fail. Their own propaganda is against them.

21

TRADE AND CULTURE

I N a branch of the Embassy on Kutuzovsky Prospekt
the Commercial, Cultural and Scientific Attachés pursued their several courses like distant satraps of a de-
clining imperial power, vague rumours of their
independent activities reaching us from time to time on
the other side of the river. Dugald Stewart, the Commercial Counsellor, in private life the head of a
Scottish clan, was indefatigable in the promotion of
Anglo-Soviet trade. His wife was an enterprising lady
who had been dropped into Yugoslavia during the war
and had succeeded with great adroitness in escaping the
eye of both the Germans and Fitzroy Maclean, head of
the British mission, who disliked having women about
the place. They had discovered early in their diplomatic
career that all roads in the modern British Foreign
Service do not lead to Rome, having been required to
spend a year with small children in the middle of the
Iraqi marshes in a dilapidated house inhabited by
huge spiders which could be heard plopping down the
stairs. Now, having stacked three strapping sons in
bunks in the one small spare room of their flat, they
gave themselves whole-heartedly to the nightly succour

of bored British businessmen, marooned on the seventeenth floor of the Ukraine Hotel and only too glad to follow their unconventional host from his office to his flat through the window as the shortest way to a drink. He and his successor earned the gratitude of many for their hospitality and for the Commercial Office's untiring efforts to further their affairs. I was only too conscious that the reputation of the Embassy at home depended largely on their efforts.

With the Ministry of Foreign Trade we used the Russian tactics of repetitious obstinacy. The Russians bought from us only about half what we bought from them. We never lost an opportunity to badger them about it. They argued that they were using their sterling to buy raw materials from the sterling area. It was all coming back to us. We told them that they could use their surplus dollars or Deutsche Marks for that; they should have a trade balance with Britain alone as they had with countries with which they traded on a bilateral basis. They argued that the strategic embargo and our refusal to buy Russian oil were brakes on our trade. We replied that this made no sense, so long as the balance was in their favour. By 1964 we heard no more of the oil argument, since by that time the Soviet oil surplus had turned into a deficit.

Khrushchev, now very set in his ways and fond of the old themes, never lost an opportunity to bring up the familiar arguments. He enjoyed attacking us on our refusal to supply one article, a very thin plastic film. The neatest reply was made by Lord (then Mr) Erroll, when he visited Moscow as President of the Board of Trade. He said, 'If your experts do not know the strategic use of this material, they are ill-informed. We have our embargo and you have yours. The only difference is that we publish ours; you do not publish yours.' We heard less of this argument, too, as time went on. The Russians knew well enough that the Europeans were always trying to get the Americans to cut down the embargo, being sceptical whether it had any value apart from material and technique directly of use for military needs, and sometimes speculating whether the embargo would not look rather different to the Americans as soon as they had made up their minds to trade freely with the Soviet Union themselves. On the other side, the Americans had presumably not forgotten that we had given the Russians the technique of the Rolls-Royce Nene engine, which was developed for the Migs used in the Korean war.

Both British and Russians also knew well enough that if the British bought large quantities of Soviet goods, mostly raw materials, it was because British importers could get them more cheaply than from any other sources and that a proportion of them were re-exported. The obvious remedy for the imbalance of Anglo-Soviet trade was to conduct it on a bilateral basis, as most other countries did; but this was contrary to the firm British principle that we must maintain the multilateral basis of trade and payments. An official of the Board of Trade, in the happy irresponsibility of his last few months before retirement, without consulting anyone, threatened the Russians that we would remove some Soviet products from the list of goods imported on open general licence, but was promptly sat on by the watchdogs in the Treasury and Bank of England. It was true that countries which traded with the Soviet Union on a bilateral basis also suffered to some extent when Soviet foreign-exchange balances were low; but we were at a disadvantage compared with them, since the Russians were well aware that our views on the advantages of a multilateral trading system made us reluctant to impose a strict balance on bilateral Anglo-Soviet trade.

We pursued our point. In 1964 Mr Heath, then President of the Board of Trade, succeeded in getting the Soviet Minister of Foreign Trade, Mr Patolichev, whose defences were temporarily weakened by indisposition during an exhausting tour in Britain, to agree to an exchange of letters by which the Soviet Government promised to use their best endeavours to achieve a closer balance. We won the argument; but the balance deteriorated further as a result of the disastrous Soviet harvest of 1963 and their consequent large purchases of grain from abroad. But within a few years, with the help of the new credits provided by the system of financial guarantees, the balance greatly improved and trade substantially increased both ways. The Russians took our arguments with good grace. It was what they would have done themselves and they respected our persistence. They knew we were active in helping our businessmen and welcomed our interest in economic affairs. The help which we could give was, as it has been described, marginal but essential. We could put the businessmen on the right track, but not sell their goods for them.

There were, inevitably, the exhibitions at which the elderly woman with the shopping-basket, trailing a child or two complete with balloons, would turn out to be the top electronics expert, the really vital visitor. There was the mammoth agricultural exhibition, bringing scenes graven on the memory of all concerned in it. The tensions generated by a large exhibition in the Soviet Union are formidable, and we were surprised that no member of the committee quite reached the point of murdering one of his fellow-members. The poultry exhibitors were convinced that a dastardly plot by the Soviet secret police was afoot when they discovered that all their White Leghorns had become speckled overnight, until it was pointed out that the coops had been painted without the birds being removed. We were privately happy to see rather too political a gesture go wrong, the presentation to Mr Khrushchev of two 'peace doves' in a silver cage, the donor having, as it was reported to me, been unaware that the first three items on the Soviet list of prohibited imports were armaments, pornographic literature and doves. In any case, since Mr Khrushchev was propelled into retirement only a few weeks after the exhibition, the silver cage did not turn out to be a satisfactory investment.

There were more memorable scenes during the entertainments which inevitably accompanied a major exhibition; Mr Kosygin at dinner looking up and saying, 'But where are Gerzog and Gerzogya Nortoomberlandski?' They had been omitted by mistake from a Soviet invitation, but nobly and graciously allowed themselves to be summoned to a second course. There was the harassed British exhibition official trying to silence 400 thirsty and loquacious British businessmen during Mr Kosygin's speech and falling off the platform in the process, and the six foot six Galloway herdsman, broad in proportion, in his kilt, turned out of the men's lavatory in the National Hotel. Like all these affairs, it was exhausting to all concerned and no one ever seemed to know whether it had done any good. I had more faith in the small specialised exhibitions of a few machines meant only for the people who would be likely to buy them.

The setting of our cultural relations was succinctly summed up by Mr Khrushchev in 1963. He said, 'We live in a period of the sharpest ideological struggle for the minds of men, for their re-education. This is a complicated process, far more difficult than retooling plants and factories. You must understand that a fierce struggle is going on in the world between two incompatible ideologies, the socialist and bourgeois. We are for class positions in the arts and take a decisive stand against the peaceful co-existence of the socialist and bourgeois ideologies.' Cultural exchanges were highly political in Soviet thinking. The Soviet ideologists were struggling to reconcile two contradictory aims. They wanted to create the image of a modern state, but at the same time to keep their people uncontaminated by bourgeois ideas. It simply could not be done. From this came the many inconsistencies in their treatment of their cultural relations with the outside world. It seemed sometimes as if the image had been completely submerged by the compulsions of ideological defence.

In 1962 it had seemed that there might be some free debate on the two systems. Sartre had suggested it on the grounds that Marxism was obviously superior. British philosophers had visited their Soviet counterparts in Moscow. A formidable team had been collected by the Great Britain–U.S.S.R. Association in response to a Soviet invitation to visit Moscow in the spring of 1963 to discuss co-existence. But a few weeks before the date fixed for the meeting the ideological thaw ended and the new freeze began. The invitation was cancelled at a few days' notice and was not renewed. Free debate was considered too dangerous.

Our policy was simple. We were not engaged in an attack on the Soviet system. If the Russians wanted that system, that was their business. We did not like their promoting Communism in our country, though we had the great advantage that we could afford a free debate on politics and philosophy. We had no desire to attack their system in the Soviet Union. All we wanted was that the people of the two countries should get to know each other, which would help us to get along together a little better. We had much to learn from each other. We therefore wanted to encourage Anglo-Soviet contacts over as wide a field as possible.

On the bread-and-butter level, cultural and scientific exchanges were regulated under the Cultural Agreement, the subject of a detailed haggle every two years, and subsidiary agreements like the arrangements for the exchange of scientists between the Royal Society and the Soviet Academy of Sciences. It was rather like a child's game; you swop three librarians for two economists and a town planner and hope you have got a reasonable bargain. The Russians concentrated on scientific and technical exchanges, trying to ensure, not surprisingly, that they got more useful information out of us than we got out of them. They had the advantage in having their factories and research institutes under strict control. Gosconcert, the Soviet State impressarios, ground out the last cent and, since they controlled all the theatres and concert halls in the Soviet Union, ensured that we should have to subsidise our orchestras and ballet and theatre companies, while they dealt with private British impressarios and made large amounts in foreign exchange out of us. The British performers earned roubles in the Soviet Union, but could not get them exchanged into sterling.

We tried to broaden and loosen up the cultural exchanges, but did not get very far. When the Soviet Government arrested a British tourist or otherwise outraged British opinion, which happened fairly regularly, someone always proposed that we should break off cultural exchanges. That was not so easy. Unlike the Americans, we were not prepared to use our passport system to stop people going to the Soviet Union and, in any case, it would not be easy to stop scientists and musicians going while Moscow was full of British businessmen. Who was to bear the financial loss which would be suffered by the cancellation at the last moment of a Russian ballet tour in Britain, under the orders of the British Government? Many carefully laid plans would be upset. We could not turn the tap on and off at will as the Russians could, with their strict control over the lives of their citizens.

In general, the cultural exchanges were useful and successful. British orchestras, musicians and theatrical companies visiting the Soviet Union were assured of immense success. Crowds besieged the theatre in the hope of getting in to see Paul Scofield's Lear, two young men getting in from the roof by a convenient drainpipe and being allowed by the management to stay as a reward for their enterprise. John Ogden became the hero of the Moscow teenagers. The Russian musicians adopted Benjamin Britten and Peter Pears. Britten brought the English Opera Group in his own chamber operas, including *The Turn of the Screw*, which the orthodox judged ideologically unsound and the musicians found admirable. At my pressing request, the Foreign Office even agreed that the Opera Group should visit the Baltic States, which had previously been forbidden territory, since we had not recognised them as juridically part of the Soviet Union; my cultural attaché, however, was not allowed to accompany them, a reservation apparently intended to provide a fig-leaf of non-recognition.

The British students were mostly resilient and cheerful and adapted themselves well to Russian conditions. One group whom I visited at Leningrad were three in a small room, with hot water available in the hostel for only a brief period twice a week. The walls were so thin that every sound could be heard from the next room where parties went on until 3 a.m. So they adapted their hours of sleep accordingly and did most of their work in the public libraries. They had no complaints, as conditions were the same for everyone. One batch seemed particularly accident-prone. One was expelled because he unwisely passed a message from a defector in England to his wife. Another lost his head when he could not marry a Russian girl and abused me on the telephone, which probably amused the police. I am happy to say that they are now married. Two systematically broke all the regulations, but miraculously survived their year of study. The police occasionally tried to get one to inform on the others, but did not trouble them greatly, for there was not much to be gained from trying to recruit a future university teacher. One teacher of English, who brought his wife and children, found himself in a poor hotel in a room without a cooking-stove and with nothing to sit on except five beds. To their credit, the family, with help from us, stuck it out. I believe that nearly all the students and teachers look back on their Russian experience as worth while. The personal friendships made up for all the discomforts of everyday life.

In every negotiation for a renewal of the Cultural Agreement we argued that British newspapers should be freely sold in the Soviet Union. The only one which could be bought in Moscow was the *Morning Star* (then *Daily Worker*) and later even it disappeared for some time when the British Communist Party opposed the Soviet attack on Czechoslovakia. After I had left, the Russians made a slight concession by allowing a token number of copies of *The Times* and a few European newspapers to be sold to foreigners in the tourist hotels. The argument continues. We published a magazine called *Anglia* limited to 50,000 copies. In exchange we agreed to 'facilitate the distribution' in England of *Soviet Weekly*, but it did not sell very well and the Russians seemed to think it was our fault. *Anglia* was a survey of British life, well edited, lively and readable, but not controversial. It fitted into the pocket and so could be carried unobtrusively. We could have sold many more copies. The American version was large, glossy and more ambitious. It hovered on the edge of controversy with articles on modern art and reproductions of 'abstracts'. It was aimed more at the young intellectual. We aimed at the average Russian. Perhaps we were too cautious; but I believe that the magazine had a favourable effect on the Russian view of Britain, which was our purpose. But it was only a drop in the ocean. The usual view of Britain in the Soviet newspapers and magazines was of a country of fat top-hatted capitalists and Dickensian slums.

Very few foreign books were allowed into the Soviet Union. The French opened a bookshop, but there was never much in it and we did not think it worth while copying them. When I went to Moscow, the B.B.C. Overseas Service was being jammed. I delivered an anodyne little piece in bad Russian. It was jammed four times, a comic effort of the minor Soviet bureaucracy. After some months, for no apparent reason, the jamming stopped – perhaps because it was expensive and not very effective, or because the machines were required to jam Chinese propaganda. There had probably been an internal argument about it, since Soviet officials, when telling me how monstrous they thought the British film *From Russia with Love*, which they had seen in London, said that the jamming was 'on a razor's edge', though if they really thought that I would try to exercise a political censorship on James Bond in order to protect B.B.C. broadcasts they had a lot to learn about Britain. We knew that some senior Soviet officials listened to the B.B.C. news, presumably having rightly not much confidence in the home-grown variety. Later political attacks on the B.B.C. showed that its overseas service was effective.

British visitors multiplied, students, schoolboys, scientists, tourists, climbers, trade unionists, technicians. A certain macabre interest was aroused by the photograph in the magazine of a British trade association of a large party of prosperous and rotund British Master Bakers grouped round their host, Mr Penkovsky, afterwards to acquire some notoriety before his life was abruptly terminated by a Soviet firing squad. Towns were twinned; Margate with Yalta, Manchester with Leningrad, Coventry with Volgograd. The connection of the cities which had suffered so severely from Nazi attack seemed particularly appropriate until one heard that Volgograd was also twinned with 'the heroic city of Port Said'. The Russians, predictably, turned down the British Council's proposal for a Henry Moore exhibition in Moscow, though other Eastern European states welcomed it. They bought British films of the 'rape and the kitchen sink' variety, in order to show the decadence of British bourgeois life. British film producers did not seem to realise it. Our Soviet friends said, to comfort us, 'We know that British life is not really like that.' *Carleton Brown of the F.O.* had the double advantage of being entertaining and ridiculing the Foreign Office, but the most popular British film star with no ideological overtones was Norman Wisdom.

In Britain, Mr Harold Macmillan, viewing *Swan Lake,* said, 'King Edward VII would have remarked, "Very pretty, very pretty"; we must be able to get on with these people.' But Madame Furtseva was deeply shocked by the orgy scene in *Moses and Aaron*. Russian musicians, dancers and actors were assured of a full house, but most Russian films were too long, boring and ideological for British audiences. Heroes of Soviet Labour were not good box-office on the Odeon chain. Isaac Newton had signed the certificate of membership of the Royal Society for Peter the Great's Menshikov and the Society's continuing ties with the Soviet Academy of Sciences were marked by the grant of their fellowship to distinguished Soviet scientists, though relations became strained for a time after the events in Czechoslovakia. Soviet tourists went to Britain in large groups by ship and were never let loose, which naturally led the British to think that the Soviet authorities were afraid they would run away or at least become ideologically contaminated. Every now and again a Soviet citizen decided to stay in Britain. It was difficult to understand why the Soviet authorities should have been so concerned to advertise the weaknesses of their system by making such a fuss about them, when it would surely have been more sensible to let them retire without advertisement into the obscurity of British life. Soviet technicians were to be found in every factory or conference to which they were invited, where there was something to be learnt. For all Soviet visitors the most important call was Marks & Spencer. I remained strongly of the opinion that it is in British interests that the British and Russian people should get to know each other and each other's countries.

22

THE GAME OF INTELLIGENCE

W E had nine service attachés, four airmen, three sailors and two soldiers. It is no reflection on these admirable public servants that I sometimes thought that the policy of the Ministry of Defence must be never to send one service attaché when two would do. Their number has now been reduced. Their job was wholly different from the job of a service attaché in a non-Communist country. They were rarely allowed to see anything worth while in the way of manœuvres, training or installations. They were licensed gatherers of military information by open means. It will be plain to readers of the British press that the Russians did not use the same methods abroad, but obtained their military intelligence principally through their agents. Whatever the difference in methods, I presumed that each side thought that it gained more than the other by the exchange of service attachés. Otherwise, there would not have been any, unless it was that both services, from long habit, thought it indecent to go about without them. The satellites were already in operation, but the 'bears who looked over the mountain' travelled

conscientiously with their friends from other NATO
countries wherever they were allowed to go in the Soviet
Union and their reports on what they saw on the other
side of the mountain were, I assumed, dissected and
filed, equally conscientiously, by the Defence Departments at home. That was not my business.

It was a great game between the attachés and the
Soviet police, who conducted a running war with the
object of discouraging inquisitiveness. The principle
underlying the battle was reciprocity. If the Russians
allowed one of our attachés to see something worth
while, we responded by allowing one of theirs an equivalent visit in Britain. If they 'bent' the route of one of
our attachés, we 'bent' the route of one of theirs. Both
had reason to appreciate G. K. Chesterton's lines,

A merry road, a mazy road and such as we did tread,
The night we went to Birmingham by way of Beachy
     Head.

The ultimate sanction was that, if they threw out one
of our attachés, we threw out one of theirs of equivalent
rank. If they refused a visa, we refused one in return.
The rules of the game were well defined and understood by both sides. The Russians doubtless thought of
it in terms of chess. There were various well-docu-
mented opening and retaliatory plays. Normally the
game ended in a draw. Occasionally, one side tried to ·
change the rules. The Russians, hoping to avoid the
capture of one of their knights, refrained from taking
one of ours, but blocked him on the board, so that he
could not move out of Moscow. We protested, withdrew our man and simultaneously expelled one of
theirs. All they could do then was formally to expel the
man whom they had blocked and whom we had already withdrawn. It was a draw in our favour, and the

proposed amendment to the rules, which did not suit us, was tacitly dropped.

So the game went on. There were various orthodox moves permitted by long custom. The aircraft on internal lines were built conveniently with one row of 'blind' seats without windows, usually reserved for foreign attachés. Even I was once honoured with one of these seats, though I would not know a missile site from a haystack. The attachés were diligently followed round museums and doubtless shared the feelings of Robert Louis Stevenson's child:

I have a little shadow that goes in and out with me
And what can be the use of him is more than I can see.

When the attachés were considered to be becoming too inquisitive, they might be denounced by an allegedly casual citizen for being near forbidden ground, or there might be an accident which would immobilise their car but not hurt anyone. They were prevented from photographing the weapons dispersing after the May Day parade, though any pressman could photograph the same weapons while they were passing the spectators' stands. We presumed this was merely a Pavlovian reaction to attachés as such. In the train the watchers once showed a sense of humour by playing *Colonel Bogey* on the loud-speakers for the benefit of the British travellers. When a little opiate was added to the drinks in a hotel in the evening, apparently to prevent the subjects travelling by the next morning's aircraft, the effect was spoilt by the efforts of the hotel staff by banging on the door to wake them up in time to catch it. This was not in the rule book, so we and the Americans protested loudly and publicly.

In the autumn of 1964 a British Assistant Naval Attaché travelled by train to Khabarovsk in the Far East with three American attachés. Their hotel room was entered at night. Some of the intruders sat on them, while others took their cameras and note-books. This was a clear breach of the rules. We delivered a battery of protests. The Russians countered with articles in the press describing the spying of the attachés, with photographs of their confiscated cameras. As usual, the game ended in a draw with mutual expulsions. At the airport a Soviet official and I were waiting to meet a visitor. I took him to a display case containing Soviet cameras and powerful lenses. I said, 'You should put a notice there. Everything for the military attaché.' He replied, 'They don't need them. They have got them already.'

The non-Communist attachés mixed socially almost exclusively with their own kind and developed a strong *esprit de corps*, with their own doyen and presentation of silver cigarette-boxes for departing members of the club. The game of chess played with attachés and policemen was accepted by both sides and did not have the slightest effect on personal or political relations. In my experience, no attaché ever came to any real harm. I did not mind the attachés showing some enterprise, without which they could not have done their jobs, but I used to say that one expulsion every six months was enough, considering that they had all been trained in the Russian language for at least eighteen months at great expense.

We were inevitably affected by the activities of that ubiquitous and painstaking body of men, the K.G.B., the Soviet secret police, by the battle of intelligence and counter-intelligence, in which every government indulges which can afford it. In November 1962, Greville Wynne was arrested in Hungary and transferred to the Soviet Union. In the spring of 1963 Penkovsky, a senior Soviet official, and Wynne were tried in Moscow with wide publicity. It was announced that Penkovsky had been shot. Wynne was imprisoned and subsequently exchanged for Lonsdale, a Soviet spy imprisoned in England. All we could do was to try to ensure that Wynne had the best defence counsel available in Moscow, since under Soviet law foreign counsel could not appear in court, and to arrange visits to Wynne by the Consul and Mrs Wynne, a lady of remarkable courage in a distressing situation.

The evidence in court included allegations against the British and American Embassies. One member of my staff, who had no conceivable connection with the affair, was expelled. We made the conventional response in London. Articles appeared in the Soviet press describing the British Embassy as a hive of imperialist spies. Guides pointed out the Embassy in similar terms to tourists in the Kremlin grounds overlooking us, and the Soviet public was warned to have nothing to do with us. The press articles about us were being published up to the day of our annual party for the Queen's birthday and we wondered whether any Russians would turn up. But attendance was practically normal, the principal guest being, as usual, a member of the Presidium. Only a few junior guests were frightened off.

During the week of the trial, it seemed to me that the Soviet leaders whom I met at parties, went out of their way to be friendly. The Soviet attitude was neatly illustrated by the remark of the chairman of a state committee who, with about fifteen of his colleagues, turned up for lunch at the Embassy on the day on which the press was full of pictures of the cameras taken from the American and British service attachés at Khabarovsk. He said: 'Every Ambassador must have his spies.' I replied: 'Perhaps he would be happier without them.' He retorted. 'No. The Ambassador must have spies.

The only trouble is when he gets a bad one.' The Russians, very sensibly, divided official life into separate compartments and did not allow a row in one compartment to spill over into another.

The underground battle to maintain personal and physical security is a tiresome feature of the non-Communist Ambassador's life in a Communist country. Attempts at blackmail are best met by understanding and mutual confidence between the Ambassador and his staff. If a man gets into difficulty and reports it, the matter can easily be dealt with by an official protest which lets the other party know that the blackmail will be ineffective. To demand of one's staff a higher moral standard than is required of the average citizen in his own country, as suggested by Mr Allen Dulles in his book *The Craft of Intelligence*, is not an effective method of defending an Embassy's security.

At the end of my time in Moscow, Gerald Brooke, a London teacher on a visit, was arrested, tried and convicted. We did our best for him. It was a constant worry during my last few months in Moscow that we could do no more. We knew from Mrs Brooke, another lady who showed a high degree of fortitude and understanding, that he had acted as a courier for an anti-Soviet organisation, bringing in secret material for them and handing it over to a Soviet citizen, who was presumably already in touch with the Soviet police. This meant that he had committed an offence against Soviet law. We succeeded in arranging early visits by the Consul and Mrs Brooke and pressed for an early trial. On the day of the trial, I happened to be paying my farewell visit to Mr Kosygin and took the opportunity to ask on a personal basis for Brooke's release, though I had no instructions to do so. Even if Mr Kosygin had wanted to intervene, I doubt whether he could have prevailed against the other State organisations involved. What was not understood at the time was that private action on behalf of an anti-Soviet organisation would be considered by the Russians to be a much more serious matter than spying for a government, which they regarded as a normal official activity. This was interference in their internal affairs.

After I had left, the affair became enmeshed in the Russians' efforts, ultimately successful, to secure the release of the Krogers, Russian spies imprisoned in Britain, in exchange for Brooke. The British Government were right in refusing the exchange in the first instance, when the Krogers had only completed a relatively short proportion of their sentence and when Brooke was to serve at most another four years. The decision some years later whether to agree to the exchange was not easy. The Krogers had by that time completed the greater part of the sentence which they were likely to serve under British prison regulations. Brooke, for whatever cause, faced a new, long sentence which might have broken him for life. There had been many exchanges in the previous few years between the Soviet Union and other European countries. I did not believe that agreement to the exchange at this time would affect the position of British visitors to the Soviet Union by encouraging the Soviet police in courses which they would not otherwise have adopted. I felt, therefore, that the Government's responsibility for a British subject in dire trouble made the decision to agree to the exchange, on balance, right.

Several well-known defectors were living in Moscow, another 'twilight brigade' as in China. They seemed to live between the Russian and foreign communities, without real contact with either. It was not in our interests that we should meet. Mrs Philby related in her book how she and her husband found themselves sitting behind my wife and me at a concert and wondered whether to talk to us. I am glad that they did not. When asked about the defectors, I used to reply that they were no longer of any interest to the British Government. I never sought news of them.

The British and foreign press correspondents in Moscow were nearly all responsible men of a high professional standard. We recognised the difficulty of the correspondents of the British popular press who were not required to send profound analyses of Soviet policy. Their editors wanted human-interest stories, which were difficult to find. Inevitably, these were often stories about members of the Embassy staff, which could be picked up in the Embassy club. Sometimes, after we had withheld information on security grounds, the story leaked in London, to the natural annoyance of the Moscow correspondents, who thought it should have been theirs. We tried to ensure that they got the stories when they could be released. We valued their opinions on the local situation and the information which they were able to give us from their own contacts. Normally, each tried to help the other.

In situations like that of an Embassy in Moscow, one learns to respect the way in which average English men and women adapt themselves to a restricted life with little freedom of movement or opportunity for recreation. My wife and I had nothing but praise for the way in which the British families in the Embassy made the best of things and helped to make life easier for their fellows.

23

THE EMBASSY

I N the Embassy Lord Hailsham, sitting precariously on the balustrade of the balcony with his back to the Kremlin, said, 'What you need for this house is a bomb. Blow it up and start again.' I leapt to its defence, resisting the temptation to push him over the edge. However you might question the old owner's taste, the house had a distinct and friendly personality and we had become attached to it. It was not a large house by English country-house standards, though, with its two separate wings, it was roomy enough to provide for a Chancery on the ground floor and a grandiose flat on the first floor for the Ambassador. In outside appearance it was like a Russian in winter, a squat, bulky figure with no distinct outline. Inside, it was an absurdly extravagant mixture of styles. The Russians used to say that, when the architect asked his client which style he preferred, he replied that he could afford all the styles. It was built on the bank of the River Moskva opposite the Kremlin, separated from the river by the road formerly known as Sophiiskaya Naberejnaya, which, while we were in Moscow, was changed to Naberejnaya Mauricea Thoreza, after the French Communist leader. Why, we asked, should we have a Frenchman? Should it not be called Naberejnaya Harrya Pollitta, after our native Communist? Its real charm, which inevitably caught every tenant and visitor, was the superb, theatrical view of the Kremlin. Winter and summer, day and night, we faced the panorama of the Kremlin, the gold and silver domes, the sun glinting on the gold crosses, the old brick towers of the Kremlin wall above the river, the essence of old Russia and modern Russia, all except Peter's Russia.

The house had been built in about 1890 by a sugar merchant named Kharitonenko. Most of the embassies in Moscow were old merchants' mansions, built either for their wives or their mistresses. Ours was clearly the official residence, being in so prominent a position. In its relatively short existence, the house had had an eventful history. Bruce Lockhart, in his *Memoirs of a Secret Agent*, describes a party given in it by the Kharitonenkos in their heyday in 1912. Writing in 1932, he remembered it a little larger than life. According to his account, it was an immense palace. A throng like a theatre queue was struggling on the staircases (though there is only one). The whole house was a 'fairyland' of flowers brought all the way from Nice. That I can well believe, if flowers were as rare in Moscow in January 1912 as in the winters of the 1960s. Orchestras seemed to be playing in every ante-chamber.

Finally, to make it a really Russian party, Lockhart's neighbour at dinner, who was acting as Russian A.D.C. to Lord Charles Beresford on his visit to Moscow, left the table, was told on the telephone by his mistress that all was over, took out his revolver and shot himself, still holding the telephone. 'It was all very sad, very Russian.' And also, I would add, very bad manners to shoot yourself in your hostess's house in the middle of her party. It could not have happened in my day, since an efficient little machine was always listening to the telephone conversations, which would inhibit an emotional exchange with your mistress, however much vodka you had drunk. Nor could we have ended our parties with a dash through Moscow in 'troikas' to the gypsy entertainment in Petrovsky Park, since the only troika left was in the stud outside Moscow known as Horse Factory No. 1 and the gypsies, having been classed as anti-social elements, had all disappeared save for a pale and licensed remnant appearing occasionally at a minor theatre.

The house was lucky to escape destruction during the Revolution, when it was said to have been for a time in the front line as a White Guard post opposite the Kremlin. After the First World War it became a Foreign Ministry Guest House, one of the guests being H. G. Wells on his visit to Moscow to see Lenin, whose forehead reminded him of Mr Arthur Balfour. 'And so back to No. 17 Sofiskaya Naberezhnaya,' he wrote, 'and lunch with Mr Vanderlip and the young sculptor from London. The old servant of the house waited on us, mournfully conscious of the meagreness of our entertainment and reminiscent of the great days of the past when Caruso had been a guest and had sung to all that was brilliant in Moscow in the room upstairs.'*

Fitzroy Maclean in his *A Person from England*, that brilliant account of adventure in Central Asia, records how Enver Pasha had stayed there, being careful to secure the key to the back-door as an escape route, his fellow guests being a diplomatic mission from Afghanistan, an American mining engineer looking for concessions, whom the Russians had taken for a millionaire banker and Mr Arthur Ransome, correspondent of the *Manchester Guardian*. After some years

---

* H. G. Wells, *Russia in the Shadows*.

as a superior boarding-house, in 1930 it became the British Embassy and thus a superior hotel. A hard-hearted British Treasury is said to have refused the request of the exiled Kharitonenko daughter for compensation.

Churchill stayed there during the war. During a lunch party in the Embassy for Mr Harold Wilson, Mr Mikoyan told me that he remembered a dinner party in the same room at which, Stalin, Molotov, Churchill, Eden and he had been present. He said, 'They had been drinking without eating. Your Ambassador, Kerr, got up to propose a toast and fell crash onto the table. But he was a strong man and got up to finish the toast.' In those rosy days, in the after-glow of the war-time alliance, there had been much friendly drinking. In my time, the Russian leaders drank very little. At Kremlin parties they imbibed only lemonade and ideology. I often wished that they lived up to the old Russian drinking tradition. It would have livened up the official parties.

The tradition had been true once. In the eighteenth century official parties must have been a great trial to ambassadors. My Danish colleague related to me extracts from the memoirs of one of his predecessors. At the Tsar's table, if an ambassador did not drink, the servant behind his chair reported to his master, who soon brought the offender to order. If the guest tried to leave the party, he was stopped by a sentry and turned back. Once, the Dane succeeded in slipping away to bed. The Tsar pulled him out of bed and made him return. The Tsar asked an elderly noble why he was not drinking. The Boyar excused himself as too old. The Tsar retorted that he was not too old to have married again recently and made him drink an enormous goblet full. The Boyar staggered and fell dead. The

Tsar, momentarily discomposed, wrote the ambassador, soon recovered himself and addressed his companions with his usual cheerfulness.

Clarke-Kerr had a relatively easy time in Moscow. He took full advantage of it, and among the older Soviet leaders was the best-remembered Ambassador. On the evening before he left, he went to say good-bye to Stalin, who asked him what he would like for a parting present. Clarke-Kerr replied that he wanted an exit permit for his masseur, Yuri, who, some time before, had been in trouble for alleged desertion from the Soviet Forces. At one o'clock in the morning, Pavlov, Stalin's interpreter, banged on the Embassy door, bringing the exit permit and a fur rug which I suspect to have been the same rug as was afterwards passed on, at a price, by every Ambassador to his successor. Yuri left with Clarke-Kerr the next day for the Far East and, owing to a mistake, was given the Minto suite in the Viceroy's house in New Delhi with nine Indian servants to wait on him. Later reports had it that he married a Scots girl and kept a fish-and-chip shop on the west coast of Scotland.

Just before he died, Stalin had ordered the British to get out of the Embassy and the Americans to leave their office on the other side of Red Square. We were too close to Russia. The Americans moved; the British, having to move their home as well as their office, delayed. Stalin died and the edict was reversed. On paper our tenure was precarious. We had only a five years' lease. There were plans to make our street into a park. All the buildings on it were to be pulled down. But there was no urgency in the air. The sacred principle of reciprocity came into it. The Russians wanted a new Embassy in London. We carried on desultory negotiations while we were shown a succession of wholly unsuitable sites for a new Moscow Embassy in the slummier parts of the city.

One day there will be new Embassies in London and Moscow. It will be a sad day for the British Ambassador when the scene is changed.

On a November evening in 1964 I was sitting in the Stanislavsky Theatre for the première of Benjamin Britten's *The Turn of the Screw*. It was five minutes before the interval. An agitated figure crept up to me and whispered, 'Nebolshoi pojàr v'Posoltsve' – 'There is a small fire in the Embassy.' I waited for the interval and went home to see what was happening. My wife arrived from London and was met by smoke and fire-engines. The fire was in one of the wings, attached to a building partly used as an infants' school. There had been an explosion. The Russian sentry had given the alarm. The fire-engines were using their hoses from the street. The firemen could not come into the Embassy compound without our permission. The Russians had let their Embassy in Ottawa burn to the ground rather than let the Canadian firemen in. The fire took hold and flames were seen coming through the roof. The Russians asked for their firemen to go on the roof. They wanted also to see the room where the fire had started. We took two of them in. By this time, the firemen on the roof had hacked their way through the roof into the room and were attacking everything in it with their hoses and axes. They directed their hoses on us and the Russians with us, and we had to retreat. By now, the fire was virtually over. We demanded the withdrawal of the firemen and protested vigorously against their entry into the building without our permission. The Russians responded with an article in the press attacking us for refusing to let the firemen do their job and thus endangering the neighbouring building. We protested against the article. Neither side gave way. The Chief of Protocol and the Head of the 'Office for the

Servicing of the Diplomatic Corps', known as the U.P.D.K., called to enquire, as if about the health of a patient. We stopped speculating how it had started and dried the place out.

To get into the Embassy, the visitor had to pass the Russian sentry. Russians produced their invitation cards. Obvious Englishmen got by without question, the only British who had any difficulty being a husband and wife of Russian Jewish origin. The sentries were on the look-out for Baptists, Jews and members of other minority classes which were harried from time to time, who might try to seek asylum in the Embassy. We did not mind their being kept out, since we could not do anything for them and, when they did succeed in getting in, all we could do was to send them out again, when they were probably arrested as soon as they were out of sight. One man, probably insane, climbed over the wall one early morning, when my wife was alone in the house and succeeded in getting up to the first storey, where he was found wandering about. Our Chancery guards were kind to him. They pushed him over the wall again and not past the sentry.

Only one Russian telephoned asking if he might come and see us. He sailed through the sentry and stayed till all hours. He was an intelligent, cosmopolitan scientist, son of a famous writer, an entertaining conversationalist in several languages, able to import the latest French novels. I had had an introduction to him in Paris from an elderly Russian émigré, who had been a member of the Provisional Government in 1917. We could only assume that he had a licence from the police to visit us, perhaps as one who would give the impression of the Russian intellectual which the authorities would like to convey to us. We enjoyed his company, and the unspoken background did not prevent a serious exchange of views. We looked forward to seeing him again. One Russian musician proposed to come and make music with me. Everything was arranged, the time and what we would play. I was not surprised when he did not turn up. Obviously there was some bureaucratic nonsense at work. When there was an official party for musicians, he was always there.

Having negotiated the sentry, the visitor entered the sugar-baron's baronial hall, furnished incongruously with medieval props in the shape of fake gothic chairs left over from the old days and spindly orange chairs, more functional than comfortable, inserted by someone on the principle that what the Ministry of Works calls 'contemporary' mixes with anything. The passage leading to my office was adorned with portraits of those predecessors, my forgotten ancestors. Not all of them should be forgotten. My favourite was Lord Whitworth, a former member of Brooks's, who was accredited to St Petersburg in 1789 during the latter part of the reign of Catherine the Great, with whom, as the history of the Club relates, he 'managed to remain on cordial terms'. The account continues that, according to Wraxall, he was 'highly favoured by nature, and his address exceeded even his figure. At every period of his life, queens and duchesses and countesses have showered on him their regard.' Near the other end of the row, separated from Whitworth by a century and a half and a certain difference of outlook, was Sir Stafford Cripps.

We always assumed that my office had its quota of microphones. But it really did not matter and it was hardly worth while looking to see. If you were going to say something really confidential, you took special precautions; but it was better to let the Russians listen to most of what you said. What was necessary was never to forget that you were talking to the machines. You could tell them a lot with advantage. Every now and again, I used to address them, saying, 'Since in this country it is difficult for me to have a really frank political discussion with the members of the Foreign Ministry, I find it useful to be able to give you my views from time to time. But, I beg of you, please report them accurately and please recognise when I am serious and when I am joking.'

I have no personal knowledge whether the principle of reciprocity applies in this domain, though I presume that the Soviet Ambassador in London makes this assumption. There was a Russian joke going round Moscow, 'Is it true that there are microphones in all the hotel rooms in Moscow?' 'Yes, but they don't work.' How well they worked I could not say. That the officials concerned were zealous in the performance of their duties was shown by the experience of a member of a technical delegation who went back to his hotel room which he had vacated, in order to look for something he had left behind and found a mechanic already taking up the floor boards to remove the precious object. There is nothing particularly reprehensible about it in diplomatic practice, however much we deplore the invasion by technical espionage of private life. It is like Victorian sex; something that everyone did, but no one talked about.

The office was used, alternately with a room in the American Embassy, for church services on Sundays. Our chaplain lived in Helsinki, since we had no accommodation for him in Moscow. When he was away, the services in our Embassy were conducted by a lay-reader with the assistance of an American Protestant clergyman sent to Moscow by the American Council of Churches, in my time first a Presbyterian and then a Lutheran. The congregation was mixed in nationality and sects. The Anglican hierarchy deplored this state of affairs, regarding it as a derogation from the pure Anglicanism which they wished to maintain. I found this an unreasonable attitude. There were only enough Protestant church-goers for one small congregation. It was surely better to keep this mixed congregation together, and I saw no reason why the Presbyterian or Lutheran clergyman should not officiate in the British Embassy. I confess that I sometimes felt a little nervous at the politics which were apt to creep into the sermons, doubtless recorded by the machines, which presumably worked on Sunday, but, after all, we had to listen to repeated doses of Communist politics and it did no harm to let the Soviet police have a little political as well as religious ideology from the other side. The high point of our services was reached when the lesson was read by Lord Home and the organ played by Mr Edward Heath. In Moscow this was *très snob*.

There had been an Anglican church in Moscow before the Revolution, an ugly example of modern Anglican gothic, since used for musicians' recordings. A Member of Parliament who frequently visited Moscow with the support of our chaplain was hoping to get it back. I used to wonder whether the Russians might not tease us by agreeing. We had no money to keep it up and no congregation to fill it and I did not relish the thought of the trouble which would be caused by a policeman stationed at the door with orders to refuse entry to Soviet citizens.

There was another periodical meeting held in my office. The Commonwealth ambassadors met once a fortnight in the embassies of each of us in turn. As time went on, and many new Commonwealth embassies were opened, it became more difficult to maintain Commonwealth solidarity. Some of the newest ambassadors were nervous of being seen to be in regular contact with the British and differences of policy became more apparent, between India and Pakistan, Nigeria and Ghana, the old and the new Commonwealth. But it was surprising to find the extent of the common outlook which was developed in these discussions. I learnt much from hearing the African and Asian point of view. Perhaps the new diplomats learnt something from us, and I thought there was no harm in the discussions being picked up by microphones and read in the Foreign Ministry.

Our first floor has already been described in the memoirs of former tenants. The visitor, having undergone the scrutiny of an ex-sergeant-major in the hall, walked up a broad wooden staircase ornamented with carved dragons and gargoyles, to be confronted by a great chimney-piece in the medieval Flemish style, furnished with a formidable steel instrument presumably intended for roasting an ox. Diverging to reach the front of the house, he was met successively by the blue drawing-room with elaborately carved overmantel in the manner of fifteenth-century Nuremberg, the red drawing-room, a sixteenth-century pastiche bearing the emblems of François I and the white and gold drawing-room, jumping in time to the Travellers' Club on the Champs Élysées. The Grand Tour concluded with the painted ceiling of the dining-room, executed in the nineties by the 'Master of the Comédie Française', depicting a party of musicians dressed in the medieval jig-saw style, improbably retaining their balance over the dining-table, and the vast royal portraits of past kings and queens, up to George V, assumed, as Sir William Hayter records, by all new Russian visitors to be his cousin, Tsar Nicholas II. This was our flat, over the 'shop'.

Other ambassadors in Moscow also had curious houses. The Americans had the largest, Spasso House, reminiscent of the concourse in a New York station, built in railway classical style and needing at least 300 guests to make it feel reasonably comfortable. The hall and staircase of the French Embassy appeared to have been copied from the scenery for *Boris Godounov* at the Bolshoi Theatre. According to local legend, the merchant who had built this house had murdered his girl friend and walled her up somewhere in the house, where she is believed to remain to this day. The German Chancery had some pretensions to historical interest. The Office for the Servicing of the Diplomatic Corps announced that they wished to do special repairs themselves, as the house was a scheduled monument, a request which, not surprisingly, was refused. The Italians lived in a gloomy mansion, lightened only by their charm and hospitality, a haphazard mixture of Gothic and Baroque, notable for the murder in the main reception room of the German Ambassador, Count von Mirbach, soon after the Revolution. The Tunisians lived in Beria's old house, but saw no ghosts. The Thais lived in a house formerly used by Khrushchev, containing eight bathrooms and a small indoor swimming-pool. Khrushchev had presumably left it for better quarters.

But, of all of them, our house, with its superb position, was the best. Behind was a little garden, a rarity in Moscow, with the only private tennis-court in the city, converted in the winter into a skating-rink. In front was the staggering back-drop of the Kremlin over the river, bustling with traffic during the summer, packed in winter with ice which was broken up daily by a special tug. We had no excuse for forgetting where power had lain for so many hundred years before Peter erected his new capital on the Neva, and again after Lenin had come back to Russia's holy city.

Popular demonstrations against embassies had been for years a feature of Moscow life. We assumed that they were organised by some State organisation and were a form of political pressure, the expression of the Soviet Party's disapproval of some act of another government. Sir William Hayter has described how, during one demonstration, he asked the policeman on duty how long it was going on. The policeman looked at his watch and replied, 'Another twenty minutes.' I told this story in New York to Mr Dobrynin, afterwards Soviet Ambassador in Washington and at that time, like me, an under-employed Under-Secretary in the United Nations' Secretariat. He replied that the demonstrators in front of the Soviet mission in New York could be seen every hour on the hour receiving their pay of one dollar from the organisers of the demonstrations, who stationed themselves only a block off, in sight of the mission's building. But the demonstrators in New York were organised by private Hungarian organisations and not by the United States Government. A former American Ambassador in Moscow told me how a Soviet official had protested to him about a demonstration in New York. He made enquiries from Washington and received instructions to inform the Soviet Foreign Ministry of the precautions which had been taken to protect the Soviet mission from damage by the demonstrators. He was received by a new official. After he had spoken, the official drew a document out of his desk and read from it. It started, 'Owing to the unsatisfactory nature of the United States' Government's reply....'

In my time, demonstrations were mostly directed against the American Embassy and carried out by

Asian students. When Belgian paratroops were carried by American aircraft to Elizabethville in the Congo, using the British Ascension Island as a staging post, there was a demonstration against the Congolese, Belgian, American and British Embassies, the damage being carefully regulated in accordance with the degree of responsibility considered to be borne by each government concerned. The Congolese Embassy was virtually sacked, while the chargé d'affaires hid under the desk in his office. All the windows on the ground floor in the front of the Belgian Embassy were broken, except one. The Ambassador, standing in the drawing-room surveying the scene, said to his son, 'Come on,' and they both picked up the stones which littered the floor and, to the astonishment of the policeman on duty, threw them through the only remaining unbroken window, from the inside. Then they felt better.

When the demonstrators reached us, only incidental participators in the affair, the last on their programme after the main sallies against the other embassies, they were kept in the road by the police at some distance from the main building and therefore succeeded in breaking only two of the main windows, probably with the aid of catapults, though most of the small windows giving on the street at the back, belonging to staff flats, were poked through with a stick, while the police looked on. It was a mild affair compared to the demonstrations in 1956 over Suez. Russian onlookers were not very sympathetic to these demonstrations and were heard commenting that it was the Russian people who would have to pay for the damage. The final, formal acts of the demonstration ritual were the protest in the Ministry rejected by the Deputy Minister in outraged tones and the speedy repair of the windows by the

U.P.D.K., which had presumably been put on notice that their workmen would be required after the demonstration.

In due course, the Russians found that they were no longer in control of the demonstrations. The students and their governments were in charge. A student demonstration against the American bombing of North Vietnam was advertised in advance in the university. The Americans asked for police protection. The police and the Army came out in force but, as usual, did not prevent windows being broken. By that time the authorities must have known the measurements of every window in the American offices which could be reached from the street by a stone. It soon became apparent that the North Vietnamese and Chinese students had their own instructions to get into fights with the police. The mounted police charged the crowd, and, when they retired to re-form, the students advanced on them singing the *Internationale*, a scene reminiscent of the 1905 revolution and duly recorded by the Chinese film-cameras deployed on the spot by the Chinese Embassy. The situation was only brought under control by unarmed soldiers interposing themselves between police and students. Some Chinese students were treated in Moscow hospitals and were sent back to Peking by air. They ran up the steps into the aircraft in Moscow, but came out on stretchers in Peking, where they were officially received by a high-ranking delegation. The Chinese press and radio poured out stories of torture and neglect in the Soviet hospitals.

After that, there were no more demonstrations while we were in Moscow. Looking back on those days, I am inclined to think that we were not badly off. The Russians may have arranged the demonstrations, but at least they saw that the diplomats did not get hurt and limited the damage to what they were prepared to repair. It is the really spontaneous demonstrations which are nowadays dangerous to the members of the diplomatic profession, whose conditions of life are changing so rapidly in this anarchic world.

24

IN AND OUT OF MOSCOW

ENTERTAINMENT, like everything else, was standardised. Officials of the department of the Foreign Ministry which dealt with your affairs would come to your diplomatic dinner-parties, and diplomats were invited once a year to spend the day in the Ministry's dacha. A delegation of doctors came from England. You asked their official hosts whom to invite among the Russian specialists in the same field. The Bolshoi ballet was going to London. An Embassy dinner was authorised. You ordered forty dancers from the Ministry of Culture. Physicists for physicists, bankers for bankers, chiropodists for chiropodists; if you tried to get away from the formula no one came. A private party was a non-event. The official hosts gave a return party with the same guests at the Praga Restaurant or the National Hotel, at which also the food was standardised. In Russian restaurants the glamour of caviar, not always of the best quality, covered many culinary sins. But, however tired you became of the Praga's menu, these parties were agreeable, since Russians are natural hosts.

You drank to peace and friendship, to the strengthening of relations between our two countries, to the

Soviet workers in botany, the chemical industry, air-craft construction or whatever was appropriate to the occasion. The thoughts that lay too deep for toasts were markedly different between the two sides, but they were best kept unspoken and did not necessarily make the toasts insincere. If your hosts were active in the Party, they wanted the victory of Communism. We wanted them to keep their Communism to themselves. But, whatever the differences between us, a little friendship on the way did no harm and could make it easier for us to live alongside each other. We could drink the toasts without hypocrisy. My wife did her part, showing great endurance and invariable good humour, finding herself, while I was in England, on Khrushchev's right at a lively dinner in the 'Royal Box' in the Bolshoi Theatre during the celebration of Shakespeare's four hundredth anniversary and valiantly offering the Soviet leaders a toast in Russian after one and a half hours of speeches tending to persuade the audience that Shakespeare was a Russian. Peter Ustinov once delivered to an admiring Russian audience a Russian speech, not one word of which had any relation to the Russian language.

As Malcolm Muggeridge reported from Moscow, diplomats and cows eat standing. Several times a week the same faces gathered round the tables at an embassy, at the Sovietskaya Hotel or at the Praga Restaurant for somebody's National Day. In the Praga you went through a series of rooms on the Chinese-box principle, starting with the lowliest, for third secretaries and other members of the proletariat, and fought your way through successive gradations of rank upwards until you reached the last box reserved for deputy foreign ministers, ambassadors and such of the top or near-top brass as, after someone's political calculation, had been selected to attend. If you cut a new embassy's National Day without good excuse, you offended your host, and the Russians, who were there in force, scored a point. The endless round of these functions was no great hardship and gave opportunities for contacts which would otherwise have been difficult to obtain, though after two years it all became a bit stale. I had great sympathy for the patient Soviet official who was condemned to the treadmill of official receptions for life.

When a colleague left Moscow, the Dean of the Diplomatic Corps gave a party known as a *coupe de champagne* for him and the heads of all the missions who recognised the departing ambassador's government. This was one of the more curious of the Moscow rituals. The departing ambassador was presented with a standard silver salver financed by a socially obligatory, uniform contribution from his colleagues. The Dean assured him that the presentation was only made because of the quite unusual esteem felt for him by other members of the corps, and the ambassador assured his colleagues and the representatives of the Foreign Ministry that his association with them had been the happiest experience of his life. If the Dean represented a government which the departing ambassador did not recognise, he was spared the party and received the salver by messenger, negotiations having been conducted through the highest common denominator, the senior ambassador, who would deal with both sides. The departing ambassador thus received the salver without compromising his political virginity. When I left, the North Vietnamese Ambassador was Dean. The salver was sent to the British Embassy and refused by a conscientious secretary, who did not want to compromise himself by receiving a parcel from so tainted a source, but was recovered. Having paid for so many salvers in my time, I required my compensation. But the standard had changed since the days when the Swedish Ambassador had been Dean. I subsequently sold my Vietnamese salver for five pounds ten shillings and could only conclude that the greater part of my colleagues' forced subscriptions had gone to help pay for the war in Vietnam.

Soviet socialism is not an egalitarian society. Great fortunes are not accumulated, but the privileged live the life of the rich through the perquisites provided by the State. In some of these we shared. There were special shops to which we could send our servants but not go ourselves, where we could get Russian provisions for local currency cheaper and in better supply than in the ordinary shops. In one flower shop my wife, on presentation of her diplomatic card, could go behind the shop and choose flowers from a much better selection than was for sale to the ordinary customer. Russians who were not so privileged did not seem to find anything wrong with this inequality. Before we left, the system of special foreign-exchange shops had been established. It is now a feature of life all over Eastern Europe and even in Cairo.

It was wrong to single out the fact that a pair of shoes made in England was sold for ten times the English price in the ordinary Moscow shops. There were other parts of the family budget subsidised by the State. Rents took a much smaller proportion of the family income than in England. It was argued that the flats were of poor quality and that the Soviet Government were building the slums of the next generation. This was not a fair criticism. Russian housing conditions had been so bad that you could not criticise a policy which concentrated on providing something tolerable quickly for as many as possible. In the new flats, even if you could hear every noise through the party walls, a family at least had a kitchen and bathroom to themselves, instead of having to share them with other inhabitants of the block.

What was important was not that so many of the ordinary requirements of modern life were still deficient, but that standards were gradually rising. However, as you looked at the patient queues outside the food shops on a winter's day or struggled to complete the appallingly complicated manœuvres required in order to buy the simplest article, you realised what a long way the Russians still had to go in organising ordinary life and what an immense amount of time and effort was wasted by their inability to make the daily round simpler, to get adequate supplies of flowers, fruit and vegetables into the shops in winter, to achieve quick service in the restaurants even if most Russians did still think three hours the proper time to take over dinner, to enable the traveller to change an air ticket anywhere in the Soviet Union without a telegram to Moscow. Workers in the service industries were the real depressed classes and at every point bureaucracy stood in the way. Increase in production was not the only way of improving economic performance in the Soviet Union.

None of us – even, so far as we knew, the Communist missions – could move more than forty kilometres outside Moscow without prior application, which might be refused. Even inside the circle, chunks were eroded from time to time, presumably as the Moscow defences strengthened. A senior Soviet official, with some sense, once said to me that he could not see any point in notifying particular areas round Moscow as out of bounds, since that showed where the defences were. In London it was thirty-five miles for the Soviet Embassy, rather more than for us, but mostly sprawling suburbs, while we could walk in the woods quite near Moscow. It was fair enough. We could not bargain tit for tat, since all the diplomats in Moscow were treated alike. When I told my staff with truth that I was freer to move around than I had been anywhere else since becoming head of mission, they replied crossly that I had had a very peculiar career.

Diplomats and other foreign residents were dangerous animals. They could not then travel by road to Vladimir; their cars and their guests could. Tourists could go by boat down the Volga, diplomats only on bits of it. Even the British wife of a Soviet journalist could not go with her husband on certain roads. On the roads the rules were strict. If you stopped on the way to the Zagorsk monastery to have lunch or retire behind a tree, a militiaman was sure to come along and move you on. On the road back from Yasnya Polyana, Tolstoy's country house, with Igor Markevich the conductor, we stopped to look at a church 200 yards off the road in a small town. A militiaman shooed us back on to the main road, a salutory experience for Markevich who had been inclined to think that movement in the Soviet Union was completely free.

Ideally, we should have liked to return like for like whenever we were stopped or followed or otherwise restricted in our movements, since the principle of reciprocity governed our lives. But in England we do not have the police to do it. When the British police followed Russians in England, they were not meticulous in observing the conventions. The Russians told me that they were profoundly shocked when a policeman at a provincial station greeted one of the Soviet Embassy staff with the words, 'I know who you are and where you are going. It would really save a lot of trouble if you would travel in my car.'

There was suspicion on both sides. The Indians had wide social contacts, but the Russians suspected that most non-Communist diplomats would use every opportunity to spy on them. The Russian people were continually warned against making contacts with foreigners. So Russians did not invite us to their private homes, though official visitors from the West would sometimes spend the day in their host's dacha. On our side, we had good reasons for not being too enterprising in seeking non-official contacts, apart from our wish not to get good people into trouble. The British students thought we were too cautious and called us the monkeys in the cage. But venturing off the rails served no interest of the Government which employed us and it was better to accept the inevitable limitations of social life. It was a little sad, since we were surrounded by so many attractive and intelligent people, whom we should have liked to know better. The suspicions will remain so long as there is no real confidence between the Communist world and the rest of us.

The Protocol Department organised a trip for heads of mission about twice a year. These trips were well worth while. You saw more than you could have seen alone, even if it was only the side on which the bread was buttered. The day was organised from early morning to late at night, though not everyone stayed the course. I made a point of doing everything, from genuine interest and so as not to be outdone by my Communist colleagues. In this way we journeyed through Soviet Armenia – including a trip on the Sevan lake in a snow-storm, for once the programme was fixed it was rigidly maintained in all weathers. We saw the one good harvest for years in the 'virgin lands' of Kazakhstan. We saw King George VI's sword of honour in a rather primitive museum in Volgograd. The trip

to Moldavia was timed to begin two days after Khrushchev fell, which caused three-quarters of the colleagues
to fall out. The Protocol Department, having ordered
a special aircraft, were so annoyed that they sulked and
refused to organise any more tours for a long time
afterwards.

Reading an account of General de Gaulle's visit to
Siberia, which suggested that he had had unusual privileges, I recognised from the memory of a Siberian tour
with Mr Erroll the same factory at Novosibirsk, the
same manager, the same questions and the same
answers. It was the normal Siberian 'milk run' for
foreign V.I.P.s: Irkutsk, Bratsk, Novosibirsk, Baikal.
It is all familiar by now to Western travellers. It is the
Soviet version of the mid-west. One comes away feeling
that the development of Siberia will be one of the
major features of world economic development in the
second half of the twentieth century.

The branch of the Soviet Academy of Sciences near
Novosibirsk was a typical Soviet enterprise, a town of
30,000 people, even at that early stage, built in six
years in the forest, with nineteen powerful scientific
institutes which had already attracted famous Soviet
scientists and mathematicians. Everything was done to
make them comfortable. They lived in what the Russians called 'cottages', which were pleasant two-storied
houses well placed among the trees. Their future
assistants were trained in the mathematical–physical
boarding school reserved for unusually intelligent
boys. The scientific town, so far as we could judge
from a brief visit, will be a formidable research-centre
for Siberian development.

The only other useful information which I acquired
on this trip is that if you are overtaken on the way to
Baikal by violent sickness, entailing several stops in the

forest, you will be taken in hand in the sanatorium by the lake by a fierce lady in a white coat, who makes you drink six large glasses of strong black tea and then instructs you to put your fingers down your throat. By that time you are incapable of resistance. Soviet medical assistance is nothing if not thorough.

The traveller goes to Uzbekistan to drink in the staggering beauties of the Muslim memorials of the past. Even on a private tour, he will not be able to form more than a superficial and perhaps wholly erroneous impression of how the old colony is faring in these days. At least, if no one stops you wandering by yourselves down the Fergana valley, Babar's birthplace in the shadow of the great mountains, there cannot be anything much that the authorities do not want you to see. The advantage of my misreading the map was that we found ourselves in Kokand, one of the old petty Khanates off the tourist route. Here I smelt my old life again. It might have been one of the smaller Indian States. In the old days the Russians had done just what we did with the Indian rulers. They took charge of the Khans' external relations, leaving them internal autonomy, and deposed them when they overstepped the mark in oppressing their subjects. The villages and the methods of farming and irrigation looked very like the northern Indian plains. Uzbekistan had been a successful colonial enterprise under the Tsars and appeared prosperous enough now to the casual observer.

In Tashkent the Muslim ecclesiastical administration survived under strict political control and provided for the Muslim visitor an example of the freedom of religion in a state professing atheism as its official creed. The mosque was full on Fridays, but the religious schools were nearly extinct, which was a more significant indication of the probable future of Islam

in Central Asia. If we were to believe our Uzbek inform-
ants, Uzbekistan retained its national character, Uzbek
was still the principal language in the university and
there had been little intermarriage between Uzbeks and
Russians. It appeared to our untutored eyes that, whatever compulsions had been exercised by the dominant
Power, the social compromises between the nationalities had been accepted, that the Russians had had the
sense to take their time and that here, at any rate, in
this republic, so isolated from the outside world, they
had no serious irredentist movement to fear, whether
based on nationalism or religion.

The Russians have learnt to value their traditional
architecture. It was reported in *Isvestiya* that a school-
mistress had encouraged her pupils to throw stones at
a church. After all, the country was atheist. But the
writer pointed out that this was all wrong. The church
was a part of Russian history and should be preserved.
And so, though in the early days of the Revolution
many churches had been destroyed, Russians now
admitted that it had been a mistake. They pointed with
pride to the tiny churches, ruined for so long, which
were now being carefully restored and preserved as an
authentic part of the national scenery below the tower-
ing cliffs of the vast Rossiya Hotel, then being built
beside the Kremlin on the river bank.

The old Russian buildings are so very Russian, from
the superb simplicity of Novgorod and Pskov, battered
in the war, but still displaying little masterpieces round
every corner, to the height of fantasy and profusion of
colour of the onion domes of St Basil or its country
cousin in Peredelkino, below which a simple flat stone
marks the grave of Pasternak, brought there by a long
procession of mourners who had filed all day past the
poet while Richter played. The monasteries of Suzdal

in the snow in their setting of old wooden houses and horse-drawn sledges might be a scene in one of the great nineteenth-century novels. The creators of these churches and monasteries had the Russian sense of the theatre. You can see it as you approach the fairy-tale silhouette of the Bishop's fortress palace at 'the great' Rostov, with its towers and domes and chapels and living-rooms built on the walls, in the square of the Kremlin churches, which makes so superb a setting for the Bolshoi Theatre's first scene of *Boris Godounov*, and in the frescoes with the weird beasts of the Apocalypse, showing the Russian origins of Chagall's imagination.

The new atheism has not converted it all into museums. The scene at the Troitsa Sergei monastery at Zagorsk is still full of life. There, beneath the blue gold-starred domes, the churches crowd on each other, huddling inside the fortress walls and, as I remember it best, in winter with the snow just falling, in the evening light, the old people feed the birds, the crowd of pilgrims wait in line to fill their pots with water from the holy well and, inside the little church of St Sergei, whose miraculous bones rest in an open tomb, the day-long chanting drones on mournfully and the rows of old peasants sit in the dim light in their padded coats and great felt boots, the men holding their fur hats and the women with their heads bound up in thick woollen scarves. If you can penetrate to the monastery of Pechora, surrounded by its formidable walls and towers, no more than twenty miles from the most easterly fortress of the Junkers, the meeting-place of the races, you walk through the fortress gate past a little monk who sits at the peep-hole in the door, peering out, oblivious of the continual stream of people passing through the other open door at his side, presumably a vestigial act with its roots in the days when the monastery was a real fortress and the door was opened only to friends.

Lenin was surely right in moving the capital back to Moscow, for he was withdrawing from the Europe of dynastic marriages and international capital, and founding a new harsh way of life which was in many ways a renewal of the old Russian ways. Peter's city, the window on Europe, has always been alien to Russia. The Western tourist loves it the most, not only because of its grand baroque palaces, superbly placed along the Neva, with their glorious pictures and those other palaces near by, so meticulously restored after the ravages of the war, but also because he finds it comfortable as a part of the Western European civilisation with which he is familiar and which has formed his taste. Leningrad is magnificent, it is a phase of Russian history; yet it is now a provincial town and the mausoleum of Peter's hopes to transform Russia into something alien to its character. But what a glorious failure!

I used to say that the picture galleries of the Russian museum in Leningrad were like a journey through Russia. You travelled for weeks through interminable, monotonous birch forests until you emerged in Vladivostok. No one can begin to understand the country unless he realises that Russians are obsessed by size, by the vastness of their country and its immense resources, the country which can swallow an invader, which must strive to outdo its great rival in space, in industry, in sheer power. It is still an empire, comprising an immense variety of peoples, scenery and art; to the north-west the Catholic States of the Baltic; to the south-west the Moldavian fruit gardens still claimed by Romania, Kiev dominated by the great cathedral on the Dnieper with the overpowering mosaic of the

Saviour high up in the apse, with its catacombs full of mummified monks, where the Ukrainian street-signs show the continuing strength of Ukrainian nationalism; to the south-east the sea-blue domes of Samarkand, the smell of the old Orient in Bokhara with its memories of inaccessibility and cruelty; to the east the interminable Siberian forest and steppe reaching to the Pacific and the borders of China; to the south the Turkish and Iranian borders, the Catholicos at Echmiadzin still pre-eminent among the Armenians of the Soviet Union and of the Armenian diaspora and the edge of the Kurdish Mountains. It is a familiar geography lesson, but we should never forget that the Soviet Union touches half the world.

Let me linger a little in the south, first in Armenia, figuring on its flag the mountain of Ararat, which dominates Erevan, yet is inaccessible to Soviet Armenians. In the early days of the Revolution the Turkish Government maintained that a Turkish mountain should not be figured in the flag of a Soviet republic, to which Lunacharsky is said to have replied that the Turks had the moon on their flag. The Russians used to say that they had three Armenians in Moscow, Mikoyan, Petrosian (head of the atomic energy committee), and Trevelyan. I disclaim Armenian descent, but can have sympathy for a people which, like my own Cornish ancestors, have been pushed around by foreigners.

But it is Georgia which holds first place in our affectionate memory. The Georgians tell how at the creation of the world all the peoples came before God to be allotted a country to live in. But the Georgians were drinking in a neighbouring inn. When they came at last to God, he said there was nothing left. Why were they not there earlier? They replied that they had been drinking God's health. This so impressed God that he said they should have the loveliest country of all, Georgia, which he had been reserving for himself. This seems to me to be a reasonable story. It is a beautiful, wildly romantic country. Take the Georgian military highway from Piatigorsk where Lermontov was killed in a duel. Put the Georgian tales of Lermontov and Tolstoy in your pocket and travel with 'the Hero of our Time' up the River Terek to the pass and down the White Araqvi, past the little villages clinging to the steep slopes and the churches, each with its tower topped by a candle extinguisher, so wholly different in form and spirit from the Russian extravagances, to the junction of the White and the Black Araqvi at Pasana-uri, where you may stay comfortably and dine in a seclusion of vines.

On the road we had been held up by an enormous flock of sheep, which effectively blocked traffic coming both ways on the narrow mountain-road. My private secretary got out of the car to photograph the scene. The shepherd asked why he was doing it. He replied that he was interested. The shepherd retorted, 'I'm bored with your interest.' The Georgians are an independent and outspoken people. They have never cared much for the Russians, even though they first asked the Russians in to protect them from the Persians. Their man was Stalin and his statue had remained in their parks through the whole period of his eclipse.

You pass on down the road to Tbilisi, the capital of Georgia on the Kura, 'our Tiflis' of the old song, where the old houses with their carved wooden balconies, almost touching over the narrow streets, are hidden behind the main streets of shops and hotels, which might be a Balkan capital of the early twentieth century or the scene of *The Prisoner of Zenda*. In the museum the magic word 'safe' takes you to one of the finest collections in the country, the Georgian enamels, rivalling the Scythian gold of the Hermitage.

On the way, only twenty kilometres short of Tbilisi, at the foot of the mountains, lies the old capital, Mtskheta, with its austere and exquisite cathedral. In it are buried the father and forefathers of a friend, coming from a famous Georgian family, whose mother was the daughter of a near relation of the Tsar. I had invited her to visit us in Moscow. I asked the wife of a senior Soviet official, herself a professor of history, whether she did not think it a good idea that I should invite a Romanov to the Soviet Union. She replied in firm tones, 'Ona ochen skoro budet sanitazyratsya', which I could only interpret as meaning that she would quickly be disinfected. At least, it showed confidence in the power of the Soviet idea.

Above the town is a little old chapel on the edge of the cliff, which touches the imagination as you look down on the river and the cathedral far below. Here, on our first visit, occurred a strange incident. We were four in the party: my wife, an Intourist girl, the Ambassador of Nepal and I – Christian, atheist, Hindu and agnostic. We peered into the chapel through the locked grill. I, being unobservant and earthy, noticed nothing. The old watchman was sent to get the keys. We went inside. 'But where are the candles which were burning?' the other three asked. We could find no traces of fresh wax, nor any warmth on the stone altar on which the candles had been seen only a few minutes earlier. The old watchman said that there had been people burning candles there early that morning, for it was a Christian festival and, though the church was no longer used, believers still marked the great days. No doubt the candles had burnt out in the natural way; but the atmosphere was so charged with history that a little miracle seemed in place. The seal was set on it by the old watchman whom we heard murmur, 'Govoryat shto neechevo nyet, no yest shto to.' 'They say there is nothing; but there *is* something.'

In a few years one collects a jumble of memories; the beach at Yalta where the people stake their claims to six feet of stony ground at seven o'clock in the morning and for the rest of the day nothing is visible but massive bodies in bikinis or under-clothes; an American family asking for real turtle soup and after-shave lotion in the hotel at Bokhara; the roof of the world seen far off from the road to Afghanistan; the peace of the fountain of Bakshisarai; the Russian forest in the silence of a bitter cold, still winter's day; the village churches in the clearings; the Christmas trees in the little windows of Moscow's wooden houses in the snow; the winter trails across the Volga ice; Rostropovich after the first performance of Britten's 'cello symphony in Leningrad, taken by that heady exaltation which Russians feel on a memorable occasion and which I can feel with them; the indignation of the Aeroflot girl at Tashkent with Mrs Roosevelt for having written that Russians never smiled, for she had given her a beautiful welcoming smile; the tawdry red velvet curtains; the lace; the net; the antimacassars; the heavy awkward arm-chairs; the bed-clothes that won't tuck in; the taps wrenched out of their sockets; the discovery that chicken à la Kiev should never be eaten in Kiev; the dire effects of standardisation of production in ensuring that lavatory seats from Riga to Alma Ata will break in the same place, and that every curtain over a distance of a thousand miles comes off its hooks in the same way immediately you try to pull it; the courtesy and real service, with only occasional glumness and inattention; the long, long meals; all the human kindness, the inefficiency, the inconsequence of the Russian provincial hotel.

In the new world of Communism one is born, one marries and one dies like anywhere else. Of births I recall only the indignation of a British father, outraged that he was not allowed to see his wife after their baby was born, for fear of infection. Soviet hospitals make no concessions to weak human feelings. One marriage was an oddity, between an English and an American student in the Baptist church after the morning Sunday service. The bridegroom and best man wore morning coats and carnations in their buttonholes; the bride wore white. The congregation, mostly working men and women, can never have seen anything like it, and tears of emotion and pleasure poured down. Alas! There was an unhappy sequel. The couple tried to import bibles, subversive literature, for their Baptist friends, and were lucky only to lose the bibles and be turned back from the frontier. Death was celebrated with elaborate ritual. High officials of the secular State are still buried, as in the days before the Revolution, beside Novodevichi's tall bell-tower, after the body has lain in a public hall on a mountain of flowers, while the pillars of the new establishment and the diplomatic corps pass by and lay their wreaths and a full orchestra plays the funeral march from the Eroica symphony. A conductor of the Bolshoi Theatre was placed in death on his old rostrum before the stage, while the curtains half-opened to reveal in the dim light the temple scenery of *Aïda*, and the women's voices softly sang the mournful music which he had directed so often in that place.

The church was still a part, if a small part, of Russian life and the churches in Moscow were well attended, not only by the old. Late on Sunday morning the young parents brought their babies to be baptised, from conviction, or to please grandmother, or as a matter of traditional practice. At Easter the people in their hundreds, surely not all believers, brought their Pashka cakes to be blessed, and at midnight came the great moment in the cathedral, packed like the London Tube in the rush hour, as the frail, old Patriarch in his mitre and diamonds, supported by his priests, moved in grand procession up the aisle after his symbolic journey round the church to the accompaniment of the chanting of the hidden choirs and the whistles and cat-calls of the young Komsomols in the street, when, the body of Christ being nowhere to be found, the congregation cried against the chanting, 'Christus voskress' – 'Christ is risen, he is risen indeed.'

But everywhere the scene was dominated by Lenin; pictures of Lenin, rows and rows of the works of Lenin, Lenin's Rolls-Royce on wheels, Lenin's Rolls-Royce on skis and caterpillars, Lenin's apartment in the Kremlin, and Lenin himself, preserved for ever in Red Square, guarded by sentries whose precision and immobility cannot be matched in the Western world, while the great line of devout pilgrims stretched far away into the distance, coming from Samarkand and Kiev, from Minsk and Vladivostok, from Riga and Erevan – all the variety of people in this immense country of birch forest and plain, mountain, desert and frozen waste, a world in itself, all come to visit the Little Father of the Revolution.

I pay my tribute to the Russian people, so full of warmth and friendliness beneath that apparently sullen exterior, so emotional, caught up in enthusiasm or cast down in depression, full of humour, delightful companions, always ready for a party. Communists or not, they remain Russians, with all the charm and waywardness, the creativeness and inefficiency of their nature, struggling to get through the door of a concert hall or to buy in a crowded shop, queuing patiently for hours for the necessities of life, maddening and irresistible, fearful liars and deeply sincere, tough and softhearted, with their Russian nature seeming to mould their ways more than Communism, a great people among whom, in spite of all the restrictions, the difficulties, the underground battles and the frustrations of Embassy life in Moscow, we are happy to have lived for a time, and whose fascination will stay with us always.

And so I come back in memory to our Moscow home; the river, busy with traffic or blocked with ice and, behind it, dominating our outlook and perhaps our thoughts, the towers, crosses and onion domes of the Kremlin outlined against the clear evening sky.

25

THE SOVIET OUTLOOK

Mr Brezhnev had said to me, 'We are Communists and we shall continue to act like Communists.' The aim of the Soviet Party is to preserve their own system, to maintain their leadership of the Communist world, to extend the area of Communism and to alter the balance of power in the world in its favour. They believe it to be historically inevitable that Communism will conquer the world and, though they profess not to export Communism, they are prone to give it a push along the road whenever they see an opportunity. Communism is a religion, an ideology, call it what you will, which fundamentally conditions the thought of the Soviet leaders, who believe implicitly in the truth of its doctrines. They are not opportunist politicians cynically using the Leninist creed as opium for the masses, in order to preserve their own power, even if they regard the power of the Party and their own position as its leaders as an essential part of the system to which they are dedicated. They believe that the main purpose of their lives is to promote Communism at home and abroad for the benefit of mankind and that to this end all other considerations of humanity, of freedom of thought and expression must be sacrificed. This is the framework within which Soviet policy must be assessed. Khrushchev's declared policy of 'peaceful co-existence' never meant to live and let live, which is what we mean by it. It means something more like to win the world for Communism without blowing it up.

The Soviet Communist regards himself as the 'progressive' who is on the right road to the future. We are the reactionaries who have not yet cast off the slough of the past. Marx and Lenin were prophets who by their genius apprehended the truth. The boys and girls of the Komsomol Institute in Moscow pass every day under the text 'Lenin was; Lenin is; Lenin will be'. Lenin was mortal, but transcends mortality. I asked the wife of a senior official of the Soviet Foreign Ministry, a lady of culture and intelligence, with experience of the outside world, how people like her judged *Dr Zhivago* as literature, apart from its political content. She replied, Do you not understand that we cannot think of it apart from its content? If we were to accept it, the whole basis of our life would be destroyed and we should know that all that we have been through in the last fifty years, the starvation, the suffering, the human misery, would have been useless, without meaning, without hope for the future. Such people see all the advantages of Western prosperity and intellectual and spiritual freedoms, but they see also that the Western way of life brings its own problems of anarchy, violence and licence. They are assailed every day by a didactic press proclaiming the Soviet truth, even though its divergence from the facts is often only too obvious. They have every incentive not to lose faith that, whatever they have to put up with at present, their future holds the prospect of a better life for all, that the rough and narrow path of Communism is the right way ahead and that the Western way of life will prove to be only the broad path leading to destruction.

The Western press records the protests of the writers and scientists against the repression of intellectual freedom by the successors of Khrushchev. This is a new phenomenon and the protests are growing in intensity. But most of the intellectuals, the scientists, the technologists, the managers, whatever reservations they may have about the actions of their masters and the way they work the system, probably still believe that, with all its weaknesses and injustices, their system is basically better than the Western way of life, which it will inevitably supplant. The conditions of life and work of a Soviet scientist or engineer are relatively good, at least since the Party gave up interfering with scientific research on ideological grounds. They get on with their work, secure enough in their ivory towers, isolating themselves from politics, able in their privileged position to collect underground paintings, if their tastes lie in that direction, visiting their professional colleagues in the West, living happily enough in their own separate world, knowing only too well the danger and suffering which would face them and their families if they chose the way of open dissent.

The young are a problem, as in any other country. The Soviet press reflects the concern of the older generation at the increasing tendency of the young to question the ways of their elders, which we in the West regard as natural and to some extent healthy. During my years in Moscow, the Party's propagandists frequently sought to deny that there was what came to be called the 'conflict of generations'. It is a real problem for the ageing revolutionaries, who have become the Establishment, that if there is a conflict of generations since the old are by definition revolutionaries, the young dissenters must be counter-revolutionaries. In terms of the doctrine this is a contradiction. Therefore a conflict of generations does not exist. 'But it does,' said my Russian teacher, 'it certainly exists in my own family and in the families of my friends.'

In our time, at least, neither the protests of the intellectuals nor the questionings of the young are likely to disrupt the power structure which rules the Soviet Union. In spite of all the grumbling and the discontents, most Russians still accept the Communist system and the power of the Communist Party as the inevitable framework of their lives. We believe that the future will show that Communism is not the right way to a better future for mankind and that it will never conquer the world, but we shall be making a serious error if we believe that the Soviet system is only maintained by the repression of a people actively hostile to it.

Russians are intensely patriotic, as the war showed. They are proud of Soviet achievements and that they are now one of the two great Powers, the only states with resources to put men into space, the Powers whose nuclear weapons enable them to control the destinies of the world. Russian national aims are an important part of Soviet policy, and the aims of improving living standards, industry and agriculture, health and education, and maintaining the security of the country, are those of any government. The Soviet leaders act like Russians as well as like Communists. As in Tsarist days, the national minorities in the Ukraine, the Caucasus, the Baltic States are kept in firm control. Central Asia is still a Russian colony, well administered, relatively prosperous and content, isolated from the currents of anti-colonialism by the simple fact that no sea separates it from the pressures of the metropolitan power. Soviet foreign policy is still devoted to the old interests, sometimes even where they are no longer relevant in modern conditions. The Polish question, the outlet to the south, the growing threat from the south-east are still lively issues in their new forms. Somehow, the doctrine and the national interests are continually reconciled.

Internally, the old ways of the Tsars continue: the pervasive power of the secret police; the suppression of heresy; prison, exile and labour camps for dissent. Only it is now more difficult to isolate the Russian people from the outside world. At no period of Russian history has there been real freedom of thought or expression in Russia. When towards the end of the nineteenth century an experiment was made in the loosening of control, the results were thought so dangerous that control was reimposed. I was waiting on the Nevsky Prospekt for a Soviet official, turning the pages of old, pre-revolutionary magazines. An advertisement of a study of Russian politics described that time as the revolutionary period of Russian history.

The debates on literature and the arts have an intensely Russian flavour. The account of the trial of Sinyavsky and Daniel, published in the West, reads like a passage from Dostoevsky, and the discussions in Tarsis's Ward 7 might well have taken place in a nineteenth-century prison settlement. Russian history did not begin in 1917, and the Soviet system would not have taken root and overcome those opposed to it if it had not followed a long history of absolute rule, in which freedom, as we know it, did not exist. As Charques writes, 'History is ... what succeeds. But what succeeds in the guise of innovation, seldom fails to reflect the continuity of the present with the past. In one sense the Bolsheviks triumphed because, in pursuit of power and the burning desire to create a new heaven and a new earth, they alone were prepared to resort to traditional methods of Russian rule.' The Soviet system is at least partly the inheritor of the system which exiled Pushkin and Dostoevsky. We are still apt to judge the Communist approach to freedom of opinion and information from the point of view of a political and social background which Russia has never known.

The Party rules the country; directs and interprets policy, allows no deviation from its current line, no criticism of policy, but only of execution of policy by subordinates – the aspect of Soviet life to which *Crocodil*, the Russian *Punch*, is almost wholly devoted. It seeks to direct all human activities – social, political, intellectual, artistic, economic – towards the building of the Communist society, though, for very human reasons, it does not always succeed. It aims at the exclusion of all influences which might weaken the basis of belief. But the world changes. Scientific discoveries and the economic development of the two most powerful countries have altered the conditions of national and international life and the balance of power, and these changes influence all aspects of Soviet policy, which is continually modified under the pressure of world events and of internal opinion, which can make itself felt even in a Communist state. The strands intermingle and influence one another, the ideology, the legacy of Russian history, national interests and all the ideals, the prejudices and the calculations of personal advantage, which make up the thinking of any political leader inside or outside the Communist world. But the basis of political and economic power remains securely in the hands of the Party.

When I paid my farewell call on Mr Kosygin, the Soviet Prime Minister, he was good enough to express his regret that I was leaving Moscow and his hope that I should not lose all interest in the Soviet Union. I assured him that I should continue to take an active interest in Anglo-Soviet relations and asked his permission to write to him from time to time. He readily agreed. Perhaps I shall write to him some day, if I feel that it will be useful and not embarrassing to the British Government or my successor of the moment, though the views of a retired Ambassador who no longer represents his Government cannot, in diplomatic terms, be of interest to another Government. Meanwhile, I put down on paper the kind of letter which I should like to, but shall not, send to Mr Kosygin.

Dear Mr Kosygin,

When I saw you before leaving Moscow, you told me that I might write personally to you and I am therefore sending you a few thoughts based on my time in Moscow and my continuing interest since that time in Soviet affairs.

I am principally concerned to consider the way in which Anglo-Soviet relations may develop in the future. It is obvious that they cannot be considered in isolation, for the issues between us concern many other countries besides our own and an improvement in our relations is impossible without a corresponding improvement in East–West relations in general.

Soviet Communists explain the doctrine of peaceful co-existence in terms of a doctrine of struggle, a struggle to achieve the victory of Communism by all means short of war. This interpretation of the doctrine increases the danger of conflict between us. The continual effort to convert one side or the other inevitably leads to a strengthening of the opposing forces and to an increase of tension, which may bring serious risks in its train. National Liberation struggles, as you call them, which I interpret as meaning struggles to ensure that what you call progressive forces will dominate a situation of political conflict, get out of hand if pushed too far and become local wars in which, as you well know, the rest of us risk becoming involved.

You have had considerable success in your propaganda against neo-colonialism, because the old colonies have not yet got used to being independent and are happy to blame the 'imperialists' for their own inability to solve the intractable problems with which they are now faced for the first time. You have naturally taken advantage of the agreeable if only temporary position of relative respectability in which the Soviet Union finds itself in the developing world. But you know, as well as we do, that nearly the whole colonial world has become independent, mostly with the co-operation of the colonial powers, and that the neo-colonial enemy is difficult to catch, since he does not exist, unless you aim to step into our old position.

You hope to change the balance of power in favour of Communism and of the Soviet Union by making non-Communist countries Communist, or at least by giving them a little gentle encouragement in that direction, but you must surely reflect sometimes that the more Communist countries there are, the more tension and conflict will build up within the Communist world. As the old Jewish proverb says, 'He who amasses wealth, amasses problems.' We in the West used to make the same sort of mistakes when we fondly imagined that all our old colonies would find the Westminster form of democracy, even including wigs in the tropics, ideally suited to their requirements and when the Americans thought neutralism a dirty word and, as was said, that every Head of State of a newly independent country subscribed not only to the Atlantic Charter, but also to the *Atlantic Monthly*. You will find that if more countries become Communist it will be very different from the Communism you know at home. The game may prove to be, as we say, not worth the candle. And, in the process, you will increasingly become involved in embarrassing and even dangerous situations without any real advantage to Soviet interests. You may then perhaps begin to wonder whether the compulsions of your doctrine have not carried you too far.

We in the West should not be over-frightened of Communism, though we shall keep up our defences and shall not allow ourselves to be swamped by your ideology, which suits neither our temperament nor our historical and political traditions. You should not be over-concerned with what you call the forces of reaction. For to see the world merely as a struggle between an unchanging Communism and an unchanging reaction is altogether too simple a concept to have much relevance to the way things actually happen and to current developments in the world. I must confess myself to be an optimist, not in the sense of your doctrine that Communism, as we know it, will conquer the world and bring about your Kingdom of Heaven upon earth, nor in the sense of those who believe that Communism will disappear from the face of the globe, but in the sense that we shall just, if only just, succeed in avoiding self-destruction and shall, eventually, if not in our generation, work out some way of living together a little more easily than at present.

In the Middle Ages it must have appeared inconceivable that Christians and Muslims could ever co-exist in peace. Can we not hope that, if we manage our affairs with common sense and prudence, future generations will look back with amazement and incredulity at the controversies of the twentieth century as those of a less enlightened age? Your ideologists bitterly oppose the view that the two societies will tend to converge. But it may happen without our being conscious of it. Our societies are in a continual process of change as new discoveries radically transform the conditions of our lives in ways which neither Karl Marx nor the nineteenth-century capitalists could ever have imagined. The doctrines on both sides continually need reinterpretation in the light of changing circumstances. All men who call themselves Christians no longer believe in the inevitable conversion of the heathen. All men who call themselves Communists can surely no longer believe that the world is inevitably moving towards the perfect Communist society.

It must be our aim so to increase confidence and the general sense of security that we can gradually come to terms with each other and in the end dismantle our alliances and begin seriously to disarm. You and the Americans, by your possession of overwhelming nuclear power, hold the destinies of the world in your hands. You know very well that you must have an understanding on nuclear weapons with the Americans, if you do not want to waste all your precious resources on sterile weapons which you can never use, instead of employing them to increase the prosperity of your own country and the poorer countries of the world, and if we are all, including you, to sleep easily in our beds. I believe that you have now gone beyond the negative concept of avoidance of confrontation to the positive policy of the two-power balance. There seems at least some hope that we may be entering a period of negotiation and that you will now be in permanent discussion with the Americans in order to build and maintain the basic system of world security.

This is not to say that you and the Americans should dominate the world. Nor do I think that you will succeed in doing so, even if the liberal academics left over from the Kennedy era, with some arrogance, are now apt to say that Europe no longer counts and therefore does not need a foreign policy. There is plenty of room for manœuvre by other states under your self-cancelling nuclear umbrella which, by its very power, stops both of you from bringing your real strength to bear on any situation outside your own backyards. The rest of Europe will inevitably grow together, sooner or later, and will not submit for ever to be divided into ideologically opposing groups. You will both have to take account of it as a major political force in the world. Meanwhile, the establishment of a permanent East–West Commission should help towards real European security.

Your Czechoslovakian adventure was presumably a defensive reaction, though none the more creditable for that, arising from the fear that to allow the Czechs to develop their own brand of socialism would undermine both the system of East European security on which you believe yourselves to depend and the social and political system which you maintain so rigidly in your own country. Of course, you knew that in the short term you would have no difficulty in bringing it off, though your assessment of opinion inside Czechoslovakia, particularly of the workers, seems to have been faulty. You also knew well enough that you had nothing to fear from the Western States. But you will remember that it was a shrewd Western politician who first sensed the wind of change in Africa and I am inclined to believe that the more you try to keep out the wind of change in the Soviet Union and Eastern Europe the more trouble you will be storing up for yourselves or your successors.

De Gaulle's phrase, Europe from the Atlantic to the

Urals, never had any meaning so long as the German problem remained unsolved. You told me that the Soviet Union would never allow the reunification of Germany and that the British would be stupid if they promoted it. In any case, in the present state of lack of mutual confidence, Germany is not going to be reunited and we can only hope that Central Europe can gradually be made more stable by the Germans themselves, with your and our help. Meanwhile, the old occupying Powers should ensure that nothing upsets the peace of Berlin and that the old arrangements by which the Western powers have free access to Berlin are immune from disturbance. We understand your fear that, even in this nuclear age, the restless spirit of the Germans can become the focus of a new conflict. The best way of ensuring that this does not happen is to make the best, not the worst, of the Germans, so that the vast majority of them, who are reasonable human beings, can keep the evil djinn from which we and they have suffered so much in this century securely and permanently corked up in his bottle. There are now welcome signs that you and the West Germans are beginning to get on better terms with each other.

China will be the great world problem for us all. Their Most Christian Majesties fought each other often enough in the past, and it is by no means out of the question that Their Most Communist Majesties may fight each other in the future. It must be tempting to preempt the conflict by using force before the Chinese develop their nuclear power. But I do not believe that you will judge this to be the right course. You know well the dangers of war between the Soviet Union and China, that you would not succeed for long in trying to impose on China a change of government in your own interests, and that if you went into China you would find it very difficult to get out again. In time, the Chinese will become a great Power. We must hope that in the process they will acquire the responsibility of a great Power towards the rest of the world. Their conception of time is different from ours. We should not forget the old Chinese saying that the first hundred years of every new dynasty are the worst.

And so I come back to Anglo-Soviet relations. They are like the British weather, alternating between showers and sunshine, with occasional severe frost which disrupts the traffic and bursts the pipes, because we are never ready for it. We in Britain should not think that détente is just round the corner, because the sun has come out for a bit, nor that we have gone back to the worst days of the Cold War, when we get a little frost or sleet. The Soviet Government should not get excited when we make exceedingly rude noises about the way they treat their writers or their propensity to use the Soviet Army to settle a quarrel with their neighbours. For us free speech means slanging our own leaders and everyone else's. It will help if the Soviet authorities keep a sensible control on the treatment of British subjects by their intelligence and counter-intelligence services. They should also realise that most Soviet defectors are of no importance and are a nuisance, but that we do not allow anyone, from our own or the Soviet services, to put pressure on them, and that if a defector returns to the Soviet Union and tells a press conference of the elaborate tortures to which the British have subjected him the British public regards it as ludicrous. And if they want to decorate their spies, which is quite reasonable, they should confine it to their own nationals. Of course, we can always retaliate by giving Penkovsky a posthumous O.B.E.

If you think that there is too much internal politics

in our treatment of foreign affairs, if you find it a bore to have to deal with new British ministers every few months, please remember that we know that our political system has many defects, but that any other system, however tidy and efficient, would suit us worse. To us liberty is more important. You know from experience that you cannot expect us, for temporary advantage, to turn against our allies and our friends. As Mr Gromyko said in London in a difficult time, let us never be tempted to destroy in a few days what it has taken years to build up. In bad times, we should both keep our heads down. In better days, we should try and build up our relationship in the belief that if we show common sense, prudence and good will we shall be able to get on reasonably well together and avoid disaster.

I apologise that I, a mere retired official, should have the temerity to preach to the Prime Minister of a Super Power. In return, you may tell me that, as our old proverb says, I am teaching my grandmother to suck eggs.

With kindest regards and memories of your personal kindness to my family and me in Moscow,

Yours very sincerely,

Humphrey Trevelyan

INDEX